The Woman God Designed

"Instead of *The Woman God Designed*, Tonia's book could be titled *The Mankind God Designed*. Though focused on marriage, particularly the woman's side of that institution, it offers insights into creation purposes and processes of a depth beyond what one might expect from a book about womanhood. I believe this book would be beneficial reading for women seeking the will of God for their lives and their marriages. It would be just as beneficial to men."

> — *Betty Robison*
> *Wife of James Robison, Life Outreach International*
> *Co-Host of "Life Today"*

"The moment I heard about *The Woman God Designed*, I knew I had to read it. Tonia challenges us to embrace the truth of God's Word concerning the role of women in today's world and gives us the tools to be transformed from the inside out. Because she has walked out what she shares, this book will motivate, equip and enable any woman who sincerely desires to be a woman, wife, and mother after God's own heart."

> — *Carol Warren*
> *Women's Education Director, Capstone Church*
> *Fort Worth, Texas*

"Your teaching, coupled with the work of the Spirit, has continued to make a wonderful difference in my life and marriage. God transformed my heart and the good fruit is evident. I could tell a major difference in my husband after 24 hours! I am increasingly convinced that the work of honor accomplished in a woman's heart toward her husband carries with it the power to set husbands free and empower them to be what God created them to be. It's thrilling."

> — *Steffani Powell*
> *Small Group Women's Ministry in Austin, Texas*

"As leader of a Women's Ministry at a 1200+ church, I have researched several books and workbooks, such as *Women Mentoring Women* and *Fascinating Womanhood*. But by far Tonia Woolever's *The Woman God Designed* supersedes all other books for teaching women of today."

> — *Toni Tomei*
> *Director of Women's Ministry*
> *New Hope Ministries, Naples, Florida*

"I found that this book addresses the exact issues that I needed in my own marriage counseling sessions. I was amazed that it was both timeless and yet

very timely in its message. This is truly an anointed work, and I would recommend it to anyone in the marriage counseling field."
> — *Pastor Don Tomei*
> *New Hope Ministries, Naples, Florida*

"This book is so anointed. In my opinion, Tonia's teachings are some of the very best I have ever read or heard. She is a gifted teacher!"
> — *Betty Freberg*
> *Author, Ten Women of God*
> *Founder & Director of Tenth Woman Ministries, Azle, Texas*

"Next to the Bible, I think this is the most important book a woman could read."
> — *Vonda Roe*
> *Pastor's Wife, Fort Worth, Texas*

"Our group of ladies is using your book *The Woman God Designed* for Bible study. We're praising God for your book. We like the book so much that many of us would like to give a copy to the other members of our families."
> — *Shirley Rice*
> *Bible Study Leader, Ida Grove, Iowa*

"Tonia, I wanted to tell you what a difference the teachings in your book have made in my life. It is like I have a whole new marriage, and I cannot thank you enough."
> — *Kathleen Francis*
> *Marble Falls, Texas*

"I am currently leading a group of women in the study of your book. We have had some wonderful conversations. The Lord led me to lead this class because I so need to learn this information myself. Thank you so much for writing this book."
> — *Eleanor J. Sprankle*
> *Bible Study Leader, Spruce Creek, Pennsylvania*

"Many husbands have come to me and said, 'I bought this for my wife, but I gained as much or more from reading it as she did!"
> — *Dr. Ron Woolever*
> *Founder & Director, Shammah Ministries*

The Woman God Designed
Copyright © 2008 Tonia Woolever
ISBN 0-9725944-1-7

Published by:

>   ScribeLife Publications
>   280 Son Shine Circle
>   Azle, Texas

ScribeLife Publications is a Division of Shammah Ministries, Azle, Texas

First Edition published in 2001.

A Study Guide for Group Leaders is available for this book. To order, log onto
www.shammah.org.
Or contact the publisher directly via email sent to: ScribeLife@charter.net.

THE WOMAN GOD DESIGNED

Living the Life He Longs to Give

By

Tonia Woolever

DEDICATION

This book is dedicated to my husband Ron, whom I affectionately call Brown Eyes. How have you loved me? Let me count the ways: Number One Fan, Best Friend, Lover, Grillmeister and Chief Bottle Washer, Enforcer of the Schedule, Enforcer of Rest...just to name a few. Without you this book would have never been written, much less finished. Thank you for always refusing to let me be less than Jesus calls me to be; though it may not always seem like it, I've come to understand that you never love me more than in such moments. Your love and Jesus' love have changed me forever. I admire you, for you are a man after God's own heart. I'm so glad Jesus kept me from throwing our life away.

Special thanks to the friends and colleagues who encouraged me with your confidence in the value of this work. In particular I thank three dear friends: Betty, my first prayer partner and faithful cheerleader; Carol Jean, whose fearless love and godward gaze always renew my spirit; and Norma, whose wonderful support made publication of this book a dream come true. Every woman should be blessed with friends such as you.

Jesus, I offer you my highest praise, because from you and through you and to you are all things.

That this book was lived and then written is a testimony to the fact that in my weakness you are always waiting to show your strength. You are the hero I was looking for.

Because of how you have loved me, I have learned how to love. Between these two bookends I have found the abundant life you promised.

A note to my daughter:

Gabriele, it is fitting to include the original artwork you drew for the first cover of *The Woman God Designed* when you were only 17. A dusty old cameo from my jewelry box came alive in all its beauty and detail under your discerning eyes and skillful hand. I cannot think of a better metaphor for what the Holy Spirit brings to our human experience on earth, and which sums up all I have attempted to say in this book.

No mother could have more pride and joy in a daughter than I have in you. You are a delightful woman, and a satisfying taste of Jesus to all who share your journey. In all the ways God intended for daughters to be to their mothers, you are my glory.

XOXORR

Table of Contents

Foreword

It is my fervent hope that this book will be read not just by women who are believers, but also by those who are contemplating whether to give themselves to God. To you I want to say, do not hesitate to give yourself to the One who will love you like no other, who is real and waiting to be the architect of a deeply satisfying life. He is real. He speaks. He understands. Your tears, your longings, your dreams, even your weaknesses, will be treated as a precious thing. No one will value your life and make it valuable, like Jesus Christ. He asks everything, and replaces all with riches of soul and spirit that you could never buy:

> "Come, all you who are thirsty, come to the waters; and you who have no money, come, buy and eat! Come, buy wine and milk without money and without cost. Why spend money on what is not bread, and your labour on what does not satisfy? Listen, listen to me, and eat what is good, and your soul will delight in the richest of fare. Give ear and come to me; hear me, that your soul may live. I will make an everlasting covenant with you, my faithful love promised to David. (Isaiah 55:1-3)

My first 30 years of life, I did it my way. I tried my best to give myself life, and ended up stealing life, not only from myself, but from those around me, even those I loved. When I considered giving myself to God, it was with an absolute aversion to the thought of becoming like many of the religious folks I'd encountered, who seemed to be essentially unchanged people who had merely overlaid the requirements of church on top of everything else, or like the radio and TV personalities that peddle Jesus, miracles and prosperity.

I wasn't thinking at all of giving myself to God because it was right or would honor Him. My motives were entirely selfish: I wanted life, authentic, satisfying, nurtured life. I craved real truth and wisdom and the ability to be the kind of woman I surely was not: life-giving, joyful, fulfilled.

I made my choice out of desperation, and because, as you will discover, God came to me, and poured his love out on me, at the moment in life when I was at my worst morally. I have not regretted my decision for even a moment, now 27 years later. Not to say I have had a perfect life or been a perfect person — only to say that God has absolutely never wavered in His promise described in Isaiah 55.

To you who are already believers, I want to answer the question, "Why another book for Christian women?" The answer is because, like all other books, this one is unique. It is a mixture of my Christian journey, with all its failures and joys, and teaching you what I have learned about how God interacts with a very imperfect woman to bring her life, and to help her become what He always dreamed of. No woman could aspire to anything greater.

This book is different because I write as a woman whose marriage failed in spite of the fact we were full time pastors and Bible teachers, filled with His Spirit, to reveal how the Lord gave us a new marriage covenant based on love, honor and Himself. I write as a Christian who came face to face with the reality that I had no idea how to really love God. I write as that woman who still, selfishly, is thirsty for the real thing, the real God who will meet with me in real life.

Mine is, admittedly, a very selfish perspective. I thought about telling you in this introduction that I want to help you become a great Christian, to help you become a disciple of Jesus Christ, faithful and true. Here's the thing: Jesus is so lovely, so satisfying, so true, that when you taste of the real person He is, the rest of these follow naturally. It's like falling in love; no one needs to tell you how. Real devotion for Him flows out of the real experience of his love.

Altogether, in these pages I offer you a course in how to walk with the Holy Spirit, as the Apostle Paul instructed us to do in Galatians 5:25. I pray you will encounter the real Jesus and his powerful love as you study, ponder and pray. I say to your spirit, your real life is hidden in Jesus Christ, you are safe in his keeping, and the joy is real.

Tonia Woolever
Azle, Texas
July, 2008

Chapter 1

A Woman's Search For Abundant Life

The thief does not come except to steal and to kill and to destroy. I have come so that they might have life, and that they might have it more abundantly. (John 10:10, MKJV).

This book is a result of my quest to find and enjoy the abundant life that Jesus promises to us all. When I surrendered to the love of Jesus at the age of 29 my religious page was entirely blank. As I began to read my Bible for the first time, beginning with the gospel of John, I was immediately enthralled with this promise and was blessed with a childlike faith to embrace and expect this with my whole heart. Wrapped in my cocoon of new love for Jesus, I had abundant life in the beginning, helped along by my natural tendency to be a Pollyana.

I jumped into church life in every way, even marrying a pastor after a few years, which thrust me into the front lines of the battle to reconcile religion with real life. For a while all was well, but gradually, in an almost imperceptible way, life and the church culture and my too intimate view of the private life of church members began to chip away at my childlike faith and my satisfied heart. Eventually my Pollyanna view of Christian life was fairly shattered.

Over two decades of being a pastor's wife, teacher and counselor, working with Christians in every denomination and even different cultures, has confirmed a tragically consistent fact: that while many have successfully mastered the social life of the church, far too few are experiencing the abundant life Jesus died to give us. God's power and anointing may exist in the church, but does not seem to reach into the living room, kitchen or bedroom. People are increasingly less willing to accept this promise that never seems to be true for them. They want the real thing, or not at all, and that's a good thing. Christians need to identify the thief of their peace, joy and fulfillment, in life and especially in their most important relationship, marriage.

I was one of these, possessing the resources for a great Christian life and marriage: full of the Holy Spirit, a genuine desire to live for God, a man I loved. Yet in the midst of this my marriage was unsatisfying and perpetually brought out the worst in my husband and I. In public ministry we were successful, in private we were lonely, loving one minute and hating the next, living from one battle of the wills to another. Most importantly, I had ceased enjoying my relationship with Jesus, and had entered the fellowship of those who do what's right as a Christian, out of duty. I hated it; I felt like a hypocrite and as a ministry professional, one who continually offered a drink to thirsty people from a well that I secretly knew was dry.

I eventually learned that this problem is all too common among Christians, which is why so many have fallen away either from church or the Lord himself. With my first love for Jesus still a vivid memory, it broke my heart. I wanted the real thing; no substitutes, no plates I had to keep spinning in the air by faith to make it work, no public professions of victory undermined by private boredom or doubt. I just couldn't give up what I had hoped in from the beginning. The hope of joy and abundant life, the promise of being deeply loved and watched over by a god who had laid down his life for me, haunted me. I went on a quest to recover this hope, and the result of that journey has become this book. I found what I was looking for, and my joy is made complete in sharing it.

My quest: can God really give me abundant life?

The teaching in this book came out of my need to prove to myself that God's Word is as powerful and life-giving as it promises. I ultimately discovered that when my experience falls short of what God promises, the failure is not in God's Word or his ability and willingness to perform his word, but within my own heart. A crucial key to possessing His life is discovering and removing the hypocrisy that exists between what we say we believe about God and how we actually respond to Him. This process begins with understanding the real motives of one's own heart.

For instance, the Lord has shown me that while my goal was abundant life, the choices I made were actually motivated by my need for security and the control necessary to achieve it — which caused me make choices that actually robbed me of that desired abundant life.

I begin this book by sharing my personal story with you, so you will have a context for the profound change the Lord has worked in my heart, my experience of life, and my marriage. I will share how God changed my life through a failed marriage, and even gave me a new one — with the same husband. Then I will challenge you to think about what kind of woman you want to be, while going back to the touchstone of God's original design in your creation, discovering and rediscovering the beauty, glory and strength God embedded in your feminine DNA, a design I hope you will embrace with all your heart.

I have made this journey myself, from being a woman shaped by the world — even as a Christian — to one whose passion is to understand and wholeheartedly embrace the design of my creator and Lord, Jesus Christ. This journey began with reading the Bible cover to cover in search of what specifically applied to me as a woman. Mind you, I did this with a determination to fully test the Lord's ways, not just memorize wisdom. I held to the belief that, as the Bible declares, the Word of God is flawless,[1] yet had learned the hard way that this matters little if one cannot genuinely apply and receive life from it. What I discovered challenged everything I had built my feminine life upon. But to my great joy it also revealed to me the heart of God and his passion for giving us abundant life through great relationships.

We live in a world that increasingly obliterates the differences between the sexes, in stark contrast to the Wisdom from heaven[2] who teaches that woman was created by God as a quite unique and distinct creature from a man. Though some areas of Christian growth are generic to both genders, I believe that the Lord transforms the feminine soul into the image of His Son by a different path than He does a man.

While I do not subscribe to the theory that a woman is only complete only if she is united to a man, I do believe that God created woman

---

[1] Psalm 18:30: "As for God, his way is perfect; the word of the Lord is flawless."

[2] According to Colossians 2:2-3, Jesus embodies all of God's wisdom.

specifically to relate to man in order to reveal the special glory God uniquely gave each. Jesus and Paul both confirmed that if any person, male or female, could remain single and therefore give God all the love and energy one would put into a marriage, it was a call and a gift to be cherished. So we know that our completion is always with God. But in this world we express God's glory through relationship, and we need to understand and live wisely in our created differences, whether married or single.

Abundant life begins with embracing the reason God made you.

God created us for relationship, and it is within relationship to God and others that we find — or fail to find — abundant life. Originally created as one being who was the very image of all God is, man was then divided by God into male and female. Therefore, the total expression of God's nature can be found in the two genders, but not identically. He divided them and made them different for one reason: because if mankind were alone, he could not have relationship, and it is in relationship that the full glory of man — and God — is revealed. This is why even God is not one, but three.

Consider this book a manual on relationship, whether with God or others. I hope to help a woman develop an awesome relationship to Jesus Christ, and if she is married, with her husband.

It may surprise you to know that in each of the Old Testament and New Testament languages, Hebrew and Greek, there are not two separate words for "woman" and "wife." The same word is used for either, sometimes being translated as woman, sometimes as wife. The Bible student must wisely use the context to know when which word applies.

Every woman who calls herself a Christian should seek to know God's will in how to relate to the men in this world, who have also been created with a distinct call and purpose. A woman needs to understand God's purpose in creating her gender and his will for her, for there can be no doubt that hidden in God's will is our highest fulfillment.

We are all daughters of Eve, and in a very real way we are still faced with her choice: will we be content with God's will for us (the Tree of Life) or will we yield to discontent and try find life our own way (through the Tree of Knowledge)? Eve's own discontent opened her up to the beguilement of the devil. He lied to her, and he is still lying to women about God, saying that God's ways will not give us the life we long for. Our enemy is a thief who has stolen from woman the glory of God's design for her. He is destroying her beauty and her strength. He wants a woman to take things into her own hands, to doubt that her soul will be satisfied with what God wants for her.

I believe that my gender wrestles continually with the issue of contentment. I certainly did. Everything in life, every relationship has been measured by its capacity to bring deep satisfaction to my soul. I have tried to squeeze satisfaction out of things and people, often in vain. We live in a world where women are crying for the liberation necessary to pursue their joy unhindered. The greatest discovery of my life has been that God can satisfy my soul in every way. In all my hungers and thirsting, God is enough. He has indeed set a table before me, even in the presence of my enemies, and taught me how to come and rest content there.

This has liberated me from the need to make my husband or anyone else, or any career, hobby or addictive substance satisfy me. The Bible is full of God's promises to satisfy us in every way. You will find in these pages my journey of testing those promises and the paths I have discovered to the promised rest of God; a rest that is, by the way, the greatest beauty secret any woman can have.

Why I wrote this book.

My goal in writing this book is to help a woman discover and embrace her God-given design, so she will receive his abundant life. I want the single woman to find the joy of knowing the Lord as her husband. I long to see every woman use her strength to help the men in her life fulfill their purpose as created by God. I particularly love to see a wife cease to struggle with her husband and her Lord and come to the place of rest so she may enjoy true contentment.

Remember that God's hopes and dreams for us are greater than our own:

> Now glory be to God who by his mighty power at work within us is able to do far more than we would ever dare to ask or even dream of – infinitely beyond our highest prayers, desires, thoughts, or hopes. (Ephesians 3:20, The Living Bible.)

Whatever you want for yourself, Jesus wants more. The greatest dream you have for your life is actually puny compared to his plans for you.

Believing this should help you dare to trust in his original, incredible design for you as a woman.

This book has three basic divisions. The first section focuses upon developing a great relationship with Jesus. I will share with you the things which I have found to be crucial for a strong, indestructible inward life and developing the kind of heart Jesus feels at home in.

The second section focuses on God's creation of woman, her special design and purpose in this world, especially as she relates to the opposite gender. We will revisit the creation story to understand God's design for marriage, and study the Biblical concept of covenant relationship. We eventually cover every major scripture addressed to women to order to understand all of God's ways for the woman He designed.

The final section covers the problematic subject of submission. Embracing the whole will of God has dramatically changed and blessed my life, but understanding God's true purpose and ways for submission was crucial in this process. God has given me a glimpse of his glory for women, that we have the high calling of showing both the church and the world how a bride honors her bridegroom. Therefore I hope to open up submission for you as to its true nature and power, and give you tools to help you sort out the issues it raises in your personal relationships.

I wrote this book because my journey has taken me both through hell and heaven on earth and I want to share what I've learned with other women, especially the one who has just come to Jesus and needs a road map for her personal path of faith to the heart of God. I write to the woman who wants to follow God but is afraid to totally entrust herself to him. I write to the woman who may be a success at church, but whose private life is quietly and desperately failing; for the woman who loves God but finds herself unable to love and respect her husband as God commands. I write especially to the woman who wants to bridge the chasm between God's promise of abundant life, and the reality in her home and heart.

Ultimately I write in obedience to my precious Heavenly Father, to serve him in his goal to bring all things on earth together under the headship of His Faithful Son, and my Lord, Jesus. I am hungry to see the kingdom of my Jesus come in its power and glory, and I want to help make a people ready for the coming of the Lord, especially those of my own gender.

Regarding the Reflection & Deeper Study Sections

At the end of each chapter, including this one, you will find a section to assist you in reflection and deeper study of the principles presented. You will see repeated references to keeping a journal to help you better process your thoughts and prayers in response to what you learn. Journaling is one of the best tools for growth you will find.

My personal experience is that a journal helps me to see the extent to which God is actively working in my life in a way that nothing else can. We think that because the Lord says something to us, we will never forget it, but this simply isn't true. The Lord uses my journal many times to remind me of a promise, a warning, or a foretelling of something special to come in my life. His direction is often more clear in review sometimes than in the present. After years of journalling I can look back and see how often he was leading me when I didn't know it, and it has made me love Him more and inspired further trust. That alone is an excellent reason to journal.

Another important reason to journal one's beliefs and thoughts is that we often don't realize what we do believe or how strongly we believe it until we verbalize it or record it in black and white. The deepest thoughts one fears to acknowledge anywhere else can be safely expressed in a private journal. It is an exercise in honesty and truth. Years of counseling have shown me that many people aren't in touch with the truth about themselves or what they really believe deep in their hearts. Many don't know how to put their own dreams or fears into words. Self-awareness is a powerful tool of growth. Journalling is an excellent tool to develop self-awareness.

Every Christian should keep a journal of prayer time with the Lord, in which to record the things the Lord says, to record praises, concerns, thoughts, and special scriptures. It does not have to be in depth, and does not have to be written in every single day. What hinders most people in journalling is thinking they have to write in it every day, like a diary, making note of every important detail of life. This will defeat you in trying to establish the journaling habit. Let it be a friend, a tool, not a burden, and give yourself permission to pick it up when you do.

My goal in these sections for further study is to help you personally apply the scriptures, to learn to hear the Lord's voice and therefore receive his personal counsel. If you have entered into relationship with Jesus Christ, your life is now defined by the New Covenant of Jesus and its promises, chief of which is the promise that you will personally know God.

Jesus referred to this promise when he said:

> *It is written in the Prophets: 'They will all be taught by God.' Everyone who listens to the Father and learns from him comes to me. (John 6:45).*

And you must come to Jesus, because "...*your life is now hidden with Christ in God.*" (Colossians 3:3).

Reflecting on Chapter 1

The purpose of this chapter is help you think about your life in relation to Jesus' promise to give you abundant life.

❖ *Read Psalm 81:10-16, and paraphrase it for yourself.*

❖ *Do you believe you are living the abundant life Jesus promised in John 10:10? If not, ponder and list the changes that you think would have to occur for your life to be described as "abundant." Include habits, people, or circumstances.*

❖ *Journal your thoughts about these things and talk to God about it.*

❖ *Prayer: Ask the Lord to reveal anything you need to know concerning his promise of abundant life for you and what might be hindering it.*

A Christian Marriage: Guaranteed to Work?

"I want a guarantee that this marriage will work!"

I married Ron Woolever in 1981, but only after he gave me a guarantee that our marriage would last. I had been through one bad marriage before knowing Jesus, and I was afraid to try again. During an episode of pre-marriage jitters in which I expressed my fears about being able to make a marriage work forever, Ron popped off, "What do you want, a guarantee?" I said, "Yes, I guess that's exactly what I want." He responded by sitting down and writing one for me. It reads:

— GUARANTEE —

To Whom It May Concern: This is to certify that a lifetime commitment between Toni and Ron will <u>not</u> fail! It will be based upon respect, love, caring, sharing and verses 4-8 of 1 Corinthians 13, and a mutual commitment to fulfilling God's purpose for them — their pledge to Him and to Each other!

— GUARANTEE—

We sure laughed about it, but I took that guarantee and put it inside my Bible to keep forever.

Wanting our wedding vows to be very personal, we each spent time with the Lord, asking Him to give us the words we would promise to one another at the altar. As a result of what I received from the Lord, these are the vows I made to Ron, my covenant with him in marriage:

"Ron, it is with great love, joy and honor that I commit myself to you. All that I have, all that I am, all that I can be, I offer to you for the rest of my life. I will strive to be the wife to you which God intended a woman to be to a man, and with His help I promise to begin each day God gives us together with new trust, new love, new hope and new faith. I will be your friend, your partner in prayer, walk by your side through all things, rejoice in your joy and share in your sorrow. I will make a home in which you can grow and return each day knowing I believe in you."

Ron spoke these beautiful vows to me:

"Toni, my love, from this moment in eternity, I commit to you my life, my unending, yet ever-growing love, my hopes, my dreams, my goals and my aspirations. All these I give freely and totally, hoping that as you accept, we can become one complete being who will walk the pathway of life in two fragile bodies. I give also my weaknesses, as well as my strengths, hoping that with God's guidance and wisdom, I will be patient and kind. I will try never to be jealous or proud. God will be foremost in our lives, but of all earthly things, you and our family will be my first commitment and my highest priority. This I covenant to you."

A few months after our wedding, a friend presented us with a calligraphy of our vows beautifully matted and framed. We hung them on our bedroom wall, his on on his side of the bed, mine on my side, so we could be reminded of them often. Serious commitments, received as a holy trust through seeking them in prayer, beautiful to behold — and we promptly forgot about them, except at dusting time, which I wasn't very good at when it came to framed things hanging on the wall.

I was thrust into the demanding and very public role of pastor's wife, which I embraced with all my heart and with high expectations of how wonderful it would be. We began our marriage in a new town, pastoring a new church in South Texas.

I jumped in quickly to do all the things a good pastor's wife does, working alongside my husband in the church office, making hospital visits with him, hosting countless congregants to dinners in our home, sitting in with Ron in counseling sessions and teaching an occasional Sunday school class. It was an intense beginning to a new marriage between two people who each had a failed marriage under their belts. If married life tests the mettle of two people, ministry married life tests it ten times more.

We hoped to blend our two families, my two children and Ron's daughter, into a happy "Brady Bunch." But we quickly realized it wasn't going to work out that way. Our "honeymoon period" was shorter than the one with the church as we realized how very different our personalities were and how much emotional baggage we had both lugged into the relationship from our first marriages.

Our strength was that we passionately loved each other and were both sincerely committed to Jesus and Biblical principles of relationship. We believed in living by the Word of God. My husband was a gifted counselor, especially good at helping married people work through their issues. I steadily developed the teaching gift that God had put in me, absorbing the Bible's treasures with joy and increasingly sharing what I discovered, especially with the women's group. We had fully embraced the Holy Spirit and prayed for him and his power to fill our lives. We believed marriage is forever and all things are possible with Christ.

The "invincible" Christian marriage.

In spite of all this, the stresses of ministry and trying to blend a family began to take their toll on our love. We often found ourselves at cross purposes and embroiled in power struggles over who should discipline the children and how. We sadly slipped into the habit of expecting the worst in each other, and judging each other harshly. Time and again we gave into the frustration over our profound disappointments in each other and how the marriage was going. After awhile both of us were experiencing that profoundly sad loneliness that should never exist in a marriage, which creeps in where two people have become emotionally estranged from one another.

Our trust in one another eroded to the point of extinction. I came to believe Ron was far more interested in fixing me than loving me, and I know I wanted to change him. Making our marriage work began to seem much too hard and beyond our ability. Though I know we both prayed about our relationship during our individual prayer times, we never prayed together. We argued over the same issues endlessly, our home becoming a battleground where we each fought for our rights, demanded our needs be met, and deeply resented each other's weaknesses. God had made us one, but our oneness had turned into two people locked in a cage match.

Marriages fail every day in America, but we didn't believe it could happen to us when we were devoted Christians who presumably possessed all the right tools to make a marriage work. Since we were the leaders of the church and expected to have it all together, we struggled through it alone, carefully keeping our problems hidden from the congregation and the community, fighting by night and counseling other couples by day in how to love each other well. Watching each other be wonderful with other people, sharing wisdom and grace and love and patience and hope, only deepened the angry undercurrent between us.

One day three years into our marriage, in the midst of a particularly vicious fight, I saw real hatred in Ron's eyes for the first time. It broke my heart. Even more, it frightened me because it mirrored something I felt in my own heart. There was no semblance of love left between us; we knew each other's weak spots and our tongues wounded well. In a few moments, our relationship crumbled. I ripped the wedding ring off of my finger and slung it at Ron; he responded by going to my Bible, found the "Guarantee" he had written to me, and ripped it in pieces. That devastated me beyond words. I ran out the door screaming about divorce, with Ron shouting behind me not to ever come back.

I pour my heart out to Jesus.

I drove off, crying so hard that before long I had to pull into a grocery store parking lot. I sat in the car weeping uncontrollably for a while, broken in a way I'd never felt before. Then I began to talk to Jesus, explaining through hot tears that I could not endure any more. I had tried my best, but I could not go back and keep my commitment to such an impossible relationship. Surely the Lord would not want us to stay in a marriage where we seemed to be sinning against one another continually. I had given up, I was no longer committed to Ron, and I just wanted out. I was sure Jesus loved me too much to ask me to stay in a relationship as painful as ours had become.

My mind was consumed with the resolve to get a divorce, even knowing that God hates it. But I hoped that Jesus would understand and forgive me; surely His compassion would prevail in how he would lead me now.

But as if there were two tracks in my mind, I was equally consumed with another thought: that if our marriage failed, the things I had been teaching others about God — particularly other women — would seem like a lie. I had been consistently outspoken about my belief in the power and willingness of God to help us through anything. Ending our marriage in divorce would make a lie out of that belief and destroy faith in Jesus in the eyes of those I had taught.

Deep in my heart I still knew that I was not wrong about Jesus and what He could do. If our marriage failed before an entire congregation, it would send the clear message that God's promises were no match for our weaknesses. I couldn't stand the idea that my failure would make God out to be a liar. The weight of carrying his Name rested upon me; I felt acutely aware of a responsibility for His reputation. If my life failed, God's Name would no doubt suffer in the eyes of those who witnessed it.

I began to be torn between the certainty that I could not endure our marriage another day, and the knowledge that if I left Ron I would betray Jesus. I loved Jesus enough that the thought of bringing reproach on His Word and Name was almost unbearable, yet I was overwhelmed with hurt and the need to protect my heart from any more. I wanted to quit, give up, get out and try to start another life. Neither option was tolerable; what on earth was I going to do?

Jesus pours his heart out to me.

I had blurted out to Jesus all of all of the things that I'd never allowed myself to admit or utter aloud in my commitment to be the a good little Christian woman, and the storm of emotions subsided enough that I finally became still, and sat there quietly in my car in the grocery store parking lot, my whole life in desperate limbo.

His gentle Spirit reminded me of the commitment Ron and I had made some time before to pray about all things, asking God when we needed wisdom[1]. If there ever was a time I needed God's guidance, it was now. I was

---

[1] Philippians 4:6 and James 1:5-6.

in a place my mother used to describe as "between a rock and a hard place." Having no idea what to do next, convinced that our marriage was hopeless, I finally said, *Jesus, what do you want me to do?*

His response was, *Toni, do you love me?*

I suddenly knew how Peter felt. *Yes, Lord, I do love you.*

Jesus then said gently and firmly, *Then go home to Ron.*

I didn't want to believe it; yet I knew it was the Lord because I had learned to recognize His "still small voice." Furthermore, the truths of John Chapter 14 were fresh on my mind from recent study, where Jesus said, "Whoever has my commands and obeys them, he is the one who loves me."[2] Now that I had His command, I knew that if I did not obey Jesus, if I did not go home to Ron, I would be guilty of not loving Jesus. No one else would have to know, but after this no matter what I did publicly as a Christian, in the secret place of my heart, where the Lord and I carried out our relationship, I would not be able to say to Him with a clear conscience, "Lord, I love you." I would have failed the test of true love for Him.

Yet as I thought about what it would mean to go back, I couldn't bear to be hurt anymore. Going back was the hardest thing in the world for me to do. I thought, *Lord, if you really have power to give us when we need it, then I have never needed it more than now.* I realized that this is where my faith in His power counted the most, in the critical crossroads of life. If it wasn't available to me in this moment of crisis, then it was useless. So I quietly begged the Holy Spirit to strengthen me to obey. Immediately, the Lord brought to my mind the words of Jesus: *I have come to give you abundant life.* Was it possible that God could give me abundant life if I went back to Ron, I wondered?

Then the Lord asked, *Do you believe I would ask you to do anything which would lead you away from abundant life?* As I let this question sink in, the words also came to me, *God is love, so whatever he gives you is an expression of that love.* I didn't realize it at the time, but I was experiencing what I later understood to be the ministry of the Holy Spirit, reminding me of the truth about Jesus and his promises.[3]

I had a decision to make, even more important than whether to go back to Ron. I had to decide what I believed about God's motives. I As far as I

---

2 John 14:21.
3 John 14:15-26.

was concerned, going back meant more emotional pain, endless frustration and struggle, and a humbling of myself to Ron I didn't think possible. Naturally, I blamed Ron for most of our problems, so nothing about that attracted me in the least. Yet God was clearly communicating to me that this was His will. He was asking me to believe that even in this command to go back He was motived by his goal to lead me to abundant life.

In a moment of stark clarity, I suddenly realized the issue wasn't Ron, the issue was Jesus, and it would always be Jesus. Would I let God be God, would I yield to his lordship over my life, a lordship I had willingly invited and whose benefits I daily proclaimed to others?

I concluded that if I really believed in God's love, I would have to trust His will, in spite of how things looked. It looked totally impossible to me, but I somehow knew that if I couldn't find my abundant life through obeying Jesus, I wasn't going to find it any other way. In this moment I had to choose between responding to my feelings or responding to my knowledge of God's love. Looking back upon a life of going with my feelings, I chose to go with God's love, and decided to go home to Ron.

It felt reckless and wild, like jumping off a cliff, yet the moment I made the decision, I was filled with His peace, the kind of profound peace that you know is a miracle, that comes from somewhere besides yourself. I wasn't happy; nor did I feel one ounce of love, trust or desire for Ron. Yet once I made my choice, strength and grace was given to me by the Holy Spirit to go home to Ron and entrust myself to God's care. I drove home not knowing what Ron would do or what I would do, not even sure what God would do, only knowing that somehow His love for me could not fail to carry me.

I arrived at home finding that Ron had gone through a similar time with the Lord. Neither of us was happy to see the other, but in mutual and cautious surrender, chastened and weary, we agreed to try one more time. At best we felt numb, yet compared to the anger and hatred we'd felt a short time before, even that numbness was a miracle, and we both knew it.

In our broken state we joined hands and acknowledged before God our inability to have a successful relationship. We confessed our sins against each another and Him, weeping together, joined in our sorrow and pain in a way we hadn't been united in months. We sought God's forgiveness and extended it to one another, sincerely, without any posturing, as the Holy Spirit invaded our broken place of submissiveness to give more grace.

A miracle happened as His peace settled in between us and seemed to flood our home; in fact it shrouded us like an iron wall for days, giving us time to heal from the wounds we had inflicted. Remembering the atmosphere of bitterness and anger that had prevailed so long, we were both stunned that our hearts could be so at rest. In fact, my heart was more than restful, it was healing with surprising speed, so that it began to be hard to remember how I had felt in those worst days. I kept thinking to myself, *Jesus, you're amazing!*

We didn't fall in love again right away, and we continued to struggle with being in "self-protect" mode. We had done a thorough job of destroying our relationship, of completely violating the faith we had placed in one another's love at the beginning of our relationship. Understand that all we had to start over with was our mutual love for and trust in Jesus and the desire to honor Him. As it turned out, that was enough.

The Holy Spirit stepped in as our teacher and counselor. In the ensuing weeks, He showed us that we had not made Jesus the center of our relationship. In spite of being filled with His Spirit, our marriage had not been truly founded upon Him but around our needs, personal goals and false expectations.

As I sat with the Lord in early morning prayer times, pondering in His presence, I began to see that I had come into marriage with very idealistic notions of what husbands and wives should be like, and that my concept of marriage was based upon unrealistic TV shows like "Father Knows Best" and "Leave It To Beaver." Since my parents divorced when I was six and I was brought up by my single mother and never saw a real marriage in action, I had false expectations of Ron, myself, and married life in general. On top of that, since Ron was an ordained pastor, I pretty much expected perfection from "the man of God." No man could have lived up to my expectations, so I had been living in a state of constant disappointment.

The Wonderful (Marriage) Counselor

The Lord told us he had allowed our old marriage to die completely and that He wanted to build us a brand new one, this time centered around the person of Jesus. Afraid of going back where we'd come from, we made a commitment to do something we'd never really done before, which was pray together daily, and seek God's personal counsel and teaching, together and individually, for how to live with and love each other, as if we didn't know everything we knew and had been teaching. Clearly, relying upon our knowledge to have a great marriage had utterly failed. Our complete bankruptcy of self-reliance turned out to be the best thing we had going, and the Lord stepped in strongly where we invited Him.

We learned firsthand what it really means to have the Holy Spirit as a counselor. As we turned to him in difficult situations in our relationship, He gave us advice. We discovered that the Lord is the ultimate expert on love, that He is very creative in weaving two very different souls and genders together, that He knows just what each of us needs in any particular moment. Looking back now it is clear that our faith that we can personally hear His voice was key in knowing Him as teacher and guide. It is what saved us from destroying our lives and helped us build a new one together.

Jesus did not deal with us in the same manner. As He taught us how to build a marriage just right for us, He did not always use identical lessons. We learned that the Lord's way of transforming a man into the image of His Son requires different dynamics than His way of transforming a woman. We are different in some very critical ways, in our needs, abilities, and weaknesses. I needed different lessons to grow into a godly wife than Ron needed to become a godly husband. We also learned that the roles of leader and helper were perfectly designed for our spiritual growth; in other words, they kept bringing us both back to our knees, to our dependence upon the Lord!

It was not easy building a new relationship; God was far more patient with us than we were with one another. We grew at different rates, so that at times it was hard to resist the temptation to point at one another and accuse the other of not being very spiritual or godly. Predictably, we both had a tendency to excuse our own shortcomings by blaming it on the other's weakness. We had destroyed our relationship trying to make each other be what we wanted. We had to learn to become lovers instead of manipulators.

The handwriting on the wall.

One day as I knelt in our bedroom praying, the Lord quietly said to me, *Read Ecclesiastes 5.* As I picked up my Bible and read, the verses about the importance of keeping your vows leaped off the page:

> *When you make a vow to God, do not delay in fulfilling it. He has no pleasure in fools; fulfill your vow. It is better not to vow than to make a*

vow and not fulfill it. Do not let your mouth lead you into sin. And do not protest to the temple messenger, "My vow was a mistake." Why should God be angry at what you say and destroy the work of your hands? (Ecclesiastes 5:4-6).

Vows. For the first time in months, I went to the framed vows I had made to Ron on our wedding day, hanging on my side of the bed, covered in dust. As I read them, the realization came that God had shown me through those vows his way to have a great marriage, and also what he expected of me as a wife. I had said them to Ron at the altar, then lost sight of them as I subtly traded in the goal of loving him for the goal of getting him to love me the way I needed.

A deep sorrow swept over me as I saw my vows in stark contrast to my behavior thus far in our marriage. Tears of repentance spilled down my cheeks. Especially convicting were the words, *"...with His help, I promise to begin each day...with new trust, new love, new hope, and new faith."* I had certainly not done that. Instead, I had saved up hurts and used them as an excuse to stop trusting Ron. I had slowly abandoned faith in my husband and our ability to make it work. "New hope" had given way to old fears. And I realized I had no idea how to start each day with new love.

And finally, the expression, *"I will strive to be the wife to you which God intended a woman to be to a man..."* quickened in my spirit, and the Lord said softly to me, *If you want to know what I intended all along for you to be as a wife, then search my Word. Only there will you find the truth.*

I took that on as a divine assignment, and over the next months I found and pondered with the Lord every scripture which describes the character and ways of the wife God designed. As I compared myself to them, I saw little resemblance. Even though I loved God and was a pastor's wife who prayed and read my Bible daily, I had actually been living more as a woman after the world's pattern than God's. The results of my search for God's design are what make up a large section of this book. Among other things, I have learned the full implications of marriage being a covenant that was created by, and lived in the presence of, God.

In spite of being an avid Bible student, the word "covenant" had barely registered in those early years. Shortly after we started our marriage anew the Lord brought a teacher into our lives who explained the Biblical concept of covenant and how it reveals the heart of God in relationship. At the time I made vows to Ron, I knew nothing about covenant, but as I see them today through new eyes of understanding they clearly contain all the elements necessary to live in a committed righteous relationship with another person.

I have come to the conclusion that righteousness only has meaning within the context of relationship to God and to other people. I was totally ignorant of the deep and lasting reality of covenant relationship, but because the One I asked for help in writing those vows is an expert on covenant, He led me to make the right promises. I can only marvel at His love and long-suffering with me, that He is faithful to not only to give me the words (the goals), but to teach me how to keep them through His daily counsel, then gracious enough to provide His own power to keep His counsel.

Our relationship today bears no resemblance to the former one. While our marriage is not perfect (nor are we), we have experienced firsthand the power and wisdom of God to help us build a strong and satisfying relationship. We are friends and lovers today. We still hurt each other and still let each other down; we are still learning how to love each other well. As a ministry family, we are constantly challenged to live what we teach and test what we believe against a continuing revelation of the person of God.

The greatest thing we learned in the process of watching God resurrect our marriage is that the strength of one's Christian life will come from hearing, and obeying, God's commands:

> Be careful to follow every command I am giving you today, so that you may live and increase and may enter and possess the land that the Lord promised on oath to your forefathers. Remember how the Lord your God led you all the way in the desert these forty years, to humble you and to test you in order to know what was in your heart, whether or not you would keep his commands. He humbled you, causing you to hunger and then feeding you with manna, which neither you nor your fathers had known, to teach you that man does not live on bread alone but on every word that comes from the mouth of the Lord. (Deuteronomy 8:1-3).

If I had not heard my Shepherd's voice that day in the parking lot, I would have surely left Ron. I would have repeated my pattern of abandoning relationships when they became too difficult.

If Ron had not heard the Lord, he would not have taken me back. Neither of us would be in ministry today, and it seems likely that I could have fallen away from Jesus altogether.

The life promised to a Christian only comes through knowing God, and knowing God only comes the way knowing any person must come: through interactive communication.

Therefore you will find a continual thread woven throughout this book about hearing God's voice. The Bible is an awesome revelation of God, but you need the Living Voice of the Living God to personally guide you each day. One of the things which distinguishes this book from so many excellent ones for women I have read is this concept: the key to God's abundant life is a relationship maintained through vital, daily communication with Him.

The Lord is our guarantee of an abundant life.

God has made Ron and I one, through teaching us to seek his counsel in prayer together, not just individually. The Holy Spirit helps us to continually renew our love, trust, and desire for one another. We have learned to forgive, sometimes several times a day. We find that when forgiveness is sincere and complete, the Lord heals us quickly of our emotional wounds. This healing and continual renewal of the heart is, in my opinion, the Lord's greatest miracle of daily life, offered to those who choose to obey his commands and do things His way.

What I have learned through the process of trying to become the woman and wife God designed is shared with you in this book. And because this teaching is based on God's Word — not my wisdom or theories — I know it will work for you, if you trust the Lord enough to obey him.

God's Word is true no matter what the circumstances, no matter who you are how or how different your story is from mine. His power is available to anyone who trusts Him and cries out for help. The Holy Spirit is entirely motivated to help you live up to those greatest commands to love God with all your might and to love your neighbor, especially your closest neighbor.

My Guarantee? It has been carefully pieced together and hangs in a special frame in our home. In its taped-together condition, it is much stronger now than it was before. It illustrates the truth that the "tape" that holds the guarantee of our relationship is the Holy Spirit, that spirit of Christ our Savior, without whose grace and power we cannot not keep our lives. It is a constant reminder that apart from total reliance upon the Lord, relationships are fragile and can be easily ripped apart; but that the relationship entrusted to God, and carried out <u>His</u> way, will be restored and made stronger than ever. Jesus Christ is my Guarantee.

Reflecting on Chapter 2

This chapter gives an intimate glimpse into the marriage of a committed Christian couple, giving insight as to why such marriages can fail, and reveals the key to making them strong.

❖ *Write down your concept of the ideal marriage and the ideal spouse. Where did you get these concepts from?*

❖ *Ask yourself, "Am I on a mission to fix my husband?"*

❖ *Start paying attention to your "self-talk" — your beliefs and thoughts about yourself, your mate, your marriage, or even God: (i.e., "You'll never change," or "If I do this, he will get angry.") Record your most persistent thoughts honestly.*

❖ *Read 2 Corinthians 10:4-5 in connection with how Jesus would have you deal with your self-talk.*

❖ *For each item on your Self-Talk List, ask the Lord to show you how to make your thoughts obedient to Him.*

❖ *Ask the Holy Spirit to reveal things hidden in your heart, which may not be thoughts with words, but which are still emotional vows you have made (i.e., "I'll never trust you again.") Talk with the Lord about what you discover, and journal these things.*

What Kind of Woman Will I Be?

I have a question for you: who and what have you allowed to shape you into the woman you are today? Who has influenced you the most? And are you satisfied with the woman you have become?

Most of us are a composite of many role models: our mothers, women we admire, friends we love. We have undoubtedly absorbed some of the daily manna we are fed by advertising media and the incessant images put before us. Our souls are also deeply shaped as a response to the men in our lives, whether fathers, brothers, friends or lovers. By this I mean we often look into their eyes to see who we are, or should be, and try to conform to that image. In the space of one day we can make the dizzying journey from wanting to please God, to wanting to please ourselves to wanting to please mother or boss or husband or daddy, and all of these even change with the seasons of our lives. It does not make for a restful existence.

I know, because I started out wanting to be like my mother. Then adolescence changed my mind, and I tried on what would make me popular in school. Then as I grew into young womanhood I wanted to be like Ayn Rand, then Eleanor Roosevelt, then Jackie O, and finally Martha Stewart overlaid on the good looks of Natalie Wood. But none of these fit, nor gave me joy. My target kept moving, and all my efforts to reinvent myself ended up with mixed results and failed to produce the kind of character and goodness and strength I longed to possess — until I made my target the Word of God. It was like coming home.

God designed a woman with a certain beauty, a manner of conduct, a character, a disposition and purpose, that is meant to bear His image, regardless of her age or marital status. Do you know what it is? Have you searched the Word of God to discover it? Or like me, have you allowed the world we live in to determine what kind of woman you will be? The pattern for womanhood revealed in the Bible is the opposite of that seen in the world, and often even dramatically different from what is seen in the church.

The woman God designed.

Scripture reveals God's blueprint for woman, designed to nurture those around her, equipped with the gift of drawing out the best in others through her loving care. He designed her for the incredible task of carrying and bringing forth children. She is intelligent, talented, and deeply creative. God created a woman to be emotionally strong and mentally wise, while remaining soft, tender and vulnerable. Possessing skills that are vital to leadership, yet not designed to carry the burden of leadership alone. We were made to seek beauty and to reveal it through trustfully receiving the leadership and protection of men: first fathers, then husbands, perhaps finally sons.

When a woman surrenders to and wholeheartedly embraces God's design, she enters a rest that is the strength of her soul and takes on a beauty that is deep and profound. She becomes satisfied, contented, and strong. As Proverbs boasts, she is clothed in strength and dignity, and she has joy.[1] But a world that has lost faith in its creator has taught women to abandon their God-given design and purpose.

The women's liberation movement of the 70's released a spirit of independence and discontent among women, a spirit still active today, showing itself in women who are determined to prove their equality and even superiority over men and throw off the restraints of patriarchal society. Women are being influenced through an absolute media onslaught to reject the pattern of femininity that God created. Women are trying to compete with men, be like men, and do jobs only fit for a man's strength and makeup. In fact, there is a move to make the sexes as alike as possible, devaluing the unique and profound differences which God built into his creation. Yet in spite of their success in throwing off the yokes of traditional womanhood, women in general remain a discontented, stressed and frustrated gender.

Most of the secular world blames God, the Bible and religion for the abuses often seen in a patriarchal society; however, what God created was in fact a wise "fathering" society designed to bless and protect women, not

---

[1] Proverbs 31:25.

subdue them, to offer their strength to women, not hurt them with it. Unfortunately what has evolved in many cultures has indeed become an overbearing, self-serving male domination that is too often cruel and abusive.

Yet this is not because of God, it is because of sin. The beauty of God's design for men and women has been perverted. The fact that even Christian men have misused the Word of God to dominate and oppress women does not make the Word of God wrong or rob His design of its power and wisdom. God is love. His will is the expression of that love, and his Word is the expression of his will — even the word that says, *"and the head of woman is man."²* Shall we turn away from the ways of God because man has perverted them with his selfish, fallen nature?

God's way is right, in spite of how man has perverted it.

It was never God's intention for woman to be dominated, abused, or treated like a piece of property that has no rights. Even Christian women are often afraid to embrace God's design for them, because they have bought the world's lie that the Biblical pattern of femininity is a complete denial of their rights. To the contrary, it was God's will from the beginning that woman be protected by men and treated with equal respect. Jesus carefully demonstrated this when he walked on the earth. He talked to, touched and ministered to women when his peers believed it would defile a teaching rabbi to do so; he rebuked men for putting their wives away in frivolous divorces; he rescued from judgment a woman about to be stoned for adultery; he gave a woman the honor of seeing him first following his resurrection.

Indisputably, men have treated women badly over the centuries in most of the cultures of the world. Men have dominated women in an ungodly manner, used them sexually, valued them no better than animals and denied them equal pay for equal work. Most commonly, they have neglected their charge to protect, guide and tenderly love women. No doubt woman's rebellion through the years has helped to fuel this vicious cycle. Both men and women have developed a pattern of relating to each other that has evolved out of their fallen nature and tends to be defensive and demanding rather than loving and giving.

---

² 1 Corinthians 11:3.

Insofar as men have abused their God-given leadership roles, one cannot blame women for wanting to be liberated. The women's liberation movement is a knee-jerk reaction to the very real suppression of their gender, but it is the devil's answer to the problem, not God's. In their quest for freedom and equal rights, women are going after the wrong enemy. Man is not the enemy. He is only a tragic tool in the hands of an evil, angry, defeated devil.

However, in their desire to break free of oppression, women have ceased to pay attention to God and have become suspicious and fearful of His ways. In their quest for freedom many women have become a sad perversion of the glorious creature God made them to be. I believe God weeps over us, and that he sent Jesus to save us in every way, including liberation from the oppression of men. God's pattern is our liberation, and we just don't know it. Salvation brings us into a relationship with God the Father through Jesus Christ, but in that salvation we are asked to lay down our worldly patterns and adopt the patterns that fit us for the kingdom of God. This is hard to do for a woman who fears that doing so will somehow narrow her existence and confine her to a lesser experience of life. I've discovered something about salvation that exposes what a lie this fear really is.

Yasha: to be open, wide and free.

The Old Testament Hebrew word translated as "save" is *yeshua*, from which we get the name Joshua, or Jesus, "one who saves." But the root word from which *yeshua* derives is *yasha*, loaded with the concept of being *"open, wide and free."* In other words, to be saved is to be released into freedom. The word *yeshua* to the Hebrew carried the concept of a life that is liberated and expansive, without hindrance, oppression or limit. This is validated in the thinking of the Apostle Paul, Hebrew of Hebrews, who penned the words, "It is for freedom that Christ has set us free.[3] Those who follow God wholeheartedly are actually the only truly liberated people on earth. True liberty only comes when one has both the wisdom and the power to be all one was created to be. Jesus, *Yeshua*, promises this kind of salvation to those who live by faith in his word and thereby walk in the Father's ways.

Women struggling with the men in their lives, are often in actuality wrestling with God. They are fearful of really surrendering to His Word and

---

[3] Galatians 5:1.

believing in his goodness; and ultimately live lives of quiet, life-robbing rebellion. In these pages I hope to help the reader stop struggling against God and surrender to Him and His ways completely. I have wrestled with God and when he prevailed, I won. And the prize was the life I always wanted, and a shortcut to the abundant life Jesus promised.

Our greatest barrier is the mind. We must indeed be renewed in our minds in order to embrace God's ways. God's kingdom is powerful, but one cannot enter and enjoy it without fully resting in its truths, having faith in their goodness. We must let God shake us loose from society's concepts of how things should be and let Him put new ones in their place. Trying to live God's promised life while living by the world's truths is like trying to travel America by using a map of Australia: you just can't get there from here. We need orientation, and it needs to begin at the beginning: with our creation.

God's glory and ours, is revealed in relationship.

The Bible says that God's purpose for creating woman was to remove man's aloneness, so he could express his created glory in relationship to her. The woman likewise was created to express her glory through covenant union with a man. While each gender is whole in themselves, man and woman together reveal the image of God in a way that is not seen in one gender alone. This is because God's glory is revealed in relationship. Everything that is most glorious about God is experienced and manifested in relating to who he is as a living person.

For instance, the Bible says that God is love, yet without someone for him to express his love to, this character trait would simply be abstract theory. I also believe this is why God is not one, but three. God's goodness is expressed in how he relates to the Son, the Holy Spirit and his creation. As made in the image of God, we display the fullness of who he is as we relate to another person in complete intimacy and faithfulness.

This is not to say that a single person is incomplete in himself or herself; God the Father is not incomplete. Yet His glory — by which I mean the fullest expression of who he is — can only be revealed in relating to his creation. So while a single person is not incomplete, their potential to express the best of who they are is also realized in relating to others. Character is revealed in us and even formed on the fly as we are tested by our responses to others. As a dear friend of mine likes to say, "The test of what's really in you is what comes out when you're mashed." Because marriage usually provides the ultimate in intensity and intimacy, it mashes us better than any other relationship.

In this context we can see that even apart from marriage, the truth remains that woman was made for man.[4] We were created as God's gift to men. The fact is that man cannot have all his glory revealed apart from being around us. Of course, we don't have to live our lives as a gift to our husbands, brothers and sons; we were created, as men, with complete freedom of will. But every woman must answer the question for herself: what kind of woman will I be?

What kind of woman will you be?

Will we be women who try to pattern ourselves after the world and then expect to magically obtain the life God promises? The wisdom of the world is not the wisdom of God; in fact, by comparison, the wisdom of the world is foolish. We have a wisdom available to us that will build us a great life, so let us choose that wisdom, so we will not be like the woman who unwittingly ruins her own life:

> Every wise woman builds her house, but the foolish one tears it down with her own hands. (Proverbs 14:1)

The Bible often uses the word "house" as a metaphor for "life." This symbolism makes the meaning of Proverbs 14:1 even clearer: *Every wise woman builds her life, but the foolish one tears it down.* Every person has the freedom to tear apart their own life or to cooperate with the Lord in building it. A woman must accept responsibility for the quality of her inward life with God. Where a child of God is concerned, abundant life is a matter of choice, not chance.

For many years I lived the life of a victim. I believed that what was wrong with my life was mostly everyone else's fault, and that if they would change, I could finally be happy or reach my goals. The day I realized my own choices and weak character were responsible for the quality of my life, I threw my hands up and surrendered to God. It was a tough moment when the Lord shined his light of truth in my heart, allowing me to see that I was

---

[4] 1 Corinthians 11:7-9.

the problem, and not other people. But without hesitation I would say that was the greatest decision of my life. I remember it in great detail and will treasure it forever, because it was the moment God set me free and rescued me from myself.

God's Wisdom is the best architect of a truly abundant life.

Unless we allow God to build our life his way, that life will fall way short of its potential.[5] If we insist on designing our own life, we end up with a mix of our wisdom and His, and then wonder why our house does not stand against the storms of life, why it does not bear the marks of blessing, contentment and abundance.

The voice of Wisdom speaks to us from Proverbs as the One who has always been at God's side and through whom all His work is accomplished.[6] This is the Spirit of Christ, the Wonderful Counselor, teacher and guide that Jesus promised would come to live with us on earth when he returned to his father's side in heaven.[7] Proverbs 9:1 implies that the Spirit of Wisdom has a seven-fold way to build life in us when it says, *Wisdom has built her house; she has hewn out its seven pillars*.

"Hew" means to carve out a material, shaping it to specific use. Your personality, your circumstances, strengths and weaknesses are completely unique. In the next seven chapters of this book I will share with you what I believe are the pillars that will support the life God wants to build in us. These pillars are actually attitudes and motives of the heart; God has to change these in order to change you.

Keep in mind that this is the work of a whole season of study and interaction with God. You cannot instantly absorb these teachings. Take time to study the accompanying scriptures and allow the Holy Spirit to teach you. Because each life is unique, we must learn to follow the Holy Spirit in His specific guidance for us, rather than imitate other people in their walk with God.

Part of the good news of the gospel is that the strength of your life depends only upon you and the Lord. Your ability to have a powerful and satisfying existence does not depend upon the other people in your life, but

---

[5] Psalm 127:1.

[6] This voice is identified in Proverbs Chapter 8.

[7] John 14:16-17; John 16:7.

upon how you respond to God. Jesus is always the issue, not other people. The center of our universe is His faithfulness, His goodness, His power and His love. Our world must revolve around these things, not the weaknesses of others.

Building your life begins with the choices you make as to what kind of woman you want to be. The choice is always up to you. You may not be free at this point in your life to change any of your circumstances or the other people in your life, but you are free every moment of your life to choose what kind of woman you will be. My prayer is that you will use your freedom to fully embrace God's will for you and take delight in his design.

Reflecting on Chapter 3

This chapter asks you to consider how you have become the woman you are, and how your choices have resulted in the life you have built for yourself.

❖ *What or who do you think has motivated you as a woman and a wife? (i.e., a need for security, success, to be like Mom, etc.) Think and pray, asking the Lord to reveal the true influences on your heart. Journal the things that come to you.*

❖ *Are you satisfied with the woman you have become? If not, what do you want to change?*

❖ *Read Romans 14:17. What does this say about the quality of life God wants to give you?*

❖ *Ask the Lord to show you any attitudes and motivations that are unwise, and the connection between these things and the state of your "house" today. Ask him to help you let go of these and prepare you for change.*

Chapter 4

I Will Be Rooted in the Love of God

I did not grow up knowing God. I was raised by a woman who was determined to do it her way and taught me to do the same. I was 29 years old before I got tired of doing it my way. Having set out to have a great life and be a great person, I had failed miserably at both. I can't honestly say I had any real consciousness that I was a sinner, but after an endless series of failures I came to realize I needed a savior, someone to rescue me from myself. Up to that point I had carefully protected myself from religious people, until I became so broken that I actually let someone talk to me about God.

I was lonely, and had taken a new job as a legal secretary. The one person who befriended me there was deeply religious. I liked her, and she made me laugh, so I tolerated her occasional mention of Jesus. What I heard was the usual: "Jesus loves you." Well-meant, but I didn't know what to do with that, honestly. I had no clue as to how to relate to this invisible God, much less figure out how to feel his love. But I knew needed that love desperately, and someone bigger and wiser than I to guide me. My life was a shambles from all of my misguided efforts to find love and happiness. My marriage had failed, my children were hurting, and I was deeply hungry in a place I couldn't even identify.

One day, at the end of my rope, depressed, broken down and weeping uncontrollably, I shook my fist at heaven and said, *"God, if you're really real, then you can make me feel this love."* Anti-religious as I was, I refused to work up some sort of belief about it in my mind. If God was real, surely he had the power to make his love known to me without me talking myself into it.

This was on a Saturday. I agreed to go to church with my friend the next day, another miracle because I hated the idea of becoming religious. Religious people didn't have any fun, and I truly suspected that God, if he existed, would ruin mine. However, I had come to the smashing realization that I wasn't having any anyway. Still, I was extremely guarded about getting sucked into that whole religious thing, so I made my friend sit with me on the back row so I could escape at the first sign that I might be taken captive.

The sermon was forgettable, the people pleasant. After having cried through most of the past 24 hours, I was emotionally exhausted. My expectations were somewhere between none and low. When the service was nearly over, I was standing with the crowd while they sang the invitation hymn, when something extraordinary happened. In that moment, an incredible "wave" of love washed over me. It was the most real and overwhelming sensation of being loved I had ever known. That it came like a wave was intensely personal, for I had grown up on the Texas Gulf Coast, where I would often lie at the water's edge and let the waves flow up over me. I loved the power of the waves and the fact that they were so "unstoppable."

This amazing wave of love felt just like that, and I knew it was from God. It is as vivid to me today as when it happened over 25 years ago. This invisible God answered my prayer so powerfully and personally that I knew in that moment that Jesus lives and does love me with all of his heart, so I gave him mine. He won me, bowled me over, amazed me, and joy overflowed. All my excuses and history and resistance lay in the dust of being swept up by this big-hearted God who wanted me.

In the days and weeks that followed, God shaped a place in my heart for himself, and from that dwelling place he has loved me faithfully from that day to this. In response to his great love I have grown to love him in return, and through this exchange of love my life and character have been changed. Though I would never claim to have found perfection, I have found wholeness, contentment, and the power to have that great life I so longed for, and my joy is to share this awesome truth with others.

In my work, first in the pastorate with my husband and now traveling across the U.S. and abroad as an ordained minister of the gospel, I have met too many Christians who have that religious existence I was so terrified of, who do not enjoy God and his love. There are multitudes of frustrated Christians who struggle to keep believing in God and wonder about this abundant life that Jesus promised. So many confess they don't really know God, don't hear his voice, don't feel his love. One of the primary goals of our ministry[1] is to change that, and to help people change the context of their relationship with God from one of religion to relationship, from legalism to love. The expert on this journey is the Apostle Paul, who penned the most compelling words regarding the foundation of our life with God:

> *And I pray that you, being rooted and established in love, may have power, together with all the saints, to grasp how wide and long and high and deep is the love of Christ, and to know this love that surpasses knowledge - that you may be filled to the measure of all the fulness of God. [Ephesians 3:17-19]*

I was fortunate enough to have my life with God quickly rooted in His love. But in our religion-saturated society, that is not always the case. Paul makes the vital but often overlooked connection between *being filled to the measure of all the fulness of God*, and being established in the full experience of God's love.

Our life is to be rooted in the love of God.

Our life with God exists because of his love, which is so great that the Bible claims it was *"because of and in order to satisfy the great and wonderful and intense love with which He loved us"* that God sent his son.[2] Paul prayed for all of us to be rooted in this love. Roots are the means through which the living plant is fed, the part that seeks nutrients to make it strong and vigorous. Their function speaks to us of hunger. Not coincidentally, the Bible says that what a man hungers for is unfailing love.[3]

This was certainly my experience. When I found God I had been searching for this love in all the wrong places. Because my introduction to Jesus came through an overwhelming experience of his love, the roots of my relationship to him were quickly formed there. The roots of a tree actually

---

[1] Shammah Ministries. The name comes from the last verse of Ezekiel, and is one of the names of God: Jehovah Shammah means "the Lord is Present."

[2] Ephesians 2:4, Amplified.

[3] Proverbs 19:22, NIV.

grow through the very act of going forth in search of nutrition. Likewise, my life with God has been a continual exploration of the depths of his love. I have put a continual demand on his love, and he has always poured it out upon me.

The church has often made the point that feelings cannot be trusted, and implied that they are somehow the opposite of faith. There is certainly a danger of following feelings rather than the Spirit, but it is wrong to classify all feelings as of the flesh. Your human spirit, that part of you where God lives and which is united to him, is quite capable of joy and sorrow and all other emotions. And some feelings are actually coming from the Holy Spirit himself, who lives within you. A Christian does not mature by denying all feeling, but by learning to discern where his feelings arise from.

What I experienced was a wave of love from the Holy Spirit, making me aware of the Father's mighty love for me. While it is true that God's love is a choice, an expression of his character and nature, do not make the mistake of thinking that His love must remain in the realm of a theological fact, that God is too distant to personally express that passion for you in a way that you can feel, in your spirit. When God sent his love to me, it was so real that my whole being experienced it as the feeling of being loved.

I understood nothing that day, and I am grateful I had not been indoctrinated with the false truth that I cannot trust feelings when it comes to God; though I feel safe in saying that would have fallen away with all my other resistance to God, so strong was the sensation. Still, though you should be open to feeling the emotions of God for you, be aware from the start that this is not something you can or should make happen. God never meant for you to just talk yourself into believing in his love by faith, and keep talking yourself into it every day. It's not your job to make yourself feel God's love; and like every other aspect of relationship with God, you can't do it without his help.

We need the power of God to know this love.

We need the power of God to even experience this love, as Paul made clear in his prayer:

> *...I pray that you, being rooted and established in love, may have power, together with all the saints, to grasp how wide and long and high and deep is the love of Christ, and to know this love that surpasses*

knowledge - that you may be filled to the measure of all the fullness of God.

Without the Holy Spirit's power we cannot even begin to fathom the depths of Christ's love. Romans 5:5 says it is the Holy Spirit's job to pour out God's love into our hearts. I now know he was the one who came to me in church that day in answer to my prayer, using his power to reveal God's love to me. I later learned that I needed that power every day to continue to walk with God and enjoy his love, to enjoy what Paul described as being *filled with all the fulness of God.*

The first few years I tried to live for Jesus simply in my own power, though I did not realize it. As time marched by and the initial romance of being a new Christian faded, I became increasingly aware that in spite of being saved, I was unable to love God with all my heart — the most basic, crucial requirement of a child of God — and unable to love others like He wanted. In spite of my earnest dedication to study, prayer and church activity, my Christian life was somewhat shallow.

I imitated and acted like Christ, but only with great self-effort, and I certainly was not being transformed into His image. I began to struggle with feeling like a hypocrite, a pretender and a failure. Once in a while if I stood back from myself and looked, I realized with alarm that I was dangerously close to becoming one of those malcontented religious persons I had once determined never to be. Eventually prayer became a chore, God seemed far off and church was boring. Not good for a pastor's wife, who has to be in church all the time! I occasionally caught myself thinking, *"Is this all there is?"* Every time I did read my Bible it led me to believe that is not how it was supposed to be.

One day in prayer I abandoned all pretense of being the dutiful child of God, voiced my honest feelings, and insisted He show me what was missing. The very next morning I found that someone — to this day I still do not know who — had left a book on my coffee table, entitled <u>Nine O'Clock In the Morning</u>. Written by Reverend Dennis Bennett, an Episcopal priest, it was his story of being a man of God who had gone through the same crisis of spiritual lifelessness I was experiencing and discovered the missing piece. That missing piece was another baptism Jesus had instructed his disciples about, not in water, but with the Spirit.

I learned that with salvation I had been marked by the Holy Spirit, guaranteeing that I belonged to God, but it was not the same as being full of him. Without hesitation I asked Jesus for this baptism, and received it. I am happy to say over 25 years later that this baptism has brought me into that experience of God I longed for, and without which I doubt I would be even walking with God today. I don't fully understand the Holy Spirit, but I enjoy him, and he has transformed my Christian life.

The Holy Spirit is the one who brought me the power that Paul prayed for, to know the width and depth and height and length of the Lord's love for me. He is the one who not only first established me in the love of God, but from that day until now, my knowledge of God's love grows deeper day by day as he shares his thoughts, guides, comforts and teaches me. Jesus promised that very thing in John 14:26:

> But the Counsellor, the Holy Spirit, whom the Father will send in my name, will teach you all things and will remind you of everything I have said to you.

Jesus also required the Holy Spirit when He lived on earth.

On earth Jesus was as human as you or I, and clearly stated that everything He did was done not in his own power, but through the power of the Holy Spirit. He taught His disciples to receive the gift of the Holy Spirit from the Father and then learn to be continually filled with this same Spirit. Each of the gospels records the words of John the Baptist:

> I baptize you with water for repentance. But after me will come one who is more powerful than I, whose sandals I am not fit to carry. He will baptize you with the Holy Spirit and with fire. (Matthew. 3:11)[4]

Jesus, Paul, and John the Baptist all clearly stated that the baptism of the Spirit is not the same as water baptism. Water baptism is a sacrament which accompanies repentance on the part of the believer. It is the public, symbolic death and resurrection of a new believer, in which he enters by faith into the experience of Jesus' death in his place. The ceremony of baptism was, for the people of Jesus' day, infused with symbolism that harkened back to the covenant ceremonies of ancient Bible times in which

---

[4] Also in Mark 1:8, Luke 3:16, and John 1:33.

one person declared himself dead to his old life in order to enter a new life united with the new covenant partner.

The baptism with the Holy Spirit is distinctly different from water baptism, and both are equally important for one who joins his life to Jesus Christ. As John the Baptist said, it is Jesus the Son who baptizes a believer with the Spirit. However, this baptism is received by faith just like salvation.[5]

This baptism has been too much misunderstood and too much neglected. The spiritual rebirth of salvation is just that: God gives you a brand new human spirit, by which you are able to be joined to him who is spirit. Your new spirit is the vessel that is able to join to and carry His Presence. But what you fill that new spirit with is your choice, now and for every day of your Christian life. Having your human spirit filled with the Spirit of Christ is absolutely necessary if a Christian wants to experience the full life, love and power of God.

Your "lamp" requires the "oil" of the Holy Spirit.

As Jesus walked the earth in human form, he was filled with the Holy Spirit, consistently symbolized in scripture as fire, oil and light.[6] This is why Jesus told his disciples that while he was on the earth, he was the light of the world[7] — carrying in his human vessel the light and fire of the Holy Spirit. Preparing to return to heaven, he told his disciples, *"You are now the light (lamp) of the world."*[8] In other words, you will now be the lamp of the Lord, the vessels that carry the light and fire of God in this earth. What I learned from <u>Nine O'Clock In the Morning</u> is that my new birth at salvation had created a new vessel — a new lamp — but I had no oil. In fact, Proverbs 31:18 refers to this same imagery when it says of the wise and godly woman, *her lamp does not go out at night.*

Hebrew lamps operated on oil and burned with a wick. To speak of one's lamp being snuffed out in their culture was to imply a state of foolishness, poverty, dire straights, or death. A wise Hebrew always had enough oil to burn his lamp throughout the pitch black desert nights. In Matthew 25:1,

---

[5] Galatians 3:2.

[6] Luke 4:1.

[7] John 9:5.

[8] Matthew 5:14.

Jesus refers to a lamp in the parable of the wise and foolish virgins, saying that the wise virgins kept their lamps burning during their wait for the bridegroom, always having plenty of oil on hand. Furthermore, the parable teaches that every woman is responsible to keep oil in her own lamp rather than depend upon someone else's supply.

Again, as he prepared to go to the cross, Jesus told his disciples that when he returned to the Father, the Holy Spirit would come take his place on earth as their Counselor and Teacher, to live with them and be in them, so they would have the life and spirit of both Jesus and the Father in them.[9] Before the eyes of His water-baptized disciples Jesus was crucified, buried and resurrected, creating what He called "the new covenant in my blood." The first thing he did after being reunited with his disciples was to mark them with the Holy Spirit, a "spiritual seal" [10] as commonly given to those who entered into covenant:

> And...he breathed on them and said, "Receive the Holy Spirit. (John 20:22).

But even though the disciples had been "marked" with the Holy Spirit, Jesus told them there would be more:

> Do not leave Jerusalem, but wait for the gift my Father promised, which you have heard me speak about. For John baptized with water, but in a few days you will be baptized with the Holy Spirit. (Acts 1:4-5)

Awhile after this announcement came the day when Jesus' disciples were gathered in one place praying, and a mighty wind came in the room. "Tongues of fire" appeared to rest upon each of them and *all of them were filled with the Holy Spirit and began to speak in other tongues as the Spirit enabled them.*[11] Thus the promised gift had come from the Father in heaven. Those who received it had the ability to speak in a tongue unknown to them, fulfilling Jesus' prediction that His followers would speak in other tongues.[12]

---

[9] John 14:16-17; 16:7-15.

[10] Ephesians 1:13-14

[11] Acts 2:4.

[12] Mark 16:15-18.

Both baptisms are vital in the life of a believer.

The book of Acts reveals that all of Jesus' followers who were spreading His gospel and winning souls to His kingdom believed that every Christian needed this baptism in addition to water baptism. It records numerous incidents showing that the apostles were careful to see to it that new believers were baptized both in water <u>and</u> in the Holy Spirit.[13]

It is clear that they knew what all Christians must learn: if Jesus needed to be filled with the Holy Spirit for his life on this earth, how much more do we! Incredibly this gift from God has been rejected by millions of Christians because of fear and distrust over issues like tongues. The fear of the Holy Spirit has been brought into the Body of Christ by God's enemy, the devil.

Satan — the thief of God's life in you — wants to keep Christians ignorant of the baptism in the Spirit because he fears it more than anything. He knows the Holy Spirit is the source of all life and joy in a child of God, the means by which we will actually become like Jesus in character and power, which will greatly multiply God's threat to Satan's dark kingdom. If Satan can keep the child of God afraid of the Holy Spirit or suspicious of his workings, he will succeed in keeping him in a dry, powerless place, frustrated and unsatisfied in knowing God.

In frightening people away from the baptism of the Holy Spirit, the devil succeeds in his goal to keep God's children from experiencing the immeasurable dimensions of God's love, a love meant to be the very foundation of our lives. We cannot be established or built up in God's love apart from the Holy Spirit filling up our being and communicating it to us every day. Bored, powerless Christians easily fall away from and lose their taste for God, or lose all faith in His promised life.

I did not speak in tongues at first, though I had no fear of this gift because I knew that God is good, and He gives only good things. I was not determined to speak in other tongues, but I was open to it. In fact, when I was baptized in the Holy Spirit, the first evidence of it was that I felt the most profound love and desire for God I had ever known. I had a new passion for his Word; I read it with more insight, and it was much more alive. All this is no surprise in light of the fact that the Holy Spirit is the author of the scriptures and loves the Father and Son passionately!

---

[13] See Appendix A for a complete list of scriptures on this topic.

A couple of weeks later the ability to speak in an unknown tongue did bubble up to the surface, at a time when I wasn't even thinking about it. It was Thanksgiving Day, we had a house full of relatives, and the usual cooking, football and board games were under way. In the middle of all this, I felt the Holy Spirit drawing me to come away with him briefly. I slipped into my bedroom, knelt down by the bed and said, *"What is it, Lord?"* In that moment my throat seemed to swell and tingle a bit; I opened my mouth to speak and out came a language I did not understand, lovely and mysterious.

Though I had no idea what the words meant, I had no doubt I was praising God, because my spirit was full of joyful thoughts of him. From that time on I have often prayed in an unknown language, as the Holy Spirit has led me, which he has never done without my permission. It is a gift clearly validated and experienced by the early church, and nowhere in scripture does it say that this baptism and its gifts would only be needed for a temporary time. Neither Jesus nor any other voice in the Bible ever taught or even hinted at such a thing. Later in this book you will learn more about the purpose of a spiritual prayer language.

In the part of the Body that has always embraced speaking in tongues, some insist that if a person does not pray in an unknown tongue he is not and has never yet been filled with the Spirit, as if this is the only proof. I personally do not believe this. I think this gift, like all gifts of the Spirit, is part of the whole package, a package which is a Person, and whether a gift is ever released or quickened in a believer is a personal matter between that individual and God. In fact, I have met so-called "Spirit-filled" people who demonstrate little of God's character, but who pray in tongues all the time. This teaches us that a person can have the Spirit, learn to exercise his gifts, yet still not be surrendered to and controlled by the Him. There are also those who are reluctant to surrender their tongues to the Lord like this (and he does not force it upon them), yet the fruit of their lives and their passion for God clearly shows they are filled with and led by the Spirit.

Keep yourself in God's love.

Jude warns us in his New Testament letter that in our time there would be scoffers to discourage us from receiving all that the Lord would give us in the Holy Spirit:

> But, dear friends, remember what the apostles of our Lord Jesus Christ foretold. They said to you, "In the last times there will be scoffers who will follow their own ungodly desires." These are the men who divide you, who follow mere natural instincts and do not have the Spirit. But you, dear friends, build yourselves up in your most holy faith and pray in the Holy Spirit. Keep yourselves in God's love as you wait for the mercy of our Lord Jesus Christ to bring you to eternal life. (Jude 17-21).

His advice on how to hold onto your faith? Pray in the Holy Spirit, because this is what will actually build you up spiritually. Typically the people who do scoff at the idea of being filled with the Spirit's power are the ones who struggle in their knowledge of God, and who rarely live their lives at rest in His love.

By the way, the expression "pray in the Holy Spirit" does not necessarily mean praying in an unknown tongue. This description would be accurately applied to any words you speak in any language, known or unknown, that are received through the Holy Spirit, inspired by Him, as opposed to what you might think of to say.

The life God promises requires the Holy Spirit's power.

We need the Spirit continually filling and empowering us to keep us in God's love and build up our faith in his power and presence. Over the years I have watched the power of the Holy Spirit ebb and flow within me. At low tide my love for God grows weak, along with my will and desire to obey God. When I am full of the Holy Spirit, then I am also full of love for God, and joy in his presence, and the wrestling of whether to trust or obey Him is stilled. I now ask the Lord to fill me new each morning. I have come to know the Holy Spirit as my most trusted friend and counselor.

Now this Jesus whom we so love and trust — if he wants to baptize us in the Holy Spirit, shall we spurn it? Shall we fear this gift from our heavenly Father, given at the precious cost of the blood of Jesus? No! It is foolish to fear something which Jesus called a stream of living water that would satisfy the thirsty soul:

> On the last and greatest day of the Feast, Jesus stood and said in a loud voice, "If anyone is thirsty, let him come to me and drink. Whoever believes in me, as the Scripture has said, streams of living water will flow

from within him." By this he meant the Spirit, whom those who believed
in him were later to receive. Up to that time the Spirit had not been given,
since Jesus had not yet been glorified. (John 7:37-39).

I urge you to embrace this gift of the Spirit, this baptism, without fear, or any expectation other than what the Bible reveals: the power to love God and know his love, to experience the heart and mind of Christ, the power to do what Jesus did, and more. If you desire this gift simply go to Jesus and ask Him for it.

As we embark on the journey of becoming the woman God designed, let us begin answering the question, *"What kind of woman will I be?"* with this answer:

I will be a woman whose life is rooted and established in the love of God. I will be a woman who is filled with the Holy Spirit each new day, who has the fountain and very source of God's life living within her.

Reflecting on Chapter 4

This chapter taught that the foundation of our life in Christ is meant to be God's immeasurable and unfailing love, and revealed the Holy Spirit's role in establishing us in this love.

❖ *Read Ephesians 3:17-19 again, and ponder: is your relationship to God rooted in His love? If not, ask the Holy Spirit to help you discover what your heart is rooted in as a basis for coming to and knowing God. The answers might be things like fear of going to hell, the desire to be a good person, neediness, spiritual ambition, or perfectionism.*

❖ *Study Appendix A. Look up and read all scriptures not directly quoted.*

❖ *If you have not experienced this baptism, ask Jesus for it.*

I Will Live By Faith

One concept is abundantly clear in the Bible: God is not just interested in saving us from hell and taking us to heaven; His plan has always been to dwell with us, to share life. The Bible says we are to live and move and have our being in God, and that he wants to live and move and have his being in us. What a miracle it is that the Creator of the Universe, who could live anywhere he wants, has chosen to dwell within the hearts of His creation!

That God has always intended to live as close to us as possible is made clear from the beginning in Genesis and never changes throughout the Bible. God put Adam in a delightful garden and came to walk with him each day. When God brought the descendants of Abraham out from Egypt, his first act after getting them safely away from Pharaoh's army was to have Moses build a tabernacle for him so that he could dwell in the midst of his people.[1] When God was forced to send the people into exile because they sinned against Him and the land in violating the Sabbath, he had Jeremiah tell the people that he would bring them back to himself under a new covenant, that would not fail, in which each person would be able to personally know and be taught by the Lord.[2]

When Jesus instructed his disciples about the Holy Spirit he said that He would be in them, "to live with you forever."[3] Perhaps Moses summed it up the best, when he said, *"Lord, through all the generations you have been our home."* (Psalm 90:1, New Living Testament.)

---

[1] Exodus 25:8.

[2] Jeremiah 31:31-34 and Hebrews 8:8-12.

[3] John 14:16-17.

Have you ever wondered why it is that even though Jesus lives in the hearts of believers, some people seem to remain largely unchanged? (Of course, you've surely never wondered this about yourself, only about all those other Christians.) The reason is this: a person may be filled with the Holy Spirit, yet not allow Him to really live (express Himself) through them. Having the mark of the Holy Spirit is not the same as having the Holy Spirit living, acting and teaching from within your soul. This only happens when one begins to respond to His indwelling presence by faith; indeed, this is what faith is for. Amazing as it seems, we can ignore this God who lives in us, because he is so gentle, humble and meek. God complained about our tendency to ignore the gentle Spirit.

You always ignore the Holy Spirit.

All day long I have held out my hands to an obstinate people, who walk in ways not good, pursuing their own imaginations - a people who continually provoke me to my very face... (Isaiah 65:2-3).

This verse underscores two realities: number one, God is with us all day long. Number two, we ignore God's presence in order to walk in our own ways and pursue our own imaginations rather than live by faith that we are in his presence and should respond accordingly. Because of this, even though God has kept his promise through Jesus Christ to live in us in order to personally guide and teach us — we, by ignoring this great gift, scorn it. Why do we do this?

Perhaps because we still want to do it our way, rather than surrender to God. We know in our hearts that when God teaches, he expects an obedient response, otherwise we are guilty of real sin, of rebellion. In fact, the Hebrew word for "hear" (as in "Hear, O Israel") literally means to hear responsively, with the intent to obey.

Just before his crucifixion Jesus took his disciples aside and taught them specifically about the relationship they were have to the Holy Spirit. Up to this time he had told his disciples, *"Follow me."* When it was time to return to his Father in heaven he told them to follow the Holy Spirit. We are not supposed to be following rules, we are to follow a Person, and that person is Jesus Christ, whose Spirit now lives in us.

Following rules lets us feel pride when we do it right, but they are easy to ignore because they are not in our face, don't force themselves upon us, and don't meddle in our lives as they sit in a book somewhere.

But following a person is a very different proposition, because the person, in this case God, just might want us to do something we don't want to do, and a person must be responded to. We can ignore a rule or find a way around it that soothes the conscience without making us change, but it is much harder to ignore a person. So, if we ignore the person in the first place, we never have to face the question of responding obediently.

I need (the Spirit of) God's grace to help me.

The bad news is that God's Word demands that we live in a way we cannot possibly carry out on our own. The good news is that God gives us the power we need. His strength carries us where we cannot go alone. Some people have defined grace simply as "God's unmerited favor," but it is so much more than that. The Bible clearly reveals grace as God's ability in us to do what we cannot. God's grace — his ability — is there to help us when we have not the power to carry out his will. The Holy Spirit is the very Spirit of Grace.

The word which is translated "grace" in our Bibles is the Greek word *charis*, the same word translated as the gifts and anointing the Holy Spirit gave Jesus and the apostles. We tend to think of anointing or spiritual gifts in connection with dramatic abilities for public ministry. But God's grace is an inward supply of his strength and ability to carry out all the decisions we are asked make in order to please him and carry out his will. We need God's grace so much that the Apostle Paul began and ended each of his letters with a prayer for the reader to receive it!

If you choose to obey God wholeheartedly, you will quickly discover two things: how desperately you need Jesus every step of the way, and how quickly He responds to help you when you set your heart upon obedience. When God comes and asks something hard of us — to really forgive that husband three times in one day for the same hurtful offense — we instinctively react, *I can't Lord; you're asking too much*. We may even convince ourselves that God surely doesn't expect us to forgive as long as it seems like someone is getting away with what they did wrong. But this is not what God says in His Word. What has God said about things we think are too difficult to carry out? His grace — his ability residing in us through the Holy Spirit — is sufficient, is enough for us.[4]

Jesus himself relied totally upon the Father's grace to say and do what he did on earth. The gospel of John reveals this most clearly, where numerous times Jesus is quoted as saying something like:

> *"I tell you the truth, the Son can do nothing by himself; he can do only what he sees his Father doing, because whatever the Father does the Son also does." (John 5:19)*

How incredible it is for the Son of God to say, *"The Son can do nothing by himself"*! He even said in John 8:28 that the words he uttered were not merely his own: "I…speak just what the Father has taught me." We have to remember that on earth, Jesus was as human as we are; he had to be in order to experience the full temptations of man and be the perfect sacrifice. The scripture says Jesus was full of the Holy Spirit. Beyond the power to do miracles, the secret to Jesus' righteous and powerful life on earth was not his own goodness, but his choice to live a life of total dependence upon the Spirit, who revealed to Jesus what the Father was saying and doing.

The biggest hindrance to sharing the life and power of God is self-reliance. This is why self-denial is a vital ingredient in being a Christian. We must learn not only to deny self's selfish needs, but self's abilities. The person who relies on self won't rely on God. God allows us to be put in situations that seem impossible so we will have to rely upon Him. If you cling to your own power in trying to live as God has told you, you forfeit His mighty power. That's a terrible trade, don't you think? We must learn to trade in the self life and learn to live the Spirit life.

One day the Lord told me to read Acts 5:20, which says:

> *"Go, stand in the temple courts," he said, "and tell the people the full message of this new life."*

The longer I live, the more I see the need for this assignment. The full message is that we are not just saved from the curse of sin and an old way of life, but saved to a new life, the life of the Spirit. Unless we embrace Him

---

[4] Second Corinthians 12:9.

and the life he alone can give, we cannot whine to God and ask why he's not doing what he promises.

The greatest promise and privilege of the new covenant is that we will all know God.[5] In order to do this we must take time to cultivate the spiritual part of us, to nurture and grow our human spirit, the part that is joined to the Lord and will live with him forever. God has removed every possible barrier and provided everything we need to know him.

1 Corinthians 2:11-12 says,

> *For who among men knows the thoughts of a man except the man's spirit within him? In the same way no one knows the thoughts of God except the Spirit of God. We have not received the spirit of the world but the Spirit who is from God, that we may understand what God has freely given us.*

Simply put, apart from the Holy Spirit we will not understand what God has freely given us. In fact, Paul once identified this new covenant as the covenant of the Spirit.[6] Jesus once described those who are saved as having been "born of the Spirit."

We must learn to relate to the Holy Spirit.

A new believer is unfamiliar with the personality of God. His soul has been saved, but still needs to be renewed in its knowledge of who God is and how he is to relate to Him. How does this renewal happen? By studying the Word of God, praying — conversing with God — and worship — the beholding and adoration of God. As the believer does these things he becomes acquainted with the Lord and begins to more easily perceive the ways and thoughts of the Spirit. We become familiar with God just as we become familiar with another person, by spending time with them. Relationship is a process, even with God.

Even after you are born again, your soul is full of the old life: old ways of thinking, judging, and feeling, which will continue to dictate how you act and live. As you read the Bible, your beliefs begin to be changed if you accept what you read. In this way your mind starts to be renewed. You learn

---

[5] Hebrews 8:10-12

[6] 2 Corinthians 3:6

how to properly relate to God and as you do, false beliefs about God and life fall away. As you relate more and more to the Lord he heals your soul of hurts and painful memories. As the days and months of life with God pass by, your soul gradually begins to look, act and sound like the Spirit who has come to abide in you.

But this doesn't happen automatically; it is the direct result of deliberately living by faith in His presence, seeking his counsel, acknowledging your need of His wisdom, becoming ever more sensitive to what offends Him. It is living life in response to who God is, in response to his wonderful love and graciousness, that we are changed. Paul speaks of this life with the Spirit when he says:

> But I say, walk and live habitually in the Holy Spirit, responsive to and controlled and guided by the Spirit... (Galatians 5:16, The Amplified Bible)

> If we live by the Holy Spirit, let us also walk by the Spirit. If by the Holy Spirit we have our life in God, let us go forward, walking in line, our conduct controlled by the Spirit. (Galatians 5:23, The Amplified Bible.)

The Bible declares that those who are "spiritual" are those "who are responsive to and controlled by the Spirit."[7] The Holy Spirit is gentle and for the most part a submissive presence. He will not force you to be good, or change, or think differently. He doesn't make you do anything. If he did, most of the Christians in the world would be very different today! The Holy Spirit has all the power, wisdom and love of God to give you, and is the very gift of God Himself given to you. But to whom much is given, much is expected. I wonder how we will be judged in the end for ignoring this wonderful gift.

In my early days as a Christian, I presumed things about God simply because the Bible said so — such as the fact that God would talk to me. I experienced precious intimacies with God that I later lost to teachers who convinced me I had to work harder at being a Christian for God to relate to me so intimately, or put so much fear of deception in me that I sacrificed his comforting voice to caution.

---

[7] Galatians 6:1, The Amplified Bible.

I have regained that precious intimacy with God and thrown away my fear. I do not walk perfectly with God; indeed, learning to relate to God is the occupation of a lifetime. As I read the Bible, again and again I see the promise of a life that is incredible, powerful and peaceful, even if not free of trouble and affliction. It is a life that is lived in the realm of the kingdom of God while one is still here on the earth. It is what I have come to call "the Spirit life."

I have not fully attained it, but it is my continual target. It is a life that Jesus made possible by his death, and to which we are called, and too few ever enjoy. Just as scientists say we only use a fraction of our brain, we only experience a fraction of the life possible with the indwelling Spirit. This life is the promised land we are meant to dwell in here on earth.

Spirit life is responding to the presence of the Holy Spirit.

The righteous shall live by faith. Most people assume that simply means to believe in God; yet the Bible says even demons believe God exists. We would never say a demon is living by faith just because he believes in God. The true definition of living by faith is to live one's life as a visible response to the invisible presence of God. A popular wall plaque says that Jesus is the unseen guest at every meal, a witness to every act, a listener to every conversation. Truer words were never spoken. God knows our every thought. He is with us and knows us every moment, regardless of how often we may feel utterly alone.

The righteous should live by faith in the fact that they now have a constant companion, a ready teacher and counselor who wants to relate to them just as Jesus related to his disciples. The church as a whole has not yet come into a right relationship with the Holy Spirit., and many live far below the life that is possible. As the man said, we always ignore the Holy Spirit. Frankly, most of us continually alter our behavior at least a little in the presence of others. If we really believe God is with us, our behavior and attitudes will change, just as they do almost effortlessly when someone significant is with you.

We live our lives as a response to other people.

We all live our lives as a response to and result of our culture, our environment, our education. But without a doubt what contributes most to the measure of our existence and reveals who we are, is the people we relate to. We all tend to look into the eyes of others to see who we are, and we inevitably imitate the behavior of those we spend the most time with whether we approve of it or not. How many of us have lamented the ways of a mother or father only to realize we have come to act just like them?

It is the very rare person who is not influenced by those around him. We are all created with the need to be accepted and loved. Over the years our personalities and character are etched by those who touch our hearts for good or evil, whether up close in relationship or at a distance in hero worship. We respond to what we see with our eyes, hear with our ears and experience with people. All of these become easily woven into the very moral fiber of a person.

We live our lives as a response to a spouse, or children, or parents, mentors and co-workers, all of which is natural enough. No one has to teach us how to do this. But once we invite Christ to take up residence in our hearts, we have another Person to respond to, one who should become the main influence on our character and outlook on life, and especially how we view ourselves. It is the Lord's eyes we should gaze into to see who we are, to seek approval and find our identity.

The journey to becoming the woman God designed includes choosing who will be the foremost influence on your soul, who will shape your spirit, whose presence you will respond to the most.

By faith, I will be personally taught by God.

My personal growth blossomed when I finally allowed Jesus to fill me with His Holy Spirit, as I began to experience the joy of being personally taught by God, which, in my typical childlike way, I took very literally. Among other things, I asked the Holy Spirit to show me what to read in the Bible each day, and I received many very personal, right-on lessons that I would never have thought of myself.

There was one incredible six-month period when the Lord directed me day after day to read only three little books of the Bible: Ephesians, Philippians, and First John. You can read them all in less than hour. After the first few times, when it became clear we were going to camp out there awhile, I began to slow down and really meditate on the words. For the first time, I experienced the thrill of having the Holy Spirit reveal things to me, taking me deeper into understanding the heart of God. Sure, I grew a bit weary of being told to read the same thing every day, yet every day, every time of revisiting the words in those few pages, I was rewarded, even delighted, with what the Spirit revealed. The truths in those letters became deeply woven in the fabric in my soul. Short-sighted as I am, it was a while before I realized how strategic this learning season was.

The Lord knew something I didn't: he was laying a foundation for my life and calling. What I thought was mere Bible study was the personal tutelage of the Holy Spirit, preparing me for a life of teaching, writing, counseling and mentoring, yet I have never been to seminary or Bible school, a fact which often surprises people. I'm not suggesting everyone should prepare for ministry this way, and higher education is very valuable. But God is intensely personal with us, and He lead me in a way that wonderfully knit together His gifts and calling with my marriage and personal circumstances, redeeming my mistakes, making my lack of finances and every other obstacle irrelevant. He's a designer God, and I'm one of His designer women.

The righteous shall live by faith.

To live by faith is to live in the awareness of God's presence, paying attention in case He might want to interact with us in some way, might want to talk some time other than the usual "God time" we have decided upon. We treat God as if we are the only ones who get to initiate a conversation, as if he is expected to sit quietly by unless we address Him, and must wait for us to visit! The best relationships are flexible, spontaneous, and by turns serious, playful, companionable, confrontative. How we quench the Holy Spirit's willingness to express himself.

How do you really live by faith? Tune in, and learn to perceive the moods of the Lord. Once I was straining hard in prayer, feeling a little guilty because I resented being cooped up inside when I really wanted to go walk in the spring sunshine, and the Lord said, *Lighten up. I'd love to take a walk with you in the sunshine!"* We thoroughly enjoyed ourselves on that walk, and I learned how deeply spiritual an encounter with God can be when you aren't on your knees.

What I'm describing to you has often been considered the domain of mystics who were known for "practicing the Presence." But this life is not

God's

just for mystics and monks; it is for every hungry soul who thirsts for a real God in real life. As you practice living in response to his presence, you become aware of how the Lord is a witness to your thoughts and feelings, and eventually it occurs to you to ask what the Lord thinks of what you think about people and things. These are the kinds of questions and answers that really begin to change who you are.

Once you get acquainted with the Holy Spirit, you will find him to be your truest friend. As you develop trust in Him and in the process, he will lead you out of the prison of your old thoughts, habits, fears or weaknesses to the freedom that is life with God, that freedom for which Christ died. Heaven awaits as our true home, but it is clear that we are not to just be "on hold" in this life, merely enduring, and basically strangers with the God to whom we now belong. God wants to know and be known by us now, and he doesn't ask us to guess how to go about it, or leave us to make out the best way we can.

How do I learn to relate to this invisible friend?

God is spirit, and we are now also spirit. We must learn to see and hear him with the eyes and ears of our spirit. These are faculties we all have and must develop. How do I know? Number one, we have all read or heard stories of people who have had a death experience and were later brought back to life. Regardless of the circumstances, these stories always share one amazing fact: the person whose physical body has died continues to "see" and "hear" people who are in the room with them, seeing their own body in its lifeless state, seeing the doctors, nurses or loved ones around them, and hearing what they are saying. *(Stopped)*

Ponder this: if the physical body that can see and hear is now lifeless and all such faculties are unavailable, how is such a person still seeing and hearing? He is seeing with the faculties of his spirit, which can also see and hear. Just as a blind person develops an intensely heightened sense of hearing, we would do well to become more blind and deaf to the natural world so that we could develop the eyes and ears of our spirit. In fact, even the Lord seems to recommend this:

> *"Hear, you deaf; look, you blind, and see! Who is blind but my servant, and deaf like the messenger I send? Who is blind like the one committed to me, blind like the servant of the Lord? You have seen many*

things, but have paid no attention; your ears are open, but you hear nothing." (Isaiah 42:18-20).

As human beings we continue to rely upon what we see and hear with our physical eyes and ears more than what we could be seeing and hearing with our spiritual eyes and ears. In Ephesians 1:18 Paul asks God to enlighten "the eyes of our hearts" so we can fully know the hope to which God has called us, and the riches of his glorious inheritance. We too must ask God to help us develop our spiritual eyes and ears.

Another useful illustration comes from broadcasting and the receivers (television and radio) which we have in our homes. Broadcast signals fill the airwaves constantly and are all around us, yet we do not hear or see them, nor do these signals blare out of our televisions and radios if they are turned off. The sportscasters are shouting, the talking heads arguing, the pop stars are singing all the time, but unless we deliberately turn the receiver on and tune it in to a specific frequency, we never hear or see it.

This is also true of the Spirit of God living within us, who is always ready to give wisdom, comfort or inspiration. By his own description his voice is still and small, and we must quiet our minds and listen for the broadcast. We must "tune in." We can be sure He is broadcasting.

The Spirit in us always knows the thoughts of God.

The Christian life is a progression of learning to live more by the Spirit than by the flesh. We can see and hear in our spirit and we can know things in our spirit, apart from the seeing, hearing and knowing that is experienced through the physical brain and body. I got a very real lesson about this a few years ago. My husband and I were on our way from our ministry headquarters in Texas to Iowa where I was scheduled to conduct a weekend women's retreat. I was asleep in the back seat and Ron was driving in the wee hours of the morning when he fell asleep at the wheel. He awoke just in time to helplessly watch as our car plowed into the rear of a large recreational vehicle.

I do not remember the wreck. My first recollection of the event was waking up in an ambulance with my head, arms and legs strapped down tight. In addition to a concussion, they feared I had broken my neck. Since I had been lying down asleep in the back seat, I was not wearing a seat belt, and at impact my body went flying, head first, into the front bench seat, practically wrapping it around my husband!

As I drifted into consciousness in the ambulance, the EMS personnel asked if I knew my name. I thought very hard, but had no clue what my name was. They asked if I knew where I lived and where we were going when we had the wreck; still no clue. No matter how hard I tried to remember, none of this knowledge came to me. My head injuries had given me amnesia.

Then EMS people started to comfort me, but I told them the one thing I knew with absolute clarity in that moment: *"I know I will be all right. I belong to Jesus and He is with me."* Incredibly, the only thing I knew was that I was saved, and safe. I knew Jesus' name. I felt wrapped in a warm cocoon of peace, knew that Jesus was with me and was going to take care of me. I had no fear whatsoever. On the hour-long drive to the hospital I drifted in and out of consciousness, and each time I came to they would ask the same questions, with the same result. I didn't even know I had a husband.

Ron was not allowed to ride in the ambulance, but had contacted our intercessors and friends to pray for us, and their prayers were powerful and effective. About six hours later they released me from the emergency room, having done x-rays, an MRI, and other examinations, finding nothing wrong but a concussion and a broken nose. By the time they released me, my memory had returned and if anything else had been wrong with me, the Lord had healed it. The broken nose had actually re-aligned and corrected a long-standing problem of not being able to breath out of one nostril that was blocked by excess cartilage! And in spite of the doctors assuring me that I would have two whopping black eyes from having the bridge of my nose rearrange a car seat, I never had any bruising on my face and my vanity remained intact as I conducted the Ladies Retreat that weekend. We had experienced a miracle.

It was only later that it dawned on me how amazing it was that even during the hours when I did not know who I was, I continually knew whose I was, whose loving care was carrying me. The only possible explanation for this is to look at the different faculties of the spirit and the body. My injured brain could provide no information whatsoever, not even a husband's face or name, so everything I did know came from by the Holy Spirit revealing it to my spirit. My brain didn't work, but my spirit was fine, and it was through my spirit that peace and knowledge flowed. My spirit could still see and hear Jesus as he comforted me.

Letting the Holy Spirit pray through us.

I spoke earlier of the prayer language that the Holy Spirit makes available to us, and any discussion about communicating with the Holy Spirit must clarify the purpose of such a mysterious thing. Quite frankly, after the novelty of praying in an unknown language wore off, I began to wonder why it is necessary. Being a very inquisitive person, I have tested God on everything, and he has not minded. One night just before drifting off to sleep, I asked the Lord to show me the point of praying in a language I do not understand.

Normally I sleep soundly through the night, but on this night I awoke abruptly at 1 a.m., instantly alert and with the name of a woman on my mind I'd never heard before. I felt the need to pray, but since I did not know her I had no idea what she needed, and God wasn't telling. I went to the living room and decided to simply pray in my prayer language. As I prayed, I saw a picture of our local city jail, so I thought perhaps this was a woman in trouble, or a police department employee. I felt deeply impressed as I prayed that she was going through a very difficult time and that the Lord wanted me to give her the message that He loved her deeply and that he was at work to heal the difficulties in her life.

After about an hour I felt the urge to pray lift. I called the police department and asked if this woman was in jail or if she worked there, but they had never heard of her. Baffled, I told the Lord he would have to help me find her if he wanted me to deliver his message. He gave me no further information, and I went back to bed. The following afternoon a lady from our church dropped by for coffee on the way home from her job as a dispatcher at the police department. Oddly enough I didn't immediately make a connection, so the Holy Spirit finally said quietly, *"Ask her if she knows this woman."*

When I mentioned the woman's name my friend's eyes got as big as saucers. *"Where did you hear that name?"* she demanded. I told her God had awakened me in the night to pray for her, and had given me a message for her. Tears filled my friends eyes. *"I do know her,"* she said. *"She works with me at in the dispatcher's office."*

"But they told me they had never heard of her," I protested.

"Not by that name," my friend said. *"Only her immediate family and I know her by that name. Two years ago she left a very abusive husband in fear for her life, and she now goes by another name."* I was astounded. I had believed, but now I really believed! And what my friend told me next only further confirmed my experience. She reminded me of a tragic accident a year earlier in which two local high school students had rolled over in a topless Jeep. One young man died, the other had since been paralyzed from the neck down. The woman I had prayed for in the night was the mother of the paralyzed young man.

I was anxious to call her, but honestly had some fear that what had been so very real to me might seem absolutely weird to her. This woman was a Christian but I didn't know how she would react to a stranger calling to say that God had a message for her. I called and introduced myself, explained that the Lord had awoken me and given me her name in the night and stirred me to pray for her and gave a message to encourage her that he was at work in her situation. She began to weep, and said, *"What time did this happen?"* When I told her the time, she said, *"Then I know God has spoken to you, because that is about the time my son woke me up and asked me to cover up his feet."*

"I don't understand."

"His feet were cold. He has not had any feeling in his legs or feet since the accident a year ago. God is obviously restoring the feeling in his legs. It's a miracle!" I cried with her, and was in absolute awe of God and what he was doing for this woman and her son.

Apparently God had used my prayers to begin a miracle. To be honest, in those days I didn't have the kind of faith that God could heal someone just because I prayed for them. God wanted to heal this young man, but needed someone to intercede so that his will in heaven would be released in earth.[8] By praying in the unknown tongue given by the Spirit, the Lord had sidestepped my lack of faith and used me to pray a prayer beyond my ability to believe. I was amazed at how God had accomplished so much with this one event: he blessed these people, answered my question and taught me an unforgettable lesson.

---

[8]"This, then, is how you should pray: `Our Father in heaven... your will be done on earth as it is in heaven.'" (Matthew 6:9-10).

I have since learned that there are other reasons for praying in a language I do not understand. One is privacy; there are simply some things I don't need to know about another person. Someone I know may have a secret sin such as addiction to pornography or some other embarrassing thing. Human beings can be very judgmental people. If God wants to set someone free of something that is none of my business, he can pray through me without my understanding, releasing his will without my interference. There are also times when we are called upon to pray and really don't know what is needed, such as hidden medical conditions. And finally, I am certain that God has had me pray in this way for people I have never met and situations I've never heard of. This is his way of using clay vessels to participate in his glorious work, overcoming all our limitations to make us partners in the work of his kingdom.

What kind of woman will I be? I will be a woman who walks with God, who learns how to live in close fellowship with the Holy Spirit, living my life as a response to His love, His words, His will, His ways, His joy, His ability to satisfy my soul. I will be a woman who lets God live and move and have his being in me.

Reflecting on Chapter 5

This chapter teaches that the strength and fulness of your Christian life comes through being filled with the Holy Spirit and living your life as a response to Him as teacher, comforter and strengthener.

❖ *The author's definition of living by faith is to live your life as a response to the presence of God. According to this definition, are you living by faith?*

❖ *Do you see yourself as controlled by the Holy Spirit? If not, ponder how your life would be different if you were.*

❖ *Ponder: Have you ever felt comforted by the Comforter? Or counseled by the Counselor?*

❖ *Ask the Lord to help you develop your spiritual senses of seeing and hearing Him.*

❖ *Considering what you have learned, set a new goal to live by faith.*

For Deeper Study

❖ *Read Appendix C, "What the Holy Spirit Does With And For You" and the scriptures listed.*

I Will Love the Lord With All My Heart

What is most important in my walk with God? Is it how much money I give? That I am in church every time the doors open, or that I pray at least an hour each day? That I become a spiritual warrior or sit at the feet of Jesus?

It is currently popular to define a mission statement for oneself, to identify a central core value, a basis from which to make decisions about how we will spend our time, our money, and our lives. But this has been done for you already, dear Christian:

> One of the teachers of the law...asked [Jesus], "Of all the commandments, which is the most important?
>
> "The most important one," answered Jesus, "is this: ...Love the Lord your God with all your heart and with all your soul and with all your mind and with all your strength."
>
> "Well said, teacher," the man replied. " ...To love him with all your heart, with all your understanding and with all your strength, and to love your neighbor as yourself is more important than all burnt offerings and sacrifices." (Mark 12:28-33).

The greatest goal of every Christian should be to love the Lord with all one's might. When the Holy Spirit brought me to this truth one day and made it personal, it was like a mighty wind had come and blown away everything that was cluttering my spiritual landscape. Suddenly I had only one measuring stick for me, my life, my choices.

When I determined to let this command be my greatest goal in life, it changed everything about my walk with God.

To begin with, I realized quickly that not only did I not love God like this, I didn't know how. Like countless Christians before me, I had tried to make myself love God, and failed. My inability to love God truly, deeply, brought me to the realization I needed more than a Bible, a church and good intentions. It seemed I had two choices: give up, muddle through and settle for the dry toast Christian life, or take a stand to settle for nothing less than a love affair with Jesus, and beg for help. My discontent combined with my helplessness formed the vacuum that God later showed me needed to be filled with the Holy Spirit — the melted butter on my toast.

Not only is our ability to experience God's love dependent upon the work of the Spirit, it is He who teaches us how to love God in return. He is the one who faithfully leads us in a path of relating rightly to Jesus and the Father, making God's will known to us, helping us to know how to obey and giving us the grace (ability) to do so as proof of our deep love and devotion.

Even so, while the Holy Spirit gives us the power to love God, the motivation to love God is up to us. What we are motivated by is what determines how we will live, what we reach for, what we choose — in short, the mission. I made it my mission to love God with all my might over twenty years ago, and in that time I have learned a few things about why "the greatest command" is the greatest.

Love knows what to do.

Often the most ordinary experiences turn out to be a revelation from God, like the time when I was passing a teenager in a mall who was wearing a t-shirt that said, *"No Rules!"* As I walked past this boy I thought critically to myself, *"There goes one rebellious kid!"* But then I heard the Spirit say, *"Read the back of his shirt."* It said, *"Rules are for those who don't know what to do."* Somehow — no doubt with the Holy Spirit's help — those words were like lightning that suddenly illuminates the dark night landscape in front of you, bright as day.

I thought of the Ten Commandments, the "rules" God gave to the Israelites, and realized that each of them gave instruction in one of two areas: how to love God, and how to love people. They are, in essence, the rules of love, and people who love deeply don't need the rules, because their love leads them to do naturally what the rule requires.

In that "mall moment" I thought of Jesus insisting that he did not come to abolish the rules, but to fulfill them; how he accused the Pharisees of not knowing the heart of the Father, caring more about following the rules than loving God. They were, Jesus complained, far from the heart of God; and in focusing on the rules they actually hurt people. While true love leads us to fulfill all the righteousness requirements of the law, it doesn't work in reverse: fulfilling all these requirements does not make us true lovers. The Pharisees demonstrated that one can do all the right things for all the wrong reasons. They followed rules for their sake, to demonstrate their righteousness, and not for the sake of loving God or the people they were supposed to lead in the ways of God.

That teenager's t-shirt proclaimed the high calling of God, who commands us to become lovers rather than religious rule followers. It is the difference between legalism and life, between the Pharisees and Jesus the son of God, between dry toast religion and life experienced near the very heart of God.

You can see the same principle at work in your own family: when the family is close and loving towards one another, the rules are rarely mentioned. But when intimacy is poor, and selfishness reigns instead of love, we have to pull out the rules: *"You will be nice to your sister. You will clean up your room and do your chores."* God never intended for obedience to be a matter of law, but a matter of love.

Obedience is the best evidence of our love.

As parents we hope that son or daughter will clean up his room simply because we ask, and that their love for us will motivate them to want to obey. The Bible likewise teaches that obedience is ultimately the only true way to prove that we love Jesus. In fact, Jesus was so emphatic about this issue that he repeated himself three times in John Chapter 14, a typical Jewish means of emphasizing importance:

If you love me, you will obey what I command. (verse 15)

Whoever has my commands and obeys them, he is the one who loves me. He who loves me will be loved by my Father, and I too will love him and show myself to him. (verse 21)

If anyone loves me, he will obey my teaching. My Father will love him, and we will come to him and make our home with him. He who does not love me will not obey my teaching. These words you hear are not my own; they belong to the Father who sent me. (verses 23-24)

In light of these words, let's rewind a moment: when Jesus said, *Love the Lord your God with all your heart, mind and strength*, He might as well have said, *Obey the Lord with all your heart*.

I have tried living by the rules, and I have tried living a life of love for God, and the two are as like night and day. It feels very different to go to the place of prayer and ask, *"How can I love you today, Lord?"* than to make myself meet with "the boss" and say, *"Okay God, what do you want me to do,"* then wrestle with whether I am going to obey. Apart from sincere love, obedience is reduced to a matter of the will, and the truth is that we will do things for love we would not otherwise be willing to do. If you doubt me on this, go back to that place of how different it feels to clean up the poopy diapers and spit-up of your own precious infants, compared to doing it for someone else's. Love not only knows what to do, it is willing to do it, and doesn't mind. It doesn't even stop to decide, it just goes into action, happy to show the love.

The obedience that flows out of love for God changes us.

I think another reason Jesus made this the highest command is because it is love — and the obedience that naturally flows from it — that ultimately transforms us. God's love for us begins the transformation, then our love for him brings it to fulness. When I first experienced Jesus' love I made immediate changes in my life as a response to that love. I began to go to church, I read the Bible in order to learn about him, I quit cussing, and tried to treat others better. Good changes all, but mostly outward and surface, not penetrating deep into the core of my character.

It was only when I began to try to practice this command to love God with all my might that a deeper transformation began to take place in my soul. As I grew in my knowledge of God and the ability to know his voice, he began to ask things of me that he did not demand of me in those first seasons of knowing him. The Lord has always been gentle and patient with me, but the day came when, for instance, he asked me to give up cigarettes, to which I was hopelessly addicted.

In the early days of being a Christian I could not give them up. But once the Holy Spirit came and filled me with a deep love for Jesus, I was able to lay cigarettes down as an act of love for him. Whether or not I quit smoking became a very personal issue between me and the Lord I loved, not just a matter of health or discipline or doctrine.

One realizes in this place that obedience is more than just the right thing it do; it is God's plan for transforming us into the image of Christ. When we know God's will and do what He wants rather than what we would normally do, we are changed. Our choices reveal our character and express our values; when our choices change, so does the rest.

Thus, in the kingdom of God and the new covenant, our behavior becomes much more than how we act, it is now an expression of reverent worship for the God we adore — or not. Romans 12:1-2 tells us that the purest form of spiritual worship is to offer ourselves to God to do what he wants.

Change is not easy for us, and even if we have the will to change our behavior it is incredibly difficult to change our values. If we try to change in the same way the world does, it becomes a self-centered exercise, rather than god-centered — rather like the Pharisees. Christianity is not just about making ourselves be good and do right, it is about making Jesus Christ the center of our universe and living a life of worship, and honoring love with obedience. Only when we do this will we fulfill all righteousness and become like him. There is no other way. The Holy Spirit gives us the power to be like Jesus, but He will not make us change. The choice always remains with us, and what we choose depends upon what is motivating our choices. Love is all about providing that motivation.

Love never fails.

Paul wrote in First Corinthians 13:13 that of all the things in the heart of a man towards God, the most important are faith, hope and love, and that of these three, the greatest is love. He had already revealed the reason behind this truth in verse eight: *Love never fails.*

Love will motivate us to do things we would otherwise be totally incapable of doing or which are out of character. Spiritual ambition fails, money fails, friends fail, faith even fails, but love never fails. If you have ever deeply loved another person you will bear witness to the fact that love gives us the power to transcend our own limitations and fears for the sake of the beloved. The heart motivated by pure love of God knows no limits. Love is the most powerful force in the universe.

There are two kinds of Christians: those who will follow Christ into the hard places of surrender and those who will not. What seems to separate them is true love for God — sincere, heartfelt, committed love. I have been both, and tell you assuredly that the incentives of being holy or righteous or good are not enough to bring you to fulness in Christ.

My love for Jesus has often produced obedience in ways I could never have done simply in wanting to be good, and in these my life and character have been the most changed. The greatest example was when I went back to Ron because Jesus asked it of me. I could not have done that just as an act of will; I was not strong enough. But I did go back to show my love for Jesus and as a result I broke a lifelong habit of quitting and running away when things got tough. It forced me to stay put and learn how to faithfully love my husband.

For the sake of showing God I love Him, I have forgiven when I didn't think I could, I have gone places and done things I was too fearful to do otherwise. Loving God has taken me outside of myself and made me more like Jesus. Trying to make myself like Jesus was awkward, ugly, often self-serving and a chore. Letting love change me has been an amazing journey of joy, and resulted in one very important thing: it has made Jesus the center of my universe instead of me.

Jesus' love for the Father motivated his whole existence.

Jesus made it clear that he was motivated in everything He did by His love for the Father when he said in John 14:30-31:

> I will not speak with you much longer, for the prince of this world is coming. He has no hold on me, but the world must learn that I love the Father and that I do exactly what my Father has commanded me.

It was love for the Father and love for us that took him to the cross, one proceeding out of the other. If He had not loved the Father so powerfully, then He would not have loved us also. He loved us because the Father loved us.

I am convinced that we overlook the power of that love. Jesus did not go to the cross for us simply because it was the right thing to do. He went to the cross because He loved the Father so much he was committed to complete obedience. He did it as an act of love for the Father and the result was that we also got loved with all his might:

> *This is how we know that we love the children of God: by loving God and carrying out his commands. This is love for God: to obey his commands. And his commands are not burdensome... (1 John 5:2-3).*

In this same way Jesus loved His Father, and us, all the way to the cross. We let the love demonstrated on the cross overshadow completely the power of the love Jesus was motivated by every day. He was able to say no to the temptations that face any human being because He loved the Father enough to say no to sin. When Jesus wrestled with temptation, his ability to overcome it came from a value inside that said to submit to (obey) sin was to betray His love for the Father and his Father's love for us. He could love and yield to sin, or he could love and obey the Father.

Every time Jesus said no to sin, He did it as an act of love, and thus fulfilled all righteousness. He had go to the cross as the spotless Lamb of God, or He couldn't go at all. If He had defiled himself even once, he could not have been the perfect sacrifice to atone for our sin. Offering himself up to death on the cross was the culmination of the sacrifice of love Jesus made every day of His life.

When you adopt the command to love as your mission statement and judge everything by that goal, it changes everything about the way you relate to God. You will become free from rules. You will be less judgmental towards yourself — and others as you realize that the response of a heart to God is a very personal matter, and no two people love exactly the same way. Your attitude about sin will change, because what you do and how it affects God — the one you love — will become much more personal. It feels very different to "break a rule" as opposed to hurting someone you love. You will realize that Christianity is much more than a religion, it is a relationship with a real live person whom you can delight or disappoint by your choices.

Love teaches us how to die.

Jesus taught that we should die to ourselves in order to find life. I tried doing that too. I looked for opportunities to put myself last and find ways to deny myself the things I wanted, just as a general principle. I didn't give a certain thing up because Jesus asked me to, but because giving things up is how one proves one is dying to self. It was all about the evidence, proving to myself and others that I was doing it right. But inevitably everything I did in that vein felt weirdly unsatisfying and in an odd way, self-centered. I didn't realize why until my focus changed from laws to love, and it became clear that I was being weird and self-centered. But when I made it my goal to love God rather than "do it right," the focus switched from me to Him, and a funny thing happened: self died while I wasn't looking. The death to self that Jesus asks of us is not one of suicide, it is one of neglect. We are called to be so busy loving God and others that self dies a natural, quiet, uncelebrated death.

It is the same with suffering. Christians are not asked to submit to suffering for the sake of suffering, as if that alone would somehow make us holy and good children of God. God doesn't insist on suffering to force character development in us, though he is certainly an opportunist in that regard — he doesn't waste a thing. We are asked to be willing to suffer because sometimes in choosing to love we will experience affliction to body or soul. Yet I hasten to say from personal experience, that in such cases God comes quickly and faithfully to heal the wounds of love.

Frankly, I am as weak as they come; I have never been able to deliberately choose the way of suffering. I can't bear to hurt myself or be hurt. But I have made some choices for the sake of showing God I love him that have caused me to suffer. Not once has God failed to comfort, restore, and heal me, and give me more life than I surrendered for love.

Love is what grows us up in righteousness and holiness.

God is not interested in perfection, he wants your heart. He wants relationship. With the mission to know him and love him with all your heart, you will become holy; you will walk in righteousness, you will walk in abundant life. These are the fruits of a love life shared with God.

The definition of being holy is to be wholly set apart for something or someone special, and giving yourself exclusively there. Holiness is the opposite of being common, which is giving yourself to anything and everyone. In his determination to love the Father, Jesus set himself apart just for Him and for you and thus kept himself holy all of his days. This is closely akin to the biblical meaning of the phrase, "to fear the Lord." By this the Bible refers to a healthy fear of displeasing Him, similar to what you experience with anyone you love deeply — a fear of offending them in a way that causes them to withdraw or violates their character and values. Such an offense is a violation of love. It is easy to imagine that Moses had this truth in mind when he wrote:

> *And now, O Israel, what does the Lord your God ask of you but to fear the Lord your God, to walk in all his ways, to love him, to serve the Lord your God with all your heart and with all your soul...* (Deuteronomy 10:12).

What does healthy fear of God look like in real life? The Bible teaches us it is simply expressed by hating what He hates — evil;[1] in other words, adopting and really living by God's values. For instance, the woman who fears god hates the evil shown on soap operas and turns away from them, from the ungodliness they feed into her soul. She won't pretend that God doesn't care if she pollutes herself with novels and television programs which stir up lust, vain romantic notions and discontent within her. She hates the evil of gossip and slander, and she hates the deceitful scheming and manipulation that some women use to get what they want out of men. She hates greed; she hates self-pity. She hates them because the God she loves hates them.

What kind of woman will I be? I will be a woman who loves her God with all her heart, soul, mind and strength.

⸎

---

[1] Psalm 97:10; Proverbs 8:13.

Reflecting on Chapter 6

This chapter explains the purposes and fruit of loving God with all one's might.

❖ *Read John Chapter 14.*

❖ *Ask yourself, "Is loving God my highest goal?" If not, ponder the question in God's presence, to discover honestly what is your mission (or missions) and write down what you discover in your journal.*

❖ *Ask the Holy Spirit to help you make "the greatest command" your measuring stick. As you notice a difference in how you make choices, celebrate these moments with God and record them in your journal.*

I Will Be A Woman Who Knows Her God

This is what the Lord says: "Let not the wise man boast of his wisdom or the strong man boast of his strength or the rich man boast of his riches, but let him who boasts boast about this: that he understands and knows me..." (Jeremiah 9:23-24)

Jesus not only saved us from our sin, he made it possible for us to personally know God. Would you be willing to boast to someone that you understand the heart of God? Few would, yet obviously it pleases God no end for us to seek to know his heart and understand his ways.

This pleases him far more than perfect religious observance or pious attitudes. God wants to be known by his creation, He wants to show off his glory as a father, lover, provider, defender and ruler. He delights for us to personally taste of this goodness, and therefore he invites us to approach him in childlike trust and presume upon his love and grace.

There is a scene in the movie "Anna and The King" that perfectly illustrates the unique access offered to a child. In this story the fierce King of Siam is surrounded by guards who are ready to execute severe discipline on those who violate the strict protocol of his court, in which no one is allowed to enter his presence, speak to him or even look him in the eye without his permission. One day while conducting the kingly business of his court, one of his young sons comes bursting in the room, runs through all the guards, the court officials and the many subjects bowed low with eyes to the ground, straight to his father. No one stops this child of the king; all court business is forgotten as the stern King scoops his son into his lap and asks with all fatherly tenderness, "What is it, my son?"

We have this kind of access to our heavenly Father, to the King of all Kings. If we shrink back in fear that he is Almighty God and we are his unworthy and unwelcome subjects, we dishonor the invitation to come as his beloved children, and we demonstrate a lack of trust in the promise that he will receive us with tenderness and full attention.

My husband is fond of asking people in a meeting, "How many of you would like to get closer to God?" Most everyone raises a hand; but it's a trick question, because he then tells them they are lying to themselves, for we are all as close to God as we have chosen to be. God has made it entirely possible for us to know him. While it is easier than we make it out to be, it does require time and commitment, just like any relationship. The problem is we really keep choosing to give ourselves to other pursuits, and I venture to say we are still, in our honest moments, rather intimidated by the very idea.

There are two primary ways we can get to know God: the first is through the study of His Word, the Holy Scriptures, and the second is through interactive communication in which he not only hears our voice in prayer, but we hear his. The Bible is consistent from beginning to end in showing that God communicates with his creation. He made his voice known to certain ones before the cross, and Scripture says that the new covenant of Jesus includes the privilege of personally knowing and being taught by God:

> *No longer will a man teach his neighbor, or a man his brother, saying, `Know the Lord,' because they will all know me, from the least of them to the greatest. (Hebrews 8:11)*

How can we be personally taught by God if we cannot hear his voice? This is not just referring to being taught by the scriptures, as some believe. Jesus clearly walked in and taught the truth that every born-again child of God has the privilege of knowing the voice of the Father, the Shepherd, the Comforter, the Counselor, in this earthly life. To have it otherwise would be a cruel bait and switch on God's part, promising so much that we could never know or do or be if left to figure it out for ourselves. Such a god would not be worthy of worship.

The Apostle Peter connected the dots for us on this issue when he wrote:

> *His divine power has given us everything we need for life and godliness through our knowledge of him... (2 Peter 1:3)*

"Through our knowledge of him." The fulfillment of God's promises depends upon a communication that enables us to know him. We must hear the shepherd's voice to find our personal path to abundant life. And as my husband is fond of pointing out, there is absolutely nothing which can hinder our growing knowledge of God, save for our own laziness or lack of faith.

Begin by reading the Bible, cover to cover, not just a few favorite verses. The Bible is like a portrait of God revealing the whole of who He is, and just as you could not perceive the beauty of a painting by viewing only a tiny part of it, you cannot understand God by knowing a few favorite scriptures. I am continually amazed at how few Christians actually study their Bibles daily or read them all the way through. Frequently those I teach are amazed at the things I show them in the Word of God, and some of the greatest treasures only come forth when you connect something written in Numbers with something written in Hebrews, which turns it all alive or upside down or amazing.

God's Word reveals His character and motives. Because it reveals how God responds to man in every possible situation and directly quotes his words again and again, it helps you learn to recognize his voice and distinguish it from your own or from that of the other spirit who, although he cannot know our thoughts as God does, is certainly also capable of communicating to us.

If you would know God, find a translation of the Bible you can understand and read every day. If you read even just a half hour each day, you could read the whole Bible in less than a year.

But again, the Bible is not the only part of the "word of God" you need. You need the living, breathing word of God. A.W. Tozer says in his classic book, *The Pursuit of God*, "*...God is forever seeking to speak Himself out to His creation. He fills the world with His speaking voice.*"[1] He goes on to say:

_____

[1]The Pursuit of God by A.W. Tozer, 2006, WingSpread Publishers, page 69

"I believe that much of our religious unbelief is due to a wrong conception of and a wrong feeling for the Scriptures of Truth. A silent God suddenly began to speak in a book and when the book was finished lapsed back into silence again forever. Now we read the book as the record of what God said when He was for a brief time in a speaking mood. With notions like that in our heads how can we believe? The facts are that God is not silent, has never been silent. It is the nature of God to speak…I think a new world will arise out of the religious mists when we approach our Bible with the idea that it is not only a book which was once spoken, but a book which is now speaking."[2]

The word of God: logos or rhema?

Some people use the phrase "God's Word" only to refer to the written scriptures, but the New Testament writers used two different Greek words in referring to God's Word: one is *logos*, and the other is *rhema*. While both are used to refer to what God has communicated, they are decidedly different. *Logos* refers to teaching. It comes from the root word *lego* (yes, as in the building blocks for kids) which means to lay forth in words, by systematic discourse, to build line upon line. *Logos* can be written or spoken.

Rhema, on the other hand, is something uttered. It comes from a root that pictures flowing or pouring forth, like water. In its Biblical usage *rhema* is usually seen in referring to the spoken, personal, breathed word, uttered or flowing into the "ears" of our hearts as it flows out of the heart of God. It carries the idea of something revealed.

Rhema is the word used in Matthew 4:4, when Jesus said, *"Man does not live on bread alone but by every word (rhema) that comes from the mouth of God."* It is used in Luke 1:38 when Mary says, *"Be it unto me according to your word (rhema), Lord,"* referring to the message just delivered by the angel of the Lord. It is used in Ephesians 5:26, which says that we are washed by the word *(rhema)* flowing out of God to us. Finally, the *rhema* Word of God is identified as the sword we are given by the Holy Spirit to use against our spiritual enemies.[3]

Logos is connected to the expression of laws, rules, statutes or teaching in general, like teaching the necessity of obedience to God. You could teach this to a crowd and it would be appropriate for them all as a revelation of

---

[2] Ibid, page 77.

[3] Ephesians 6:18.

what he requires in general. In contrast, *rhema* is when God says to you, *"You need to do this thing today."* It is personal and relevant at this moment, in these present circumstances, a living word. *Rhema* is what flows from one person to another in personal expression. *Logos* is what God requires, *rhema* is what God requires of me. *Logos* is the right way for a Christian to act; *rhema* is the right thing for me to do in this situation as God personally reveals it.

When you read the Bible from cover to cover, you will find things that seem to conflict. On the one hand, you are told to love an enemy; on the other, to shun those who do not live according to God's righteous laws. How do you know when to do what? That is what *rhema* is for. It is the personal instruction that flows from the Holy Spirit when you need it. Jesus said the reason his ministry was so powerful and effective was that he only did what the Father told him to do and say.[4] He sought the *rhema* of his Father continually.

Logos is teaching; *rhema* is personal counseling. *Logos* is right for everyone; it is a truth like two plus two equals four. *Rhema* is right for me, and takes into account all the factors in my life and the other lives which touch mine right now. When Jesus stood on the hillside and taught, he gave forth the *logos* of God. When he personally took Peter or John aside and counseled them, it was his personal *rhema* to them.

The Bible tells me everything I need to know about God, about how to be saved, what the kingdom of God is like. It is God's *logos* truth to all of us. But it does not tell me who to marry, what job to take, where to go to school, how to care for my body, how to pray for a specific situation. For that I need *rhema* from God. And the *logos* of God becomes *rhema* to us when the Holy Spirit quickens God's words to our mind and spirit as the writer of Hebrews explains:

> *The Word (logos) of God is living, and active. Sharper than any double-edged sword, it penetrates even to dividing soul and spirit, joints and marrow; it judges the thoughts and attitudes of the heart. (Hebrews 4:12)*

We all have well-entrenched beliefs, attitudes and traditions of thought, some so internalized that we may not realize they exist; yet they dictate how

---

[4] John 5:30; 8:27-29; 12:49-50; 14:30-31.

we act, how we feel about ourselves and others, and how we think of God. As you study the Bible, keep a notebook handy to record the beliefs and attitudes which you discover are contrary to God's truth. Next to it record what God's Word says about that subject.

How will I respond to the Word of God?

When Paul tells us to renew our minds it is referring to the need to exchange your truths for God's. You may not always like what God's Word says, but if you agree that it is flawless[5] and divinely inspired[6] — as you should — you must accept its' authority to govern your life. We must guard against manipulating the Word of God to suit our views or maintain our comfort zones. You should adopt the attitude of the psalmist who said, *Your statutes are my delight; they are my counsellors* and *I have chosen the way of truth; I have set my heart on your laws.*[7] If you learn to love and revere the Word of God as the flawless, beautiful, life-giving revelation that it is, you will be availing yourself of a priceless treasure.

The Word of God says, *Blessed is the man who fears the Lord, who finds great delight in his commands.*[8] If you are going to live by faith you must live as if you believe that every command God gives you — in the *logos* written word or in the *rhema* uttered to your heart — will lead to the fulfilling of his promise to give you abundant life. God is love, and His every command is an expression of his love coming to his children.

Seek God's counsel.

James 1-5-7 teaches us to turn to God with our questions and expect to *generously* receive all the wisdom we need:

> *If any of you lacks wisdom, he should ask God, who gives generously to all without finding fault, and it will be given to him. But when he asks, he must believe and not doubt, because he who doubts is like a wave of the sea, blown and tossed by the wind. That man should not think he will receive anything from the Lord; (James 1:5-7)*

---

5 Psalm 18:30.
6 2 Timothy 3:16.
7 Psalm 119, verses 24 and 30 respectively.
8 Psalms 112:1.

Essential to a fruitful Christian life is faith in the fact that God is willing and waiting to communicate with us in a way that we can clearly understand. Yet in our ministry work in the U.S. and overseas, we have found this to be the most neglected covenant blessing in Christians of every background. When we ask for a show of hands as to how many know God's voice, only about 10% respond in the affirmative. This is heartbreaking, in light of what Jesus died to give us.

Why do people believe that God can be all-powerful, create the universe, save us from sin and change our character, but not make his voice known to us? The problem often lies in the fact that we do not doubt God's ability, but our own, still thinking we have to earn this privilege or achieve a certain level of spiritual stature to hear Him. This was certainly not my experience. When I came to the Lord at the age of 29, I had never read a page in the Bible and knew nothing but that I needed a savior. The first gospel I read was John, and quickly ran into *"My sheep know my voice."* So I believed, but was tentative in trying it much until another book came my way called *Talking To/With God* by Lewis Shaffer, a saint who loves Jesus and had, together with an accountability partner, built an amazing ministry through listening to God's personal guidance. His book and the Bible were my primers, and I began to practice living by the voice of God. It was a thrilling, delightful and occasionally slightly terrifying experience, and the greatest choice I made in my life after surrendering to Jesus' love.

Communication is the essence of relationship.

My beloved dog Lady went completely deaf in her fourteenth year. She adored me, she lived to be in my presence, and the Lord often used her to teach me about His undivided devotion and unconditional love. But when she could no longer hear me, our relationship changed significantly, and she became much less responsive and increasingly agitated. In her hearing days I had been able to sooth her with my voice when she was stressed, such as when I gave her a bath or took her to the vet, but once she lost her hearing I could not comfort her that way. She became increasingly fearful and uncooperative, no longer able hear my commands and obey, so I had to use a leash to lead her on to get her to do certain things.[9] A certain sadness and frustration entered our relationship and I understood for the first time how

---

[9] This reminds me of Psalm 32:9, which says, "Do not be like the horse or the mule, which have no understanding but must be controlled by bit and bridle or they will not come to you."

important the sound of my voice had been to the quality of our relationship. It is no different with us and God.

In hearing God's voice I hear tender love words, I am comforted in times of trouble, I learn His will, and I am taught. This book is punctuated with personal things God has spoken to me, without apology. You too, can hear his voice. In the back of this book you will find Appendix B, entitled "My Sheep Listen to My Voice," to help you study this subject for yourself.

"Whoever has my commands…"

Jesus said, *Whoever has my commands and obeys them, he is the one who loves me*.[10] To achieve the goal of loving God with all one's heart, we must know His voice so we may possess His commands to obey. The commitment to love means seeking daily to *understand and firmly grasp what the Lord's will is*.[11] Even more important is God's desire that we know and understand Him, as He said in Jeremiah 9:24.

It is absolutely impossible to know God through other people's experiences. Each Christian's relationship with Jesus Christ is entirely unique. No one else can get together with the Lord to determine His personal will for you. I often think of Jesus looking at Peter, who wanted to know what the Lord's plans were for the Apostle John. Jesus basically said that was not to be his concern, but rather, *"You follow me."*[12] The Word says, *"For you died,"* says the Word, *"and your life is now hidden with Christ in God."*[13] In other words, this life is hidden in the heart and spirit of Jesus Christ, and is only accessible through personally knowing him.

This is not as mysterious as it seems, for this is also true of all human relationships. It is only through increasing intimacy with someone that they begin to open up and offer you their pearls, the treasures of the heart, the things we do not give to passers-by, but only those who remain with us and want to build life together with us, and who will treasure the pearls we offer.

---

[10] John 14:21.
[11] Ephesians 5:17, The Amplified Bible.
[12] John 21:21-22.
[13] Colossians 3:3.

The more you respond to God, the more you will hear.

Jesus shared an important principle about hearing God's voice: the more you respond to what you hear, the more you will hear:

> *"If anyone has ears to hear, let him hear. Consider carefully what you hear," he continued, "with the measure you use, it will be measured to you — and even more. Whoever has will be given more; whoever does not have, even what he as will be taken from him." (Mark 4:23-25)*

The person who receives personal guidance from God and responds in a way that demonstrates that he values what he hears, will continue to receive, and perhaps even more so. On the other hand, when a believer ignores or treats with small value the communication of God, he should not be surprised if God's voice would to cease to speak.

I suspect that one reason for this is the mercy of God, who may not be willing to continue putting his child in a position to deliberately sin. After all, James taught that when a man knows what to do and doesn't do it, he is sinning against the Lord.[14]

In the Hebrew language and culture, the concept of hearing means more than just listening, it means *hearing responsively.* To the Hebrew, the command to hear means to hear with an obedient response. This is like when a parent tells his child to do something, and the child does not comply. The parent may say, *Did you hear me?* but what he really means is, *I know you heard me; why didn't you do obey?*

God is merciful, and a better parent than you or I; He is not a punitive or petty person, and doesn't stop communicating the minute you fail to obey. It is when a Christian repeatedly fails to honor the voice of the Lord that He may go quiet until you have a change of heart. He will not cast his pearls before swine, so don't be one.

When you make it your goal to hear God's voice you must commit to trust and respond in faith to what you hear, and leave the results up to God. Though caution and discernment is always in order, don't be overly afraid of hearing wrong. When God sees that you have put your faith in hearing him, he adds his grace to your efforts, and will help you hear him in truth.

---

[14] James 4:17: "Anyone, then, who knows the good he ought to do and doesn't do it, sins."

Not to say that you will never experience times when God is quiet, or allows you to hear your own thoughts or those of some other spirit; but even then He is in charge of the process, and he allows this only as an occasional way to test and instruct our hearts. Not for the purpose of passing or failing, for God does not set us up to fail. We are tested only to reveal what is in our hearts (to us — He already knows), and to strengthen our intimacy and dependence upon Him.

We "hear" God's voice with our spiritual ears.

When we speak of hearing God's voice, we are not speaking of hearing with your physical ears or in your physical mind, but hearing in your spirit, which often sounds very much like what I call one's "thought voice." Communication from the Lord can come as pictures (visions), or just as a certain knowledge that arises in your spirit. With practice you will understand which is which. Until you mature in this area of discerning His voice, let the peace of Christ rule in your heart, or in other words, judge the matter. If what you hear seems out of character for God or makes you anxious, lay it aside and wait before acting upon it. If it is important, get someone else to pray with you.

As in all things, it is only practice that makes perfect, which is why you must not shrink back in the fear that you'll hear the wrong voice. Be willing to fail or mess up, as your Father is bigger than your mistakes and can redeem all. It is sad to see how fearful people are about this, so much so that many would rather not try to hear God than to risk hearing in error. The devil loves this fear because he knows that hearing God will enable you to walk in step with God, to know his thoughts, to know His will, so you can release his will on earth as it is in heaven. When you hear God, Satan's lies can be exposed and defeated. God's words bring light that invades and destroys the darkness of the devil, so we can clearly see and become wise to his schemes.

The Apostle Paul spoke of God revealing his very thoughts to us:

> However, as it is written: "No eye has seen, no ear has heard, no mind has conceived what God has prepared for those who love him"— but God has revealed it to us by his Spirit. The Spirit searches all things, even the deep things of God. For who among men knows the thoughts of a man except the man's spirit within him? In the same way no-one knows the thoughts of God except the Spirit of God. We have not received the spirit

of the world but the Spirit who is from God, that we may understand what God has freely given us.

This is what we speak, not in words taught us by human wisdom but in words taught by the Spirit, expressing spiritual truths in spiritual words. The man without the Spirit does not accept the things that come from the Spirit of God, for they are foolishness to him, and he cannot understand them, because they are spiritually discerned. The spiritual man makes judgments about all things, but he himself is not subject to any man's judgment: "For who has known the mind of the Lord that he may instruct him?" But we have the mind of Christ. (1 Corinthians 2:9-16).

The phrase *"the man without the spirit"* is more accurately rendered *"the natural man"* in the King James Version; we could read this, *The natural soul of man does not take hold of spiritual things.* This is a critical point because we often assume this verse refers only to unsaved people. It is saying that anyone who tries to understand God through his natural senses rather than the senses of his spirit, will fail.

Again, when Paul says *the man without the Spirit does not accept the things that come from the Spirit of God*, the Greek words refer to one who fails to reach out for something and take hold of it. The Spirit is always holding out what we need. We must learn to quit relying on our natural senses to perceive His activity and develop a sensitivity through our spirit instead.

I believe that when we are truly seeking God and his will, he will make sure we hear his voice. The best guarantee of hearing rightly is to make it your goal to love God, because love purifies the hearing ear. Of course you should always judge what you "hear" in prayer by what God says in the written word, because the Holy Spirit will never contradict Scripture.

Nourish yourself so you can nourish others.

Knowing God carries extra importance for the Christian wife and mother, who has a responsibility to teach her children to know God. She does not just feed her family physical food, but nourishes them emotionally and spiritually as well. What she offers to her husband and children out of her character and spirit becomes a part of them. Jesus acknowledged this truth when he said, "I am the bread of life," and "the one who 'feeds' on me will live." He was referring to the transference which occurs between people in close relationship. Proverbs 31 describes a woman's duty to feed on Jesus often so she has something to feed the spirits of her family:

> *She is like the merchant ships loaded with foodstuffs; she brings her household's food from a far country. She rises while it is yet night and gets spiritual food for her household.... (v.14-15, The Amplified Bible)*

The word "food" is translated from the Hebrew word *lechem*, which means "bread." Undoubtedly the bread represents Jesus, *"the true bread from heaven."*[15] The nourishment Jesus gives comes through feeding on His Word and His Spirit through regular, personal communication.

To say that a woman is "like a merchant ship" implies that she brings in wonderful treasures from faraway places that cannot be locally obtained. The Bible tells us that our treasure is found in Christ, *"...in whom are hidden all the treasures of wisdom and knowledge."*[16] We cannot get true wisdom from the world. We must reach out to heaven for the words that give true life, understanding that *man does not live on bread alone but on every word that comes from the mouth of the Lord.*[17]

When you are nourished by God in your spirit, you have a precious treasure of wisdom to share with your family. The bread God offers you through His Word, written and spoken, is meant to be distributed. It offers real help for real problems in real life, and the woman God designed should have plenty of such nourishment to offer. As your children witness you placing value in and actively living by God's Word, they will develop this same value, and learn to be nourished on His Word themselves.

It is not the church's job to train your children to have a relationship with God, and this could never be accomplished in one 45-minute period per week anyway. Furthermore, if you tell your children to read the Bible, yet they don't see you doing so, they won't either. They imitate what you do, not what you say.

---

[15] John 6:35 & 41.
[16] Colossians 2:2-3.
[17] Deuteronomy 8:3

Don't make the Lord do it by a formula.

In a relationship with a living being, every encounter is unique. Many people approach God with a rote formula each day, and the Lord's prayer was never intended to be the only prayer one recited to God, but a model of the kinds of things one would talk to God about each day. Some days in prayer will include all of these elements; others may be spent on one. Some days will be pouring out your heart to God, some will be mostly listening to God pour out his.[18] Other times will be spent just worshipping him in joyful silence and drinking in the knowledge of who He is. Some days He will have you open the Bible to personally teach you. Keep a journal handy at all times, and write down the precious things He says to you. Expect to hear His voice. Let Him set the agenda for each prayer meeting: *Jesus, what do you want to talk about today? Who shall I pray for this morning?*

There will be times when you will ask questions and not seem to get an answer. Perhaps He wants to discuss another subject. Some prayer times will be really brief, others will be extravagantly long. Let Him determine when prayer time is over. Don't pray by the clock, but by the Spirit.

Then when you leave the place of prayer, keep on praying. When the Word of God says, *pray without ceasing*[19] it is not telling you to withdraw from life to pray like a monk; it refers to a life of uninterrupted fellowship with the Lord. It is developing the awareness that you are always in his presence, that he often wants to communicate with you even after that little half hour you give him in the morning; it is being available for listening any time.

I will be a woman who knows her God.

What kind of woman will I be? I will be a woman who studies His Word, searching for treasures in every part. I will hear the voice of my shepherd and be personally taught by him, feeding on the bread of heaven and sharing my bread with my family. I will be a woman who knows and understands her God.

---

[18] Proverbs 1:23.

[19] 1 Thessalonians 5:17.

Reflecting on Chapter 7

This chapter explains the importance of personally knowing God through His written word and hearing His voice.

❖ *Read Appendix B, "My Sheep Listen to My Voice."*

❖ *Ask the Lord to increase your faith to hear his voice.*

❖ *Commit to a schedule to read your Bible all the way through. If you use devotional books or other Christian literature, be sure to read them in addition to, not in place of, reading the Bible.*

Chapter 8

I Will Be A Lover

People tend to view their relationship to God in isolation, apart from their other relationships, as if all that matters is what happens between them and God. But Jesus negated this when he said the command to love others is as important as the command to love Him with all one's might. He called the Pharisees (the religious superstars of his day) hypocrites because they carefully observed laws like tithing, but neglected what he described as the more important matters: justice, mercy and faithfulness. All are related to relationship.

The Apostle Paul further clarified the matter for us when he said in Galatians 5:14, *"The entire law is summed up in a single command: "Love your neighbor as yourself."* God's highest priority is for you to learn how to love. He never qualified his command and never listed any exceptions. In fact, he goes so far as to tell us to even love our enemies. Ironically, most of us do make a real effort to love those we consider to be enemies while failing to put the same effort into loving those who merely offend us or let us down: relatives, friends, neighbors, pastors, and spouses.

Some of the most religiously active people I've met have one or more relationships in serious trouble — marked by discord, unforgiveness, perhaps bitterness or even emotional estrangement. The problem is that while you may believe that the level of your religious activity earns God's approval in spite of the state of your personal relationships, you would be mistaken. In light of all that God demands regarding love and faithfulness in relationships, He could not possibly find pleasure in anyone's walk who allows their relationships to languish, no matter how many Bible classes or prayer meetings they attend.

God's kingdom will be built through love.

Great relationships are not just a step to some other goal, they are the goal. Committed, righteous relationship is the very essence of the kingdom of God, the cellular structure of the Body of Christ. Living in right relationship to others is how we show the world that God exists and what he is like. One of the reasons God lives in us is so he can express Himself to the world through us.

> *No one has ever seen God; but if we love one another, God lives in us and his love is made complete in us. 1 John 4:12*

Although Jesus dwells in all who are saved, in some of us he merely exists, while in others he really lives, meaning he is able to freely to express himself. That's what this scripture is telling us: that only when we love others well is God allowed to really live and move and have His being in us, when His character has become your character.

God's love for people finds its complete expression only as we surrender our hearts and minds to his purposes — and judgments — in responding to others. To a great degree the Body of Christ still fails to let God do this. When we rightly represent God's heart to others the world will flock to Him — and His Body — to find rest for their restless souls, instead of food, drugs, sex and other consuming pursuits.

We are not representing the heart of God rightly until we learn to love others as God has loved us. We who have received God's love will be judged by how well we took what was freely given to us and distributed it to others:

> *And so we know and rely on the love God has for us. God is love. Whoever lives in love lives in God, and God in him. In this way, love is made complete among us so that we will have confidence on the day of judgment, because in this world we are like him. (1 John 4:16-17).*

Jesus made it clear that at the end of time, when all men face him at the seat of judgment, the final exam will be: how well did you love?[1] Christians know how to "act" loving towards others, but God wants more than an outward show; he wants love and faithfulness to be our constant occupation:

---

[1] See Matthew 25:31-46.

*Let love and faithfulness never leave you. Bind them around your
neck, write them upon the tablet of your heart. (Proverbs 3:3)*

People who marry usually come together through romantic love that is
blind to the flaws of the other person. But when the challenges of life cause
romantic love to fade we have to face the truth about the person we have
married. At this point affairs and divorces often happen as disillusioned
spouses try to recapture the intoxication of being in love, or they give up
entirely and divorce. Women may try to recapture romance through reading
romance novels or watching soap operas; many hide from their profound
disappointment by turning away from the husband emotionally and
immersing themselves in children, hobbies or careers. Clearly, we pursue the
goal of "being in love" rather than becoming lovers.

Is the issue their character, or yours?

How we treat others is, and should be, an expression of our character,
not merely a response to the other person. We need to realize that God
doesn't love us because we're lovable; he loves us because he is a lover. That
is his character, and the steadfastness of his character is his glory, a glory that
is best revealed in relationship. The fact that God is loving, merciful and just
has little meaning outside the context of relationship. Likewise, as made in
God's image, our glory — or lack of it — will be revealed in how we relate to
others.

God's plan is that our character be established through our fellowship
with Him. The idea is that if we hang out with God and see how our Father
treats us, we learn to how to treat others. God essentially says, *"I treat you
not as you deserve, but for the sake of my name, as an expression of my goodness,
my faithfulness, my mercy."* The Bible says of the Lord, *"...he does not treat us
as our sins deserve or repay us according to our iniquities."*[2] Our behavior can
certainly diminish God's pleasure in us and even put him in a position to
resist blessing us, but His love never fails. His love for you is not based upon
your performance or depend upon your character, but upon his. So it is and
should be with all who are made in his image. The task of a Christian is to
become a recognizable son or daughter of God. Paul said that all of creation
is waiting for this.[3]

---

[2] Psalm 103:10.

[3] Romans 8:19.

If love is part of your character, then you love by choice, as an act of faithfulness, not as a result of how you feel or how the other person behaves. The way of the world is to let other people's behavior determine how you will behave, so that who you are changes depending upon who you are with, or the mood you are in. The less mature you are, the more likely this is to be so. If you are really a lover, the ability to love doesn't disappear when you are in the presence of someone who is difficult to love. If kindness is part of your character, your kindness will be evident no matter who you are with.

An immature Christian treats others as they seem to deserve, rather than the way God treats them. We are so sure that God wants us to fix everybody. But does he do this with us? No, God just loves us to life.

If someone gets left behind in a relationship, we tend to assume that they did something to deserve it. But in God's eyes if you fail to love someone it is not a statement about them; it is a statement about you: you don't fully know how to love. In fact, on a subconscious level what may cause us to move away from a relationship often isn't the other person's flaws, as much as the fear of having to face our inability to love. This is yet another reason why we need Christ so much: His love never fails, and He has poured into us his ability to love through the Holy Spirit.[4]

God is the continual witness and judge of our treatment of others, especially our marriage partners. In relating to a married person God's favor and pleasure in us is not based upon who we are all by ourselves. God relates to us in full view of our covenant relationships, because he is a covenant God. God clearly states in Malachi 2:14 that he stands as a continual witness between a husband and wife to see if they are faithfully loving one another, a fact which the New Testament makes clear is true even if the spouse is an unbeliever.

One of the purposes for marriage is to teach us on earth how to live faithfully in covenant with Him. God, who declares *never will I leave you or forsake you*, wants us to be able to live as if this is also our highest priority.

---

[4] Romans 5:5.

The "golden rule," or the divine rule?

The "golden rule" says we should treat others according to how we want to be treated. It's a good rule, but God has a better one: treat others according to how God treats you:

> "*A new command I give you: Love one another. As I have loved you, so you must love one another.*" *(John 13:34)*

How has God loved me? Let me count the ways. I am continually amazed at God's long-suffering with me. He came and gave his love to me while I was still a sinner and wholly unworthy of his love. He continues to give me his love even though I still let him down. The constancy of His love is what gives me the desire to keep trying to know him. When I fail, he doesn't shut me out in judgment, he offers grace — a grace that doesn't approve of sin, but insists that it cannot rip us apart. His graciousness gives me the courage I need to keep pressing in because I don't have to fear the loss of his love if I mess up.

Grace is God's insistence that his love for me does not depend upon my perfect performance. His love comes to heal my flaws, not punish them; to cover them with his garment, not magnify them. God accepts me completely, the bad and the good. He does not condone the bad, but keeps walking with me so I can learn to be like him. His new mercy comes to meet me every morning. His undeserved favor is his love leaping over my flaws to stay close.

He calls us to be like him — extending grace to others, especially those we live with every day. The very strength of our relationship to God is his graciousness towards us, his willingness to suffer long with us while he waits for us to become more like Him. Grace is what we give our children while they grow up and learn how to handle themselves in the world. We show them when they are wrong in order to teach them wrong from right; but our love doesn't waver and doesn't depend upon their perfect performance.

Love chooses to look up to others.

How you treat others flows out of what you really think about them in your heart. It is easy to think of ourselves as better than others, especially those whose flaws we know the best. But Paul counsels us in these excerpted remarks from Philippians 2:1-8:

> If you have ... any fellowship with the Spirit ... then make my joy complete by ... having the same love. Do nothing out of selfish ambition or vain conceit, but in humility consider others better than yourselves. Each of you should look not only to your own interests, but also to the interests of others. Your attitude should be the same as that of Christ Jesus: Who, being in very nature God ... made himself nothing, taking the very nature of a servant. And ... he humbled himself ...

Paul implies that a person shows he is filled with the Spirit by having the same attitude Jesus did, who though he was the son of God, did not view or treat people as less important than himself. Jesus related to others in a way that elevated them above Himself; He chose "to look up to" them. The Son of God chose to look up to people.

Jesus did not just put on a show of being humble; he honestly saw himself as lowly. How do I know? Because incredibly, when someone addressed Jesus as "Good teacher," he responded, "Why do you call me good? No one is good, except God alone!"[5] His humility ran deep.

Andrew Murray once said that humility is best illustrated by the fact that the heaviest laden branches of a fruit tree bow down to the lowest. Jesus showed his love for people by being more concerned with their problems than his own. He loved people fearlessly. He touched the untouchable. Jesus was respectful; by the way he treated even the most social outcast of his day, he honored others, treating them in a way that verified that they had worth and value. He was the greater one, yet he honored them. That's what love looks like.

Simple things like courtesy, kindness and politeness are wonderfully honoring. It is easy to only do these things when we want to impress people or are impressed by them, and more difficult to do with those we live with every day. Jesus never treated someone a certain way for his sake; he always treated others a certain way for their sake. This is the unmistakable mark of a lover.

---

[5] Mark 10:17-18.

Marriage tests your character.

The true measure of spiritual maturity is not revealed by your behavior at church, but in the quality of your personal relationships. If you don't have the fruit of Jesus' character at home where it is needed the most, then any "fruit" you display out in public is really just for show. The issues of forgiveness, mercy, self-sacrifice, love, patience and humility are tested more thoroughly in your family than anywhere else. Where else would you have opportunity to forgive the same person seven times in one day?

The old saying holds that visiting relatives are like fish, becoming unbearable after three days. But the problem is not really with the relatives; the truth is that three days is usually the limit of our ability to pretend we're more patient, gracious and forgiving than we really are.

Who is "the least of these" in your life?

Jesus told his followers, *As you have treated the least of these, you have done it to me*.[6] Most of us do strive to treat people kindly for God's sake. We are gracious to unsaved acquaintances in order to draw them to Christ; we extend kindness to our saved friends because they are in the family of faith and because — be honest — we want them to think well of us. We easily dig down and find goodness to offer those we consider to be somehow less than ourselves. But because the husband usually doesn't fit in any of these categories, he is often left in a kind of spiritual "no man's land," where it is all too easy to offer him less consideration than we do others.

I see reputedly spiritually mature women who never miss a church service or Bible study, who know how to pray and operate in spiritual gifts — yet who go home to the husband in a spirit of scorn, disapproval, and spiritual haughtiness. This should not be. If such a woman thinks God is pleased with her, she is deceived.

God's plan is that the one He lives in should offer human hands, feet, mouth and heart for Jesus to express His love to the world. A woman who preaches to her husband that God is merciful, yet shows him no mercy, will never convince that man of God's mercy. If she withholds love, patience and goodness from her husband, giving these courtesies to others while denying

---

[6] Matthew 25:40 & 45.

him, then she has withheld a true taste of Jesus from him. We should be able to say, as Jesus did, *"It is the Father living in me, who is doing his work."*[7]

One reason a woman is called to submit is so an unbelieving husband may taste of the goodness of God and hunger for God himself.[8] The fruit of your life with God should be given first to your husband and family as much or more than it is distributed to others in your community.

Barriers to love.

What hinders us in loving others? Often the problem is not an unwillingness to love them, but the fact that we simply love ourselves more than we love them. In making choices that protected or served my comfort or pleasure, I have hurt people I never intended to. Hence the command, no doubt, to *love your neighbor as yourself.* Selfishness is a barrier to loving others, a wall of concern about myself that is so high around me that I cannot see your need.

By far the greatest barrier to love is offense. We all become offended occasionally by others; no one is immune to hurt feelings. Also, a major problem is rejection or alienation, which has reached epidemic proportions in our society. Rejection is a major barrier to loving others, since we tend to give love responsively; that is, to work at loving only those who seem to love us and make us feel good about ourselves. If we sense the slightest rejection we tend to turn away from others and cease trying to love them.

Alienation is the sense of being loosely connected or completely disconnected from others, a sensation increasing dramatically as we become a society that is more face-to-face with computers, cell phones, video games and television than with other people.

Quite possibly the greatest hindrance to loving others comes from the judgments we form about them, and oddly enough, becoming a Christian only tends to increase the problem. Once we are exposed to God's Word and His ways, we acquire a heightened sense of right and wrong, and get more easily offended at everyone else's "wrong."

---

[7] John 14:10b.

[8] 1 Peter 3:1-2.

Love leaves judgment to God.

When we judge another person, we come terrifying close to displacing God on His throne. Women are especially notorious for trying to fix their husbands. Women often want to tell me what their husbands are doing wrong, even pointing to his failures as an excuse to disobey God in the matter of honoring a husband's leadership. If we all waited for the other person to behave righteously so we could act righteously, no one would ever do it. We must never point at someone else's behavior as an excuse to disobey God. We who have the very Spirit of Christ living in us should set the example in all things. Why should a woman of God show respect to a husband who doesn't deserve it? My answer is that God has called us to be those who treat others with respect — again, an expression of our character, not a reward or punishment for someone else's.

While God has called us to judge things in the sense of discerning them accurately, He has not called us to judge things in the sense of dispensing justice. This he reserves for himself alone. The woman God designed does not live in judgment of other people and knows it is not her place to fix them.

Love doesn't mean one never corrects another; real love is not blind, but it is guided by wisdom and compassion. Has it ever occurred to you that Jesus corrected the Pharisees because he loved them? Sometimes the most unloving thing we can do is leave someone in their sin or not tell them that they have spinach in their teeth. The point is, love for another person should motivate whatever we do with them. Our prayer should be, *"Lord, how can I love this person?"* And even if we do not utter this particular prayer, we can be can be sure that whenever we are obeying the Lord we are most effectively loving others at the same time.

All your life you will see others make mistakes, especially those you live with. Judgment kicks in so easy when we live up close and personal. How should we handle this? First, accept the fact that only God is a truly "just" judge, discerning the motives and conditions of a person's heart perfectly. Until you walk as closely with God as Jesus did, you cannot know and judge the heart of another human being. And even though Jesus did have such discernment, he chose not to rely upon his own judgment as he lived among men on earth. He did not treat people according to what he thought or felt, but always sought His Father's knowledge and will:

You judge by human standards; I pass judgment on no one. But if I do judge, my decisions are right, because I am not alone. I stand with the Father, who sent me. (John 8:15-16).

The phrase "human standards" is the Greek word *sarx* again, referring to the natural flesh and its senses. Jesus refused to trust his natural senses in judging others and always sought the Father's wisdom in relating to others. Because of this Jesus knew what to do when the religious leaders dragged before him the woman caught in the act of adultery. According to His Father's own law given to Moses, he had a right — even an obligation — to stone her with the others. Yet he did not. Instead, to the amazement of the crowd, he pondered a moment, then said, *"Let whoever among you that is without sin be the first one to cast the stone."* No one did, of course. It was one of many things Jesus did and taught to reveal the way things would be in the new covenant, but most importantly, we know Jesus said what he did because he sought the will of his Father. He judged the sin, but left judgment to his Father. The Lord alone was a witness to all that had led this woman to that moment, and he apparently was after much more in that moment than judging one woman's sin. He exposed the hearts of a whole community.

By saying the words the Father gave him to say, Jesus showed mercy at just the right moment and thereby effectively judged the hidden sin of a whole crowd. He could have responded legalistically; instead he responded righteously. Righteousness is not found in obeying the law, but in following the Holy Spirit. The bottom line is that it is not all about you or all about that person's failure; it is all about what God is doing and the kingdom he is building. Are we better able to judge than Jesus? If Jesus, the very Son of God, filled with the Holy Spirit, thought he needed to seek the Father's wisdom in relating to and judging people, how much more do we need this?

I remember a season when my husband was acting pretty jerky most of the time. He seemed to be in a perpetual bad mood and took it out on me. I went to the Lord often to find help in forgiving him. One day the Lord prompted me to ask Him how to pray for my husband. When I did, the Lord told me to pray every day for the wounds in Ron's heart to be healed. I was unaware of any wounds because I had been focused entirely upon Ron's outward behavior. That was my issue; but the Lord was focused on the condition of Ron's heart. I saw in this that my goal wasn't to love Ron, but to judge him. How self-righteous I had been as I had proudly came to him repeatedly for the strength to forgive Ron's actions!

I began to pray for Ron's healing, with two results. The immediate result was a change in my own attitude. I began to draw Ron out and felt compassion towards him instead of judgment. The second was that as the Lord healed Ron's heart his joy returned and his behavior changed. Part of living by faith is learning to respond to others by faith in what God says about them rather than judge by the outward appearance of things.

Do you know what "season" today is in your husband's heart, and what he needs the most? You are not called to fix your husband, but to love and serve him, in Jesus' name. If your heart is set on changing your husband, then it is set upon the wrong thing and weariness is likely present. You will find great rest for your soul when you resign from the job of fixing your man — or anyone else, for that matter.

While there are times that the Holy Spirit will use us to correct another person, we are not meant to go looking for opportunities to do so. While there are seasons for this, God calls for it far less often than we realize, and rarely needs our help. God usually uses me to judge someone else while I'm not trying. In other words, when I am simply focused on loving God and others, my behavior or attitude may cause the heart of another to be judged without me even being aware of it.

There was no greater opportunity for judgment than on the day they persecuted Jesus without cause, and his judgment would have been just. First Peter 2:23 tells us that when Jesus was at the height of his suffering, he did not judge his persecutors, but *"entrusted himself to the one who judges justly."* Jesus knew that one day he would judge the world, and this was not that day. If Jesus had judged on that day instead of loved, where would we be? The season called for mercy, love and sacrifice. The wise author of Ecclesiastes wrote:

Since a king's word is supreme, who can say to him, "What are you doing?" Whoever obeys his command will come to no harm, and the wise heart will know the proper time and procedure. For there is a proper time and procedure for every matter.... (Ecclesiastes 8:4-6)

Jesus continually tuned his ear to the Father's heart as he related to others. Is this possible for us? You bet. Remember, we have the mind of Christ and can know the thoughts of God. The Spirit has been given to us so that we may walk as Jesus walked, not in our own understanding, but in God's. For as Proverbs Chapter Three goes on to say after urging us to stay preoccupied with the issues of faithfulness and love:

Trust in the Lord with all your heart and lean not on your own understanding; in all your ways acknowledge him, and he will make your paths straight. Do not be wise in your own eyes... (Proverbs 3:5-7).

I cannot count the number of times I have taken issue with my husband, certain that I was perfectly right and just in my judgment, only to discover later that I was wrong. I invite you to take your "judgments" to God and ask *"Lord, what do you think of my opinion?"* or *"Lord, how should I respond to this person's behavior?"* The Holy Spirit would love to show you whether to hug or hurl a stone.

What to do with your anger.

Have you noticed that God's offer of forgiveness is conditional: "I will forgive you *as you forgive others."* When we withhold forgiveness from others, God withholds forgiveness from us. As the parable of the unmerciful servant in Matthew 18 reveals, God is forced to stand against us in judgment while we presume to judge. He asks us to leave judgment up to him, and demands that we forgive — quickly, often and completely.[9] This is what God does with you. Don't keep account of offenses in your mind, because *love keeps no record of wrongs.*

It is difficult to forgive as long as we remain angry about an offense, and must deal with the anger before we can go there. Sometimes our anger is just, sometimes it is not; either way, what are we to do with it?

God is our Father, let's see how he handles his anger, which is always justified. The Bible is filled with expressions of God's anger over betrayal and injustice. While God is slow to get angry, when his anger is aroused it can become great indeed because his love runs deep and his measure of righteousness is so perfect. So what does God do with his anger?

To begin with, the Bible says of God, *"For his anger lasts only a moment, but his favor lasts a lifetime."* (Psalm 30:5). Why is it that God's anger lasts only a moment? (No, it's not because a day with the Lord is like a thousand

---

[9] Note that forgiveness and reconciliation are not the same. Forgiveness is the act of one person and can be done whether the other person knows it or not; reconciliation requires two people and only happens when the behavior which has destroyed a relationship has been repented of and changed. For instance, you must forgive a husband for abusing you, but the relationship cannot be reconciled until he changes his abusive behavior.

years.) God's anger lasts only a moment because he makes a choice to turn way from it. Psalm 85:3 tells us this, that he actually sets his wrath aside.

God turns away from his anger, though justified, in order to allow His love for you become his focus again. He gives himself to his love, not to his anger. In this he does not excuse sin, but reveals his value to guard and preserve the relationship. There is no doubt this is very difficult for us mortals, but still the lesson and the value must be pondered, and the strength to do this must be sought for in prayer.

The Psalmist counsels us:

> *Be still before the Lord and wait patiently for him; do not fret when men succeed in their ways, when they carry out their wicked schemes. Refrain from anger and turn from wrath; do not fret—it leads only to evil. For evil men will be cut off, but those who hope in the Lord will inherit the land.* (Psalm 37:7-9).

Again, we have the thought of turning away from anger. In order to stay angry we have to stay focused on the offense, looking at it, meditating upon it. If we do this long enough, the accusations we make and the fury we feel is written on the tablet of our hearts in place of love and faithfulness. Making the offender answer for our anger displaces the goal to love. If left long enough, this anger can become a lifestyle, and bitterness the character of the offended.

Jesus said in John 15:13, *Greater love has no one than this, that he lay down his life for his friends.* The word "life" in the Greek actually means "soul." Jesus is saying, *Lay down your soul or die to your soul* — often defined as your mind, will and emotions. Sometimes, like our Father in heaven, we must be willing to lay down our thoughts and opinions, our deep desires, and our feelings, in order to continue to faithfully love and preserve our relationship with another person.

But hear this, even though God calls us to die to self, He does not ask us to commit suicide. Jesus said a lover would *lay down his life.* The idea is to lay something aside, no longer paying attention to it, so one can give oneself to other pursuits. In this case, we are to pursue love. The point of taking up our cross to follow Jesus is not so that we can die like he died, but so that we can love like he loved. The suffering that we are called to is actually a by-product or consequence of the choice to love. As has been said, the commitment to love others will force you to forget self at times so that self dies a natural, quiet and humble (unnoticed) death.

In order to really forgive a husband several times a day for the same offense and not shut down on him emotionally, a wife may have to deny or turn away, at least temporarily, from some personal desire; such as the need to be treated differently or for him to be her hero. Dying to self means laying aside the need to make others change right now, and abandoning your demand for immediate justice.

Make no mistake, this hurts, and these are painful sacrifices that feel as if you are letting a part of yourself die. And so you are. But God treats your sacrifice as holy, and comes quickly to offer you new life in place of what you have laid on his altar.

Isaiah 58 actually calls this a type of fasting, saying this is the kind of "fasting" the Father wants: not abstaining from food, but from our judgments and anger in order to show love to others. This kind of fasting is far more apt to draw the Spirit of God near and build Christ's character in you than only abstaining from a few meals.

I am not suggesting that you never work through things with your spouse, that you become a mouse, a doormat or Suzy Stoic. Not at all! Learning to work through problems is a crucial part of building great relationships. We do not honor God by ignoring problems, but in learning to handle them as He would. But His goal is always to build righteous character in you while strengthening and renewing the relationship. Too many Christians, in a spirit of self-righteousness, refuse to stay for the lesson and let the relationship go by the wayside, because they judged themselves innocent and in the right. As my husband loves to say, it is better to be righteous than right, and godly relationships are the very stuff of which God establishes His kingdom:

> *Righteousness and justice are the foundation of your throne; love and faithfulness go before you. (Psalms 89:14)*

Jesus can show us how to do all that God requires because he has lived in a skin suit. He may be in heaven, but the Spirit of Christ who lives with us bears forever within him an intimate knowledge of the human experience, and He understands. Jesus was tempted and tested in every way we are. Sometimes it is hard for us to really believe this, because Jesus did not experience marriage, child-rearing, advancing age, menopause or womanhood. So how can Jesus possibly relate to what you, dear lady, are going through?

He can relate because life is not just experienced as events but as the deeply felt emotions that events burn into our souls. How would Jesus conduct himself in a troubled marriage? Though unmarried, Jesus loved people deeply and experienced the indifference, selfishness and betrayal of those he loved and gave himself to. He experienced frustration and betrayal.

The woman overwhelmed by work to be done, small children demanding attention can know Jesus experienced this from the crowds that pressed in so closely and relentlessly that he often could not even eat or sleep unless he hid from them.

How about rejection and alienation, the inevitable wounds of divorce? Did not Jesus feel this deeply this when his own family did not understand his ministry, and his closest friends abandoned him?

And then there is fear. Which of us has wrestled with fear and anguish so deeply that we sweat drops of blood? But God can satisfy the needs of our hearts in all these things, as we will learn in the next chapter.

God quickly heals the wounds of love.

In my commitment to love others, I have been wounded, and not infrequently. When the heart hurts, the temptation to shut down, go away and give up on people can be overwhelming. This I know from personal experience; yet I have learned not to be afraid of being hurt anymore, because God quickly heals the wounds of love. He has healed my heart again and again, so that I may love others another day in a way that does not fail, that keeps hoping, trusting, persevering.[10]

We must quit making excuses for our failures in love and go to the throne of grace to receive God's ability to carry it out. God has convinced me that the most important job in my life is to love my husband. In fact, he told me once that if everyone would love just one other person truly well, it would change our world. If I fail at this, nothing else much matters.

God knows we need to be taught how to love like this. Titus 2:4 says *train the younger women to love their husbands and children.* One of the main

---

[10] 1 Corinthians 13:7-8.

purposes of this book is to teach a woman how to love her husband. After the crisis in my own marriage and years in the ministry I see the real need for this. Many people have never been taught how to love with mercy and grace, so that we now have generations who were not loved well raising children they do not know how to love.

We need the Holy Spirit's help to love like God loves.

The command to love is yet another reason we need the power of the Holy Spirit in every day life. We make the choice, God provides the power and the wisdom. The Holy Spirit stands ready to empower you to love your neighbor, especially if that neighbor lives in your home; He waits for us to turn to him and ask for help. He loves to help us love. Pray for the power to love as God loves. The power of God serves no greater purpose.

What kind of woman will I be? I will be a lover. I will love others like God has loved me, and trust Him to heal the wounds of loving.

Reflecting on Chapter 8

This chapter teaches us to obey Jesus' command to love others as He has loved us, and how to deal with the enemies of love such as anger, judgment and unforgiveness.

❖ *Ponder: is there is anyone you have failed to forgive, forcing God to resist forgiving you?*

❖ *Discover what your husband needs to feel loved by you in this season.*

❖ *Read Proverbs 3:3-8.*

❖ *Pay attention to the judgments you make about significant people in your life and how these interfere with your ability to love them. Begin taking your judgments to the Lord and asking him to show you the truth.*

❖ *Ask the Holy Spirit to give you the ability (grace), understanding and wisdom you need to love like God loves.*

Chapter 9

I Will Be Satisfied By God

"Come to me, all you who are weary and burdened, and I will give you rest. Take my yoke upon you and learn from me, for I am gentle and humble in heart, and you will find rest for your souls. For my yoke is easy and my burden is light." (Matthew 11:28-30).

The word "rest" which Jesus used here in the Greek has a prefix which implies repetition or intensity. He was not referring to an invitation to come only once, but again and again, whenever we need to return to a state of rest in the soul.

It's not just that we need this rest; God himself longs for us to enter into it, and the author of Hebrews implores us to make every effort to come into it.[1] So what is it exactly? According to Scripture, rest encompasses and is described as the various benefits of being in covenant with God, such as safety from one's enemies, a tranquil inner life, security in a relationship, and contentment. Of the rest that comes through contentment, a thoughtful study of Scripture reveals this to be a state of the soul in which there is a complete absence of neediness — not to be confused with having everything we think we want or need. There is vast difference.

Rest: an absence of neediness.

Contentment exists when there is no striving to fill a need; it is not about outward circumstances, but a heart at rest. Often our own desires are the source of discontent, such as when we want something we do not or cannot have. The striving in one's soul can seem impossible to still. But if

---

[1] Hebrews Chapters 3 and 4.

you are truly willing, God will change the desires of your heart, and thus end your struggle.

We focus on wrestling down the desire, straining to say no to a thing, when the shortcut is to give God permission to change your heart, the place where desire is born. Instead of trying to kill it, you carry it to Him and offer it as an act of love and trust, showing that you love Him more than that thing you want, and trust Him to give you what is best. Peace reigns in the heart that is satisfied in God, trusting God to either douse or blow on the fires that burn within the soul.

Our inspiration comes from the Psalmist who discovered the antidote for all of his soul's neediness: the Lord himself. In fact, he commanded his soul to find its rest — its complete satisfaction — in God alone:

> My soul finds rest in God alone; my salvation comes from him. .... Find rest, O my soul, in God alone; my hope comes from him. (Psalm 62:1 and 5).

Like any human being, the Psalmist might have tried to satisfy the hungers of his body and soul in various ways; but he had discovered the true hunger of his heart and refused to turn to other things to feed his need:

> O God, you are my God, earnestly I seek you; my soul thirsts for you, my body longs for you, in a dry and weary land where there is no water. I have seen you in the sanctuary and beheld your power and your glory. Because your love is better than life, my lips will glorify you. I will praise you as long as I live, and in your name I will lift up my hands. My soul will be satisfied as with the richest of foods; with singing lips my mouth will praise you. (Psalm 63:1-5).

The word translated as "rest" in both these Psalms is *damam*, one of seven Hebrew or Greek words translated as rest in the Bible. *Damam* is beholding God in quiet surrender, waiting upon Him in full trust. It is the rest that comes from gazing at God instead of the world. The psalmist chose to give his hunger to God in the real belief that God would satisfy him.

Scripture insists that God knows us completely in our humanness and meets our every need. Only a very cruel God would create us with needs and then ignore them. So while it is clear that God has the will and the ability to satisfy us, the question remains, are we satisfied by Him? Not necessarily.

Would a perfect life satisfy us?

If any woman ever had the perfect life, it was Eve. She had it all: the perfect man, no children to chase, no dust bunnies under her bed, no financial worries. Surely God created her with a perfect figure, she had no wardrobe problems, no calories or fat grams to count, no runs in her pantyhose, no other women with whom to compare herself. Yet for all this ideal existence, Eve was not satisfied with what she had. How do I know? If she had been content, the devil would have been unable to entice her to go for more. The greatest tool the devil uses to lead us astray from God's life is our discontent.

The women's movement was born out of this discontent. Lucy Stone, one of the pioneers of the women's movement, stood before a national women's rights convention in Cincinnati in 1855 and uttered these words out of her bitter soul: "In education, in marriage, in religion, in everything, disappointment is the lot of woman. It shall be the business of my life to deepen this disappointment in every woman's heart until she bows down to it no longer."

True, women had few rights in those days, and that needed to change; but my point here is that undoubtedly Lucy Stone found a field ripe for harvest in the souls of women, who seem to have a particularly difficult time staying satisfied. When women congregate it doesn't take them long to reveal what they are longing to have that will now make them happy — anything from a new dress to a new house to a different husband to a different body. We mistakenly think that if we could just have that one thing, we would be satisfied.

Satan's strategy with Eve was to convince her that she needed something more or different than what God had given her. In order to have influence over mankind, Satan had to entice him to take what he offered rather than what God provided. He first had to plant the seed of doubt in Eve's mind about God's words and His will:

> Now the serpent was more crafty than any of the wild animals the Lord God had made. He said to the woman, "Did God really say, `You must not eat from any tree in the garden'?" (Genesis 3:1).

Eve replies that God has put one certain tree off limits with a warning that if they eat of it or even touch it, they will die. She clearly knows what

God's will is. But the devil plants the seed of doubt in God's goodness by insinuating that God has deceived Adam and Eve, apparently motivated to keep for himself the secret of knowledge:

> *"You will not surely die," the serpent said to the woman. "For God knows that when you eat of it your eyes will be opened, and you will be like God, knowing good and evil." (Genesis 3:4-5).*

The devil succeeded in convincing Eve to take something God said she did not need and should not have — the fruit of the tree of knowledge. Thus we see that discontent was already lurking in her soul, for the Bible teaches that temptation has no power over us if desire is not already present.[2] Therefore, Eve could not have been successfully tempted by Satan if there were not already within her a desire to have more than what God had given her. It is this dissatisfaction with God's provision, with His expressed will that made her vulnerable to deception and ultimately led to rebellion against her Lord:

> *When the woman saw that the fruit of the tree was good for food and pleasing to the eye, and also desirable for gaining wisdom, she took some and ate it. She also gave some to her husband, who was with her, and he ate it. (Genesis 3:6).*

When God gives us something it is good, very good, and is all we need, because everything God gives — or withholds — is an expression of his great love for us. To doubt God's provision is to doubt his character, to question His goodness. The devil knows if he can get us to lose faith and trust in God's goodness or his motives, we will be open to temptation, easy suckers for the deceptive food Satan offers. Eve had a choice to make: trust God and rest content with what He offered on His Tree of Life, or turn away from God's provision and reach for something else to satisfy her hunger for more.

We are still making Eve's choice.

We are still making Eve's choice, every day of our lives. We have been restored to the Tree of Life, which represents all that God has given us for life, through the atoning sacrifice of Jesus Christ. We can choose to seek our

---

[2] James 1:13-14.

life from the Tree of Life by complete and utter reliance upon God, and a trustful submission to his ways and will, or we can choose to eat from the Tree of Knowledge by trying to satisfy ourselves with the "food" offered by the world.

Discontentment makes us vulnerable to the offerings of the devil. That is why Paul said that godliness with contentment is a great thing for us to achieve.[3]

To be honest, most people don't really know what they are hungry for, they just live in a state of vague but perpetual discontent, a fact that has made the advertising industry obscenely wealthy and increasingly bold in their drive to capture our hearts and pocketbooks, often redirecting us from what would really add to life. They do not love us, and that is why we should not heed them. Nor does the devil love us, but continually preys on the hunger of God's children to tempt them away from the Tree of Life once again, to stir up in them a hunger for meat instead of manna, the bread of heaven.

Our response to this chronic discontent is usually to fill it with food, shopping, hobbies, games, work, even relationships. We can fall into the habit of trying to make other people satisfy us, becoming manipulators continually motivated in our relationships to get others to do or be what we need to be happy. While it is God's will for us to love others so well that we do satisfy one another's needs, it is not his way for us to demand this of them.

What are we really hungry for?

We are all looking for abundant life. Most of what we really want are what I call "heart things": love, security, justice, goodness, well-being, respect. But the majority of us actually feed ourselves on food, entertainment, material possessions, and power. Years ago a pastor friend confessed from the pulpit that he had been through a season of being constantly hungry and fell into the habit of eating all the time, adding twenty pounds to his frame. He had, he confessed, developed a problem with gluttony. When he finally cried out to God for help, the Lord showed him that his "hunger" wasn't physical at all, but emotional and spiritual. As he

---

[3] 1 Timothy 6:6.

discovered and responded to his true hunger, he lost the overwhelming desire to eat, lost the weight and found peace.

One thing we are all hungry for is righteousness. Jesus spoke of this hunger when he promised: *Blessed are those who hunger and thirst for righteousness, for they will be filled.*[4] This verse is typically understood as the Lord promising to give us the ability to be righteous as he is righteous. Certainly this is true, yet I think there is more here, and like many verses has more than one layer of truth to it: I think it also speaks to the human need to be treated right by others.

You are hungry for righteousness.

Righteousness by its most basic definition is doing the right thing, at the right time, for the right reason, in relation to God and others. Of all the things God commands of us, he most wants us to love Himself and others with all our strength; these two things express what righteousness looks like. Righteousness is having the character and wisdom to give mercy at the right moment, to know when to discipline, when to kiss and when to refrain from embracing, all for the sake of effectively loving the other person.

We each experience this hunger for righteousness in all of our relationships. We all hunger to be treated rightly, to be loved faithfully, to be dealt with justly. We long for tenderness and understanding. We hunger for connection. We long to know goodness at the hands of others. And when we are wronged by others, we crave justice. And God made us this way — in his own image. We long for these things because he longs for them.

Yet God demands that we forgive, knowing that forgiveness will require us to die to the desire to be avenged. This is difficult because the desire for vengeance may be righteous (a right reaction to a real injustice). Anger at injustice is a godly emotion; God experiences it all the time. Since we're made like God it is natural for us to also want to be avenged of wrongs committed against us and those we love.

Our problem is that God claims all rights to vengeance[5] because he alone has perfect judgment and knows the truth about every heart. We do not possess the wisdom and knowledge needed to administer perfect justice.

---

[4] Matthew 5:6.

[5] Romans 12:19: *"Do not take revenge, my friends, but leave room for God's wrath, for it is written: 'It is mine to avenge; I will repay,' says the Lord."*

God's ways are for us to love our enemy (which sometimes means the one who loves us, but is acting like an enemy), return good for evil, and leave vengeance and justice up to Him. In order to obey Him in these things we must abandon our need to have a specific desire filled by a certain person in a certain time on a certain way. This can leave us sincerely hungry and unsatisfied.

The reason it is hard to forgive is that we fear if we do, they will get away with what they did to us. The heart cries for justice, and choosing forgiveness requires that you deny your soul's need for justice. Yet God demands that we do forgive, unconditionally, as often as we are wounded, even if by the same person many times.[6]

Forgiveness: a great test of God's ability to satisfy a soul.

We have God's promise that He can and will administer justice in due time, and according to the words of Matthew 5:6, will satisfy the soul's hunger for justice.

Having experienced this personally many times, I know that this is not just a promise for someday in heaven, this is for now. This is what it means to enter God's rest. We bring our hearts to rest in his will and trust in his workings, allowing the soul be content. When you make the decision to forgive, you ask God for the strength to carry it out and to meet your hunger. Your prayer might sound like this: "God, I long for righteousness in this situation. They have betrayed me, but I choose forgive. Give me the ability to carry it out as I release all judgment to you. I bring you my hunger for justice in this matter, and ask you to satisfy my soul and give me rest, in Jesus' name."

At His throne of grace you can be comforted unto a complete work of forgiveness. When God satisfies our hunger for justice, we are then liberated from anger and resentment, free to love again.

God is always ready to pour out His grace and power to help you forgive. God delights to meet our need when we chose the way of love. This is a work of the Spirit, and as in all things, not something you can make happen, only something you can choose. Your choice, His power.

---

[6] Matthew 18:21-22 and Luke 17:4-5. Note that immediately after Jesus describes how they should forgive, they cried, "Lord, increase our faith!"

Wounds of offense become wounds of love.

The world has a totally different way of dealing with offenses. Rather than forgive, the world encourages us to stand up for our rights. It sounds good to us because it really does hurt to give up such "rights," as if we are pouring salt on a wound. But because God is the one who demands that you forgive, he takes on the responsibility for your wound. It's an exchange: the wound caused by the offense is not gone; but it now remains as wound caused by your love for and obedience to God.

God promises that when you are wounded for his sake, he himself will bind up your wounds and bestow new life where you have died. You sow seeds of righteousness by doing the right thing, and He will see to it that you reap a harvest of joy:

> *Those who sow in tears will reap with songs of joy. He who goes out weeping, carrying seed to sow, will return with songs of joy, carrying sheaves with him. (Psalms 126:5-6)*

What is your harvest? The immediate reward is renewed rest and freedom. The "return" multiplies through the months and years as better health, richer relationships, and pathways to richer life you might have missed otherwise. I speak from personal experience. The harvest is far greater than anyone gives up to obtain it.

The way of God is not to demand rights, but to plant them as seeds in the soil of the kingdom. I have reaped the greatest contentment when I have given little parts of my self — certain needs, rights, beliefs — to God. For instance, my need to have a certain treatment from my husband — my "right" to be understood, or my need for his tenderness or patience. When I quit trying to get these things out of my husband and simply turn to the Lord and say, "Lord, I need this, would you satisfy my heart in this matter?" He always answers, without fail. God satisfies every hunger in my soul as long as it is offered to him.

Your self-protective heart can hardly stand not to help itself. The flesh is weak because it is self-centered: it wants to protect self, nurture self, satisfy self; the devil hopes to keep you busy serving these strong instincts in hopes that you'll never discover that God is infinitely more able to protect, nurture, and satisfy your self than you are!

We would be sadly amazed to discover how many "good" things in life actually choke the abundant life of God out of us. These things are not inherently evil, but they can become Satan's tools to rob us of God's best. These are the fruit of the tree of knowledge, representing everything of this world we reach for to give ourselves abundant life.

Our Heavenly Father is waiting for us to give up the cheap trinkets we cling to for dear life (our "rights" and desires) so he can give us the treasure of himself and his love. We try to cling to our junk while expecting God to give us his treasures, but God is not having any of that. God asks us to trade in our trash for his treasures. Such exchanges are the way of the kingdom. And there's really only one reason we would refuse to trade in our treasures: we honestly don't expect to be satisfied in God gives us. We don't expect true fulfillment to come in any real way that we can feel, and fear the only reward for our sacrifice will be some sort of spiritual merit badge from God.

Can God satisfy your soul?

While we easily fall into Eve's temptation and struggled to be satisfied with what God offers, the scriptures do teach that God is able to truly and deeply satisfy every living thing:

> The Lord will guide you always; he will satisfy your needs in a sun-scorched land and will strengthen your frame. You will be like a well-watered garden, like a spring whose waters never fail. (Isaiah 58:11).

> ...for he satisfies the thirsty and fills the hungry with good things. (Psalm 107:9).

> ...who satisfies your desires with good things so that your youth is renewed like the eagle's. (Psalm 103:5).

My favorite is Psalm 145:16, which says of the Lord, *"You open your hand and satisfy the desires of every living thing."* When God opens his hand to me and I receive what he offers, I am no longer needy. This is not just a reference to some mystical state of nirvana, and it's not about ignoring our real needs or denying what is going on in life.

Personal experience has taught me that Jesus Christ has the ability to satisfy my deepest longings and bring my heart to rest in, through, and in spite of all that life brings or fails to bring.

A.W. Tozer wrote in his classic, <u>The Pursuit of God</u>:

> *God is so vastly wonderful, so utterly and completely delightful that He can, without anything other than Himself, meet and overflow the deepest demands of our total nature, mysterious and deep as that nature is.*[7]

Take your deepest demands to God. Trust him with all the needs of your soul while you wait upon him. This is the secret strength of the ancients, of Abraham and those who often died waiting for their hopes to be fulfilled. We have life today because Abraham believed God's promise, but we forget that what sustained him while he waited for fulfillment was God himself, who said to him, *"Do not be afraid, Abram. I am your shield, your very great reward."*[8] My paraphrase: "I give you Me, and in having Me you have everything."

I would have abundant life, if only...

Like Eve, we often think life will be better if we could have more: more money, a better job, more education (knowledge), or, and here's the really big one: if some person in your life would change. At my women's retreats I often ask participants to fill in this blank: "My life would be abundant if _____."

What are your "If only's"? Fill in the blank for yourself, with as many answers as you like. Then, make note of how many of your answers involve getting other people to change; for instance, "I would have abundant life if only my husband shared my faith."

Quite frankly, while he often changes circumstances when you pray, Jesus does not make anyone do anything; he does not force people to be different. If having abundant life depends upon such things, Jesus made a promise he cannot keep — which is unthinkable. It follows then that God's ability to satisfy your soul is not connected to external conditions,

---

[7] The Pursuit of God by A.W. Tozer, 2006, WingSpread Publishers, page 42.
[8] Genesis 15:1

circumstances, or other people. The best "if only" we could have is, "If only I can get to Jesus and rest in his arms."

What do you reach for instead of Jesus?

What are you clinging to for contentment? When I gave my life to Jesus, I was hopelessly addicted to cigarettes, and had been since the age of 18. Although I made many changes when I got saved, giving up smoking wasn't one of them. Not that I didn't try; I tried quitting countless times but always failed, because I thoroughly enjoyed every cigarette I smoked.

Five years after I was saved I was still smoking, even though by then I was a pastor's wife. Although it embarrassed me to be mastered by something other than Jesus, and I knew it was a terrible example, I could not find the strength to give them up. I knew it was God's will for me to quit smoking but since he did not speak to me about quitting during those years, I continued. I was going to get away with it as long as I could. Understand, I am not justifying the fact that I smoked as a Christian, I am just stating the facts.

Finally the day came when the Lord told me to quit. I asked him to help me again and again, to no avail. One day I asked him to show me why I wasn't succeeding. He said, *"Toni, why do you smoke?"* So I thought about it, and realized that I looked to those cigarettes to satisfy me in many ways. I smoked when I was contented, as after a good meal. I smoked when I was nervous to help me calm down. I smoked when I was bored. I smoked when I was enjoying a good telephone conversation. I smoked because it tasted good with my coffee. Basically, I was celebrating all the moments in my life with a cigarette. They were like a constant friend that I reached for.

The Lord said to me, *"Toni, I want to be the one you reach for in these moments. I am jealous of your love for these cigarettes. I want to be the one you reach for when you're upset. I want to be the one you enjoy your coffee with, the one who helps to calm your nerves."*

I was giving to those cigarettes what belonged to Jesus: the opportunity to satisfy me. I determined to quit smoking again, only this time I had a very different motivation. I wasn't trying to quit for a negative reason (because it was bad for me) but for a positive reason: there was Something better to reach for, who would really satisfy me, and who would give me life and not death. So I gave my love for cigarettes to Jesus.

This time, with God's help, I succeeded. I honestly felt like I was giving up a good friend, and even grieved over them; I cried many times the first few days. But every time I wanted a cigarette, I reached for Jesus instead, asking him to satisfy my need. He answered me, no matter how many times a day I asked.

The first two weeks were hard, but one night when I lay down for bed I suddenly realized I had not thought about a cigarette once, and my day had been wonderfully satisfying. God could have just taken the desire away from me, but that would not have taught me the lesson of reaching for him in my need. By leaving me in my need for a season I repeatedly experienced his provision each time I asked, and so I learned to be satisfied in God.

Every time your soul leaves the place of peace, don't run to the cookie jar, the mall, or the computer game, or try to force some flawed human to do what only Jesus can. Reach for Jesus, and test his promise; give Him the opportunity to satisfy your heart and bring contentment in God's love.

The Lord alone is the giver of abundant, satisfying life.

That the Lord is capable of satisfying us is repeatedly portrayed in Scripture, especially in John's gospel, beginning with the Samaritan woman:

> *Jesus answered her, "All who drink of this water will be thirsty again. But whoever takes a drink of the water that I will give him shall never, no never, be thirsty any more. But the water that I will give him shall become a spring of water welling up flowing, bubbling continually within him unto, into, for eternal life." (John 4:13-14, Amplified Bible)*

Jesus says he will satisfy our thirst with living water. What is this living water? Jesus explained in John 7:37-39:

> *On the last and greatest day of the Feast, Jesus stood and said in a loud voice, "If anyone is thirsty, let him come to me and drink. Whoever believes in me, as the Scripture has said, streams of living water will flow from within him." By this he meant the Spirit, whom those who believed in him were later to receive.*

Jesus reveals that this "living water" is the presence of the Holy Spirit, who is given to believers through Jesus Christ. He is experienced like an abundant fountain. However, the mere existence of a fountain does not satisfy our thirst; we must be responsible for going to it to drink. An amusing event from my days as a young mother illustrates the relationship between our hunger and God's abundant provision.

I nursed my daughter for the first year of her life, which was one of the most beautiful experiences of my life. I had an ample supply of milk, and I loved it that by God's wonderful design, the milk stayed in place until my baby asked for it, not being released until the baby was put to the breast or cried. If my baby cried before I picked her up to feed her, I had to hurry because the milk would really start to flow!

One day I decided to squeeze in a hot shower before feeding time, which I could tell by the clock and the fulness of my milk supply was past due. Upon getting out of the shower I stepped to the bedroom door, still drying myself with a towel, to look across the bedroom at my daughter in her crib. When she saw me she cried out, and to my amazement the milk in my over-full breasts literally shot across the room in response to her cry!

Later in my prayer time, the Lord said to me, *"That is how I respond to the one who cries out to me in his hunger!"* A picture is worth a thousand words. The "milk" of God is there all the time, but is not released until the cry comes. But once it comes, the milk not only comes, it comes in abundance.

Yet we humans are notoriously independent. One of the numerous complaints of a broken-hearted God to his tribe (the Israelites) when the time came to send them into exile for their repeated sin:

> "My people have committed two sins: They have forsaken me, the spring of living water, and have dug their own cisterns, broken cisterns that cannot hold water. (Jeremiah 2:13)

How do we get to the place of being satisfied by God?

Being satisfied by God is not something you can work up; it is not something you can force yourself to do, but it does begin with believing in God's willingness and ability to satisfy your soul. The next step is to test God in this by turning away from the temptation to satisfy yourself, taking your hunger to him and receiving what he offers:

I am the Lord your God, who brought you up out of Egypt. Open wide your mouth and I will fill it. But my people would not listen to me; Israel would not submit to me. So I gave them over to their stubborn hearts to follow their own devices. If my people would but listen to me, if Israel would follow my ways, how quickly would I subdue their enemies and turn my hand against their foes! Those who hate the Lord would cringe before him, and their punishment would last for ever. But you would be fed with the finest of wheat; with honey from the rock I would satisfy you. (Psalms 81:10-16)

Learn not to determine for yourself what abundance is going to look like, but let God surprise you.

In our work we often spend as much time away from home as we do here, with our usual ministry trips lasting three or four weeks. While I love the work, I am at heart "a homebody," most naturally content in my kitchen, my garden, on my patio, in my cozy prayer place. Not my husband — his thrill is to be out on the road, doing the stuff, being with people. He thrives on it. He once set up a ministry trip that required us to be on the road for six weeks! I wasn't really happy about that and it was one of those little tests of whether I would honor my husband in my secret thoughts and attitude about the whole matter.

I made the choice to accept it without grumbling, to trust Ron and God, to even be thankful. This too is a path to contentment, and because I always ask the Holy Spirit to help me in these things, they are not done by the grit of my teeth, as He helps me come to the place I have chosen so it is genuine. Still, as I packed for this long trip I realized I had mixed emotions, on the one hand excited about the ministry, but wondering how I would in fact cope over the long weeks ahead of being away from my beloved home. On the morning we drove away, I gave my need to God, and asked him to somehow satisfy my longing for home.

To my joy, I found myself as content in that right front passenger seat through countless hours, as I have been happily puttering around my home. In fact, I felt such a deep current of continual joy that it was actually <u>better</u> than what I usually experienced at home! To have such contentment in one's heart is a great gift from God, and I praised God for it. The Lord said quietly in my spirit, *"The reason you are so happy is because I AM your home, and I am with you always."*

One of the hallmarks of a godly woman is that she is clothed with strength and has a joyful existence.[9] She is not needy, she is contented, and in this contentment she is not easily given to the temptations of the enemy. Her life is not destroyed by her own desires, unlike the woman Paul described as being easily swayed by all kinds of various desires.[10] She no longer has interest in the Tree of Knowledge, but trusts that all she needs is to be found in Jesus Christ.

Proverbs 15:15 says, *"All the days of the oppressed are wretched, but the cheerful heart has a continual feast."* The greatest joy of becoming a Christian has been the discovery that I can live at the feasting table of the Lord, which He has set before me even in the presence of my enemies.

What kind of woman will I be? I will be a woman whose soul is deeply satisfied by her God.

Reflecting on Chapter 9

This chapter teaches how to bring your heart to experience the contentment and rest of God. Contentment is God's gift to those who give their hunger to him.

❖ *According to Psalm 81:10-16, being satisfied by God is found through obedience and submission to him. Read John 15:10-11. According to these verses, what does Jesus want of you, and how do you go about doing it?*

❖ *What do you reach for instead of Jesus when your heart is needy? As the Lord reveals the things you are hungry for, record them in your journal. Ask God to tell you the truth about whether they add to or subtract from contentment.*

❖ *Ask the Holy Spirit to help you become aware of times when you are reaching for the Tree of Knowledge instead of the Tree of Life.*

---

[9] Proverbs 31:25.

[10] 2 Timothy 3:6.

I Will Be A Liberated Woman

We all love freedom, and even our sisters in the women's liberation movement would agree that the goal of freedom is a life where nothing stands in the way of pursuing life as we want to live it, and becoming who we really want to be. For women, who have frequently been oppressed by men and the world in general, freedom seems especially sweet. The problem with freedom, however, is that when we don't have it we think it is the cure for an unhappy life. "If only I were free," one reasons, "I could do what I want and nothing could stand in the way of my pursuit of the good life."

No one wants us to find freedom more than Jesus Christ; the Bible says that it was for freedom that Christ set us free.[1] As a persistent seeker of freedom, I can tell you this: freedom is a team player in the game of life; all by itself, it cannot win the game. In order to deliver the goods it promises, it must have the help of character, strength, self-discipline and truth. I learned the hard way that outward freedom is useless unless I have a heart that is free.

How does one come to have a heart that is free? It begins with having the truth:

> To the Jews who had believed him, Jesus said, "If you hold to my teaching, you are really my disciples. Then you will know the truth, and the truth will set you free." (John 8:31-32).

But as this verse makes clear, it is not just having the truth, it is holding onto it that leads us to freedom: "If you hold to my teaching..." The word Jesus used for "hold" in the Greek means "to abide." It means to remain

---

[1] Galatians 5:1.

somewhere, not just visit. Jesus is saying *"If you hold onto, remain in and live by my truth, you will be free."*

Without truth, freedom can actually enslave us. That is what happened to me. I made many foolish and hurtful choices in my early life in the quest for freedom, only to find that I did not have the wisdom to make the most of my freedom. Not only did it happen to me before I knew Jesus, but to the extent I walked in my own understanding rather than God's truth, it happened to me as a Christian. Through Jesus Christ we have been given the ability to possess truth, but God had to lead me through the process of changing my mind and the truths I lived by.

Like many women I meet, I was a victim of my own thoughts and beliefs, which I have learned are the root or source of all emotions. Emotions don't just come up by themselves; they are a response to what we believe, and not only in our conscious mind, but in the deepest places of our mind where words do not live, only memories. It is emotions that color the landscape of the feminine life and by which its quality is measured: joy, grief, excitement, compassion, contentment. Therefore, any discussion of how a woman can be truly liberated must include a discussion of her emotions and how they relate to God's life within her.

The Emotional Life of the Woman God Designed.

God designed a woman as the more emotional half of creation. In understanding God's design for woman we must explore the relationship between a woman's emotional life and her spiritual life. A woman who is saved is not automatically set free from the tyranny of her emotions — their tendency to rule her existence. This only changes as God's influence upon her heart begins to challenge the deeply-held beliefs lurking there.

It is frustrating to the new Christian, being assured that he is a new creation, to find the "old self" continually popping up with all of its hurts, thoughts, beliefs and habits. How can it be true that we are born again, made brand new, and still feel like the old person? The answer lies in the fact that a person is "saved" by accepting Jesus Christ as Savior, but still has an unchanged soul. In order to understand this we must understand what salvation really means.

When scripture speaks of salvation it is actually referring to two things: one is an event, the other is a process. The event is when you are saved from the curse of death, through faith in the blood of Jesus and his atoning death. At this moment you are given new life by God, by means of a new spirit that is created within your soul. Jesus called this being born a second time, not a flesh birth, but a birth of the Spirit.[2]

You now have a brand new human spirit, connected to God, through which you may know Him and be influenced by Him. So while your soul is no longer alienated from God, your soul itself is not reborn. Simply put, your saved soul now inhabits (or is inhabited by) a newly born spirit eternally united to the Spirit of God.

The spirit is not the same as the soul; we know they are two different things because Scripture says they can be divided.[3] The reason Jesus died to save our souls from death was to transform the human soul into a suitable habitation for the Living God. It was his Father's will from the beginning to have relationship with his creation and to dwell "in the midst of" his people.[4]

On the other hand, the process of salvation is what happens as we live day to day in this relationship with the Living God, a process that goes on until the day we go to heaven — perhaps even after we go there. Here the Spirit of God is at work to help you to develop and grow your human spirit. As your spirit grows stronger, your soul is gently and gradually "saved" from wrongful thought habits, painful memories, fears, unforgiveness, self-pity, bitterness, and every other thing that destroys the beauty of your soul in God's sight, and that robs it of life. The person who actively cooperates with this process eventually has a spirit bigger than his soul, that guides his soul, rather than the other way around.

The soul is the place from whence we experience life on the conscious and subconscious levels. Though God can make himself known to us in any way, we commonly experience His indwelling Spirit through the filter of the soul. Because the soul is the expression of the mind, will and emotions, these things affect our perception of the Spirit of God, especially in the early, less mature stages of being a Christian. Like any newborn creation, our spirits have to grow up, as Peter inferred when he said: *"Like newborn babies, crave pure spiritual milk, so that by it you may grow up in your salvation."* (1 Peter 2:2)

---

[2] John 3:5-8

[3] Hebrews 4:12.

[4] Exodus 25:8.

What is this pure spiritual milk? Milk is what an infant feeds upon to grow strong. The Bible says that we do not live on bread alone, but on every word that comes from the mouth of the Lord.[5] So our spiritual milk is to feed upon God's word, the Bible, and to learn to hear the words that come from his mouth. Do I sound like a broken record yet?

Growing up in our salvation also includes learning to develop our spiritual eyes and ears, becoming ever more sensitive to the Spirit of God, so that we can walk with Him through life, learning to live by faith as a response to his presence, rather than being controlled by our desires, emotions and thoughts. The woman who is still a slave to fear, anxiety, anger, bitterness or depression is not free, no matter how liberated she is from oppressive authority figures, rules, social conventions. If you are enslaved by your feelings and ruled by thoughts (which may not even be true) you are not liberated at all.

Controlled by emotions, or by the Holy Spirit?

The woman who has not grown up much in her salvation is generally still a slave to her thoughts and emotions, not free to enjoy the life Christ died to give her. While it is true that with determination, education and discipline a woman can learn to control her emotions, the fact is that when life deals a blow and her emotions become intense, they will invariably rise up again to rule through her soul.

Emotions in themselves are not bad; the God in whose image we are made experiences emotion with great intensity, particularly love, joy, sadness, anger, and jealousy. Such emotions are part of our God-given DNA, meant to enhance our experience of life in imitation of the very nature and life of God himself. Our emotions are a response to what we ponder and believe, as well as a register of our experiences, especially with other human beings.

But there are also emotions which reflect the nature of the devil (and fallen man), rather than God, and they are destructive to us. These emotions are fear, bitterness (unforgiveness), depression, hatred, self-pity. These emotions will, if allowed to prevail within the soul, damage our physical health, emotional health, even change our appearance. Doctors estimate that such destructive emotions are the true source of 60-90% of all illness.

---

[5] Deuteronomy 8:3.

Thus we see that what God gave us for good, the devil wants to turn for evil. Emotions can lead us astray very easily from God's will. They can rule over us like relentless task masters demanding to be soothed and responded to. Aside from her obvious lesser physical strength, I believe the tendency to be led by her emotions is one reason the Bible refers to woman as "the weaker partner."[6] Emotions are not wrong; but if they are to be enjoyed as the gift God gave, they should be under the control of the Spirit of God rather than something that causes her to actually struggle against God.

The emotions of a woman of noble character.

The woman of noble character is not enslaved by her emotions. Instead:

> *She is clothed with strength and dignity; she can laugh at the days to come. (Proverbs 31:25).*

This is the soul of a woman designed by God, whose heart has become a home for God's Spirit. The dictionary defines "dignity" as "stateliness and nobility of manner; the state or quality of being excellent, worthy or honorable." The King James Version translates this word as "honor." This is a far cry from the woman who lives in a state of stress, who is "clothed" with anxiety or self-pity or depression. In fact, the Hebrew word actually means "magnificence," being translated elsewhere as *beauty, excellency, majesty,* or *splendor,* often in describing God himself. The Amplified Bible reveals even more:

> *She looks well to how things go in her household, and the bread of idleness (gossip, discontent and self-pity) she will not eat. Her children rise up and call her blessed (happy, fortunate and to be envied); and her husband boasts of her and praises her, saying, 'Many daughters have done virtuously, nobly and well, with the strength of character that is steadfast in goodness, but you excel them all. Charm and grace are deceptive and beauty is vain, [because it is not lasting], but a woman who reverently and worshipfully fears the Lord, she shall be praised! (Proverbs 31:27-30)*

Are you getting the picture? This woman is not habitually depressed or wallowing in self-pity. She may have a "down day" when her hormone levels

---

[6] 1 Peter 3:7.

plunge, or a skirmish with anxiety when bad things happen, but her lifestyle or disposition is not one of agitation, anxiety, depression or fear. She does not place her value in and derive her joy from her physical attributes or her wardrobe; rather, she is clothed with excellence, with beauty, with splendor. She is "steadfast in goodness" — you don't have to wonder who you're going to get when you enter her presence. Does this describe you? It can, through yielding to the guidance and power of the Holy Spirit.

The woman God designed is not captive to her emotions.

The main reason that a woman of God can laugh at the days to come is because she is free of fear. She'll have problems, to be sure, but she won't be overcome by them or live in fear of them. Her soul has come to rest under the safety of God's wing, by her faith in Him to take her through every difficult situation. She says to herself, "My life is safe in God's hands. God is in control, and he will work everything out. I have nothing to be afraid of. I belong to the One who's in charge and he loves me beyond measure." When fears want to take over her mind, she seeks the counsel of the Spirit of Truth, either through reading her Bible and putting her faith in the truth she finds there, or by prayer and hearing what God would say to her about what she is believing.

The woman God has designed does not have an angry soul. She is not angry at herself, at others, or at life in general. Neither is she angry at God, a more common problem than most people realize. We all experience these kinds of anger, but they should be moments in our lives, not a way of life, for we should never let the sun set on our anger.

Most anger or fear stems from the desire to have control over one's life and the deep frustration at being unable to do so. Fallen man wants to totally control his life and therefore, by necessity, control others in his life. We want to control how others treat us and even how they feel about us.

The woman God designed has given control to God and given up the illusion that she has any power or control over circumstances or other people. Things which may interrupt her peace no longer have the power to destroy it. How does she deal with anger and make it go away? Again, she seeks the counsel of the Spirit of Truth. Hearing the truth of God has quenched my anger many times, especially where my husband is concerned.

When our son Shawn was 17 years old, he ran away from home. It was his senior year of high school, and his last chance to party before going into the Army after graduation. Apparently he wanted more freedom than we gave him and was weary of being under our authority. In his hunger for independence he moved in with a buddy from school, whose parents offered the liberty he was looking for.

This took place just before Christmas, and we were heartbroken. But at a time when we needed to cling together, my husband and I became completely divided over how to respond to Shawn's actions. I wanted to go reason with our son, beg him to come home, and show him sympathy. But Ron declared that we would not call him, go see him or have any type of communication with him until he repented of his actions and came home.

My reaction was deep anger, resentment, and fear that this would do unalterable damage to our relationship with our son. I tried to reason with Ron and change his mind, believing he had made his decision out of what I assumed was a typical father's need to maintain his authority, not wanting to back down in the face of his son's rebellion. While I was hurt and angered by Shawn's actions, I was even more upset with my husband. In a town of 8,000 it was inevitable that we ran into Shawn occasionally, which made honoring Ron's decision even more difficult.

Believing as I did that Ron was wrong, I was overcome with grief towards our son and anger at my husband. At a time when we really needed one another's comfort, none could possibly flow between us as long as I continued to take a stand against my husband while sympathizing with our son. This, of course, only deepened Ron's hurt.

Finally, I became so completely sick at heart that I did what I should have done in the first place: I sought the counsel of the Holy Spirit. By now I had learned not to go tell God all the things I thought he should know. I simply asked him, *"Lord, please show me the truth about this situation and about Ron's decision."* The Lord's answer was quick, brief and extremely clear: *"Ron has made this decision because it is MY will that you not contact your son. Ron is in my will."*

That statement produced the most dramatic implosion of anger I have ever experienced; it flew out of me like air out of a punctured balloon. Needless to say, in light of this truth, my resentment was replaced with repentance, and I apologized to God and Ron. We were at peace once again, able to stand together and comfort one another.

And the end of the story? For nine months we had no communication with our son. I still felt grief, occasionally had a good cry, especially at times like his high school graduation. But amazingly every time I took it to the Lord and asked him to satisfy my soul, He always comforted me deeply. In fact, I was astounded to see that my peace actually returned, and I was able to go on with life, and it was good. To be honest, I almost felt guilty about being so okay when things were so not okay in our family.

This did not happened because I wrestled my feelings to the ground and stood on faith statements; it happened because I had come to trust that God is good and that if it was his will for us to not have contact with our son, then that was the best for all of us, and would lead us back to life. And so it did. Nine months later we received a phone call from Shawn, who apologized, and later a letter letting us know when he would graduate from Army boot camp. We went to that graduation and had a wonderful reunion. Shawn had learned how much his family meant to him, and he also told us that he now deeply appreciated the discipline he had received at home, as it had prepared him in beginning Army life. It was the beginning of a better relationship than we had before.

I can only imagine what that season of our lives would have been like if I had walked in my own beliefs and the emotions they caused. God's truth liberated me from a powerful anger that was ruining my joy and my relationship to my husband. There is no doubt in my mind that the old, unrenewed Toni would have easily ended up in depression.

The woman God designed is not bound by depression.

Depression can develop when anger or fear exists for a long time in the soul. Such long-term negative emotions usually come from deep and profound disappointments, old hurts, perhaps a childhood trauma which left a sense of rejection. A negative emotion that lingers on usually comes from unforgiveness, either towards others or oneself, or even anger at God for not showing up in the way we expected. A good counselor can really help here.

Depression can also be an advanced case of self-pity, which is a very subtle, destructive emotion. Self-pity is actually a deeply selfish indulgence because it is entirely preoccupied with self, either self's needs or self's inadequacies. Self-pity keeps us from loving others and God. In fact, for the Christian, self-pity is actually an expression of dissatisfaction with God. It is the opposite of living with thanksgiving in your heart. If you habitually feel sorry for yourself, then on some level you are probably dissatisfied with God himself.

Self-pity can be addictive. I have noticed after years of counseling that those given to self-pity may have a hard time giving it up. Self-pity is a way of comforting ourselves, easily indulged in if we are unable to get comfort from anyone else. The Christian who indulges in self-pity has not learned how to offer their need to God and receive comfort from Him.

The woman God designed is full of strength.

A truly liberated woman has the power to be all she can be. You may be surprised at what Scripture reveals about the power that godliness gives a woman. Proverbs 31:10 says, *A wife of noble character who can find?* The Hebrew word translated as "wife of noble character" ("virtuous woman" in King James) is *chayil*. This word is also used to describe Ruth as the *"woman of noble character."*[7] But get this: it is also the same word translated as *"capable men…who fear God"* in Exodus 18:21. Clearly this word has nothing to do with gender.

The most surprising thing about *chayil* is that it is most often translated in the Bible as "army"! This is the word used in Ezekiel 37:10 to describe the "vast army" which came to life from a pile of bones, and used again in Ezekiel 38:15, as "a mighty army." So why is the same Hebrew word used to describe a vast or mighty army, and to describe a good wife? Because the emphasis is on the strength or power of what is being described, whether a man, a woman, an army, resources or character. The writer of Proverbs 31:10 carefully chose this word to convey the great strength that is found in a woman who fears the Lord.

In fact, *chayil* is often translated as *strength* in Scripture when referring to *the strength given by God.* For example:

> *It is God who arms me with strength* (**chayil**) *and makes my way perfect. (Psalms 18:32)*

> *You armed me with strength* (**chayil**) *for battle… (Psalms 18:39)*

---

[7] Ruth 3:11.

The Sovereign Lord is my strength (**chayil**)*; he makes my feet like the feet of a deer, he enables me to go on the heights.* (Habakkuk 3:19)

Chayil is derived from a root word that carries the idea of *force*. To understand why this word is used, consider that it is possible to have an army, which is not a powerful army. We witnessed this in the Persian Gulf War when Saddam Hussein tried to frighten off allied forces with myths about the true strength and numbers of his army. The news media, reporting what Hussein wanted them to report, gave the impression that a formidable enemy might be waiting to meet our armies. Instead, our forces came face to face with an untrained, ineffective and truly powerless cadre of soldiers. They were called an army because they looked like an army and had the size of an army, but possessed no true force or power. The ones with real power "liberated" Kuwait from oppressive rule.

So when *chayil* is used to describe an army, we know it describes an army with actual power or force, not just a numerically large collection of soldiers. Likewise, when *chayil* is used to describe a woman of good character, it is meant to convey the powerful force of that character.

Interestingly enough, the "word picture" for *chayil* in the Hebrew language is a woman's body writhing in the act of giving birth. Apparently to the Hebrew mind, the labor of bringing forth children evoked the ultimate in life-giving strength. Moreover, a woman giving birth demonstrates a strength that results in true fruitfulness.

This is a literal picture describing a spiritual reality: the woman God designed possesses character that is both noble and powerful; she is, in fact, clothed with strength. She is not just virtuous when her hormones balance, she is pregnant with goodness, carrying these virtues within her, ever nurturing them. The woman God designed is strong because God has made her strong. Christianity isn't a title she wears; it is a force within her. She doesn't just quote scripture, she lives by the Word. She doesn't just make faith confessions, she lives by authentic faith in the goodness of God, so her disposition is steadfast.

The Disposition of a Woman of God

Your disposition is how you conduct yourself and how you respond to life. Regardless of factors such as physical circumstances, income level, education or surroundings, how we experience life ultimately depends upon what is going on in the soul, where we really live. The woman God designed lives her life as a response to the presence and unfailing love of God, aware, like the psalmist, that *"... your love is ever before me...."* (Psalm 26:3).

The woman God designed has a steadfast soul, even in stormy times. One of the compliments I treasure most came from my father a few years after I gave my heart to the Lord. While visiting over lunch one day he looked at me with admiration and said, "Daughter, I do believe you have an unconquerable soul."

Having watched me go through some difficult situations, he was amazed at my well-being. Having watched me practically catapult from a godless life to one of being crazy about Jesus, he had been watching several years to see what would really happen in me. I loved the fact that he could see that Jesus had made a real difference in my life. I once heard a speaker ask, *"Does your life show that Jesus can be trusted?"* What a profound question! I felt like in the eyes of my Daddy, the answer was a resounding "Yes, Jesus can be trusted."

The woman God designed has a steadfast soul because she has learned to live from within that place where she shares life with Jesus Christ, the ultimate lover of her soul. She lives in the counsel of the Holy Spirit. She is able to laugh because her heart rests safely in the hands of a good God.

Balance and moderation in our emotions is the goal.

In all things we must be balanced. There is a time to mourn, there is a time to rejoice. Every emotion has its healthy place in the life of a Christian; but when emotions rise up in us and become a stronger influence than the Holy Spirit, we must run to God with them rather than let them separate us from Him, as anger and self-pity tend to do.

A good test of proper emotions is to look at the fruit they produce in your life. When an emotion separates you from God and his love, from your ability to love others, it is not good. If it divides and alienates you from others, it is wrong. If it leads you into sin, it's obvious that the devil has used your emotions to lead you away from God's influence.

Our emotions should always cause us to reach for Him more, not less. There is a time and a place for sorrow, for grief, for anger. Don't stuff these emotions down, but open them up to Jesus Christ to examine and explore together. We don't "master" our emotions, we examine them in the light of God's truth.

As women, we are by God's design going to experience life much more through our emotions than men do. I benefit from a good cry just as much as the next woman, I get angry, I have to resist being fearful or anxious at times. I am not teaching you how to master your emotions, as those of the world are taught to do. I am teaching you to surrender them to the Spirit of God for His mastery. It isn't enough to just quote a scripture against your anxiety or say things like, "By faith I won't be afraid!" These may be helpful to some degree, but never get to the root of the problem, which is what you believe in your heart. All emotions arise from what we believe. Sometimes we need someone to help us sort out the connections between what we believe and reality, and that's what a good counselor is for.

Jesus, Wonderful Counselor

In the Spirit of Christ, you have been given a Wonderful Counselor.[8] God intends for you to have a talking relationship with him, so that if you need to know something, need wisdom about any situation, you can ask God and expect him to communicate freely with you. James 1:5 tells us this in no uncertain terms:

> *If any of you lacks wisdom, he should ask God, who gives generously to all without finding fault, and it will be given to him.*

"*…who gives generously to all…*" These words do not describe a God who wants to make it hard for you to know his voice, who sits back quietly until you have all your spiritual P's and Q's together. God wants to share his wisdom with you; I'd venture to say it thrills him for you to ask.

God can reveal to you the root cause — the underlying belief — of any emotion which may have gripped your heart. He can reveal to you the truth about people and situations, so that you always walk in his truth and light. The Apostle John wrote, *I have no greater joy than to hear that my children are walking in the truth.*[9]

---

[8] Isaiah 9:6.
[9] 3 John 1:4.

You have an enemy, the devil. He wants to destroy your life, your joy, your strength, your relationships, just as he tried to do when our son ran away from home. How do we fight him? How do we defeat the enemy's plans to destroy us? Scripture tells us that our weapon against him is to exchange our thoughts for God's:

> *The weapons we fight with are not the weapons of the world. On the contrary, they have divine power to demolish strongholds. We demolish arguments and every pretension that sets itself up against the knowledge of God, and we take captive every thought to make it obedient to Christ. (2 Corinthians 10:4-5).*

Believing my husband was wrong in this situation was a belief that stood against God's truth and my knowledge of it. When I asked God for the truth, he sent his thoughts into my spirit, I believed him, and in order to be obedient to the Spirit of Christ, I "took my thoughts captive" and discarded them. Until then, they had taken me captive. God's truth demolished my arguments in a moment. He changed my mind — an event which is think may be more miraculous at times than healing cancer!

God's truth changes minds.

Not only does God want us to set us free of unruly emotions, he wants to improve our relationships with others. When our son first brought home the woman he would marry, my first reaction to her was somewhat negative. She talked about herself a lot and spoke as if she knew all about every subject that came up, though she was only 19. Her manner put me off, and I remember thinking, *Nobody could teach her anything new.* Not very gracious, I'm afraid, but as I was facing having her in my life permanently, I suppose I was in the mode of giving her the future daughter-in-law analysis.

However, when I got up and excused myself to use the bathroom, the Lord prompted me to ask Him what He thought about her. So I did, sitting there where the Lord talks to me so often because I'm alone and still for a few minutes — am I being too frank? "Okay, *show me the truth about her, Lord.*" His answer stunned me: "*Her heart is like the softest piece of clay in my hands.*" As we hadn't discussed faith together, I had no thought as to whether her heart was in God's hands — nor would I have guessed, as his words implied, that she was thoroughly teachable.

When I returned to the living room five minutes later, my whole attitude towards her had changed because God had changed my mind. I then did something I would not have dreamed of doing a short time earlier: I invited her to come in the kitchen with me and help me make stir-fry, since it was time to cook supper. She leaped up out of her chair and said, *"I'd love to! I need someone to teach me how to do stir-fry!"*

What the Lord said turned out to be so very true. I later learned that she was brought up in a home divided by divorce, by a mother who worked all the time and struggled with an addiction to alcohol. Like most who come out of dysfunctional family situations, our daughter-in-law struggled with feelings of rejection and low self-esteem. She had come across the way she did only because she was so anxious to gain our good opinion of her. My faith in what the Lord said quite possibly saved us from getting off on the wrong foot.

I found to my delight that Sharon, our precious daughter-in-love, does have a heart just like God described. She is hungry to learn about how to be a good woman, wife and mother. During a short season when she lived next door Sharon asked me to teach her how to study the Bible, how to pray and how to relate to Jesus in her everyday life. It was a precious time.

Furthermore, it is clear now, all these years later, that since God has given her the gift of teaching, it was in her God-given DNA to carry on conversations in a way that sounded like she was teaching the rest of us — though in her untrained, still immature manner. I had been foolish to judge her (form an opinion of her) as I did. God saved us both from that mistake by telling me the truth.

I could give countless examples like this, of how hearing God's counsel has changed my life and relationships. We must accept the fact that we do not know the hearts of men. We rarely know what has hurt them or is motivating them to do what they do. There is only one hope for us to respond righteously to others, to treat them as Jesus would, and that is to seek and walk in the same truth that he knows about them. This is living by faith, and not by sight.

> *My son, if you accept my words ... turning your ear to wisdom and applying your heart to understanding, and if you call out for insight and cry aloud for understanding ... then you will ... find the knowledge of*

God. For the Lord gives wisdom, and from his mouth come knowledge
and understanding. (Proverbs 2:1-4, 6)

> Then you will understand what is right and just and fair - every good
> path. For wisdom will enter your heart, and knowledge will be pleasant to
> your soul. Discretion will protect you, and understanding will guard you.
> Wisdom will save you from the ways of wicked men, from men whose
> words are perverse. (Proverbs 2:9-12).

I will be a liberated woman.

I am not a perfect woman, and I do not have a perfect life; but I have
learned life is not about being perfect. My husband still makes me cry. Life
still hurts and disappoints me. I still disappoint me. But I don't live there. I
try to dwell next to the heart of God, listening to his voice, believing that I
have access to the mind of Christ, ready to hear the real truth about the
world and the people around me, and the truth about myself.

I am determined to live "the Spirit life": that life of continual awareness
of and responsiveness to the Spirit of Christ that lives within my heart. I
have learned that He is wonderful, trustworthy, the lover of my soul.

As for me, I will be free. By walking with the Spirit of Truth, I will be
free of all that spoils the freedom in my soul, the joy of life, and my
relationship with God and other people. I will be a truly liberated woman,
for I know that it is God's will…

> …that the creation itself will be liberated from its bondage to decay
> and brought into the glorious freedom of the children of God. (Romans
> 8:21).

Reflecting on Chapter 10

This chapter teaches about the source of true freedom: walking in the truth of God, allowing godly emotions and attitudes to be formed in you.

❖ *To free yourself from an emotional stronghold you must deal with the underlying belief. Identify strong emotions you think may be ruling your heart, and ask the Holy Spirit to reveal the truth about what you believe, or about the situation, or the person. Journal what you learn.*

❖ *Meditate on the excerpts from Proverbs 2 in this chapter.*

❖ *Make it your goal to seek the wisdom of your "Wonderful Counselor," to hear God's voice.*

The Woman God Designed

Who will I pattern myself after as a woman?

Like most women, I self-examine. Am I a good wife? A good mother? Am I attractive? Does my husband really value me? Am I more desirable to him than other women? Am I in style? I measure myself against a standard that changes constantly. Over the years I have compared myself to other women, and imitated that which I admired. Every time I stood in the supermarket lines my desire to be more than I am hooked me into buying women's magazines full of articles that tell me how to dress, love, parent, make a home and be a great lover. I tried out different things; some worked, some didn't. What pleased my friend's husbands often didn't please my husband. What pleased me...only pleased me until I encountered a woman who seems better than I. I try to be like her, but on me it doesn't work.

Where is an unchanging pattern, a certain and admirable standard I can trust in completely to help me walk in the full potential of who I was created to be? Who in the world can show me the truth? As I came to realize in utter despair one day, no one in this world can. At the age of 30, living in a free country with every possible means at my disposal to grow and develop, I was not a woman I could admire, love, or teach my daughter to be.

As I crumbled in brokenness in that moment of realization, I invited Jesus Christ to take over my life. When His Spirit came to live in me, He gave me an intense hunger to read God's Word. From the first time I read the Genesis account of the creation of man and woman, I was excited: God had a specific design, purpose, and plan for me, the woman he had formed in my mother's womb. The Lord had a specific blueprint for me as a woman, and blueprints I understood.

My father, a home builder, always had blueprints in the car, in the house, and at his office. I loved to visit his construction sites and marveled how the flat blue lines turned into beautiful and functional rooms. But it didn't happen by accident; it was Dad's job to make sure the contractors followed the specs on those blueprints so that the house became what the architect had envisioned.

God created mankind with a specific design in mind. Man and woman existed first in his mind's eye, seen by him to be, look and act as He purposed and desired. He honored us by making us in His image, and we are different from all other creation in that we have free will. This means that we have the freedom to be, look and act in a way other than God designed! What shall we do with our choice in being?

At the age of 30, I happily dumped my eclectic, mismatched set of blueprints from so many different "architects," and gave myself to God's design. I made a commitment to embrace with full trust whatever the Scriptures revealed about how to be a woman and how to relate to my husband. This book is the sum of what I've learned so far. The wholehearted embrace of God's truth challenged and changed my attitudes about many things, and none more than the first revelation: that woman was created for man.

Woman was created for man.

While giving instructions on how to conduct ourselves in church, Paul makes these startling statements:

> For a man ... is the image and reflected glory of God, but woman is the expression of man's glory (majesty, pre-eminence). For man was not created from woman, but woman from man; neither was man created on account of or for the benefit of woman, but woman on account of and for the benefit of man. (1 Corinthians 11:7-9, The Amplified Bible.)

I've never seen this verse on any woman's refrigerator, yet it seems for us who call ourselves women of God it might be pretty important to understand what this means. To be sure, it does not mean we were made to be his prize, his pet, his subservient slave, sex object, cook or housekeeper. But before we define what it does mean, let's read on in Paul's explanation in 1 Corinthians 11:

Nevertheless, in the plan of the Lord and from His point of view, woman is not apart from and independent of man, nor is man aloof from and independent of woman; for as woman was made from man, even so man is also born of woman. And all, whether male or female, go forth from God as their Author. (verses 11-12)

Paul implies that regardless of the order or purpose in creation, God has made neither gender superior to the other; that in fact, man and woman are interdependent, needing each other equally. Paul clarifies his first statement by pointing out that each one needs the other in reaching their created potential. Just as the Father, Son and Holy Spirit have equality and yet defer to each other in a certain way to fulfill all righteousness, man and woman must learn to do the same.

Man and woman have equal value in the Lord's sight. They have the same ability to be born of the spirit, to abide in Him, to receive and operate in His gifts and power. In Christ, there is neither male nor female. Spiritually, you are the same before God. Even so, these truths do not negate the rest of God's clearly revealed design for how a man and woman should relate to each other in their calling as a partnership — which is to subdue the earth and fill it with godly offspring, filling the earth with His glory. To understand this better, let's take a detailed look at the story of our creation.

Revelations in our creation.

Genesis 1:26, the first reference to God's creation of man, reads:

Then God said, "Let us make man in our image, in our likeness, and let them rule..."

Having used the word "them" we know the Lord is speaking of mankind here, not yet referring to male or female. The Hebrew word translated "make" is *asah*, which means to yield out of one's self; in other words, referring to the fruit one produces out of oneself. The glory of God, or anyone, is that which he is able to produce out of his being. God has brought out of himself the universe, the magnificent galaxies, our world, and mankind. His power to do this speaks of how glorious he is.

When the Bible says we are created for the praise of God's glory it means that God wanted to show off his best stuff in us. Not content to just be God, he wanted to exercise his full potential as an Awesome God. So he created "mankind" as the expression of His glory. A few verses later, we see that God gave mankind the task of revealing the fullness of His Glory by filling the earth with more of God's fruit (his little image in mankind everywhere), enjoying and managing the rest of God's creation (earth). This was to be done in the character, wisdom and power of God.

This first telling of creation shows the creation of mankind, a creature like God, in relation to all the rest of God's creation: glorious, but not made in His image. Of all creation, mankind alone, as distinct from the animal or plant kingdom, or even the universe, received that amazing honor.

The second telling of man's creation in Genesis 2:7 serves a different purpose, to reveal the details of how and why there are two genders within "mankind":

> And the Lord God formed man from the dust of the ground and breathed into his nostrils the breath of life, and man became a living being.

In both of these scriptures, the word translated as "man" is *adam*, which one Hebrew scholar says literally means "red dirt," an idea underscored by the fact that the word "ground" in this same verse comes from the word *"adamah,"* derived from the same root. A great majority of the world's soil is actually some shade of reddish brown. In other words, the Lord God formed *"adam"* out of the *"adamah,"* man from the dust.

Now Genesis 2:18-25 says,

> The Lord God said, "It is not good for the man to be alone. I will make a helper suitable for him." Now the Lord God had formed out of the ground all the beasts of the field and all the birds of the air. He brought them to the man to see what he would name them; and whatever the man called each living creature, that was its name. So the man gave names to all the livestock, the birds of the air and all the beasts of the field. But for Adam no suitable helper was found.

> So the Lord God caused the man to fall into a deep sleep; and while he was sleeping, he took one of the man's ribs and closed up the place with flesh. Then the Lord God made a woman from the rib he had taken out of the man and he brought her to the man. The man said, "This is now bone of my bone and flesh of my flesh; she shall be called 'woman,' **for she**

was taken out of man." *For this reason a man will leave his father and mother and be united to his wife, and they will become one flesh. (emphasis mine.)*

Again, the Hebrew word used for "man" in the first two occurrences is *adam*, a generic term referring to the species we call mankind, not referring to the male gender.

Then, the writer suddenly switches terminology in verse 23 when it says, "*...for she was taken out of man...*" Instead of using *adam*, he uses the word *iysh*, which refers to man as opposite of woman, or man distinguished in his manliness.[1] This is the first time "man" is used in contrast to "woman," translated from the Hebrew word *ishshah*. Ishshah is the feminine form of *iysh*. In other words, she shall be called "*iysh*" because she was taken out of "*ishshah*."

Then in verses 21 and 22 the word "rib" literally means "part of the man," or "side." We could translate this, *God took part of adam [mankind], and he made woman [ishshah, the feminine part].*

The verbs describing how man and woman were made give further insight, as they are not the same. The word *"formed"* is used regarding *adam* in Genesis 2:7, translated from *yatsar*, meaning *"to create from scratch,"* or make something out of nothing, an entirely different word from that describing woman's creation in Genesis 2:18, where *"make"* is the Hebrew *banah*, which means *"to build."*

In *adam's* [mankind's] case, we have something created. In the woman's [*ishshah's*] case, we have something built, from the created materials already existing. So we could read this, God took part of the adam, the "red dirt creation," and he built woman (*ishshah*, the feminine counterpart to man) out of that part. What is left, by implication, is the masculine, or *"iysh"* part of creation.

It is important to understand that as made in God's image *adam's* soul was one complete being, with both feminine and masculine qualities. This is not to say, as some New Age doctrines declare, that God is both a man and a woman, only that the whole image of God includes what we perceive as masculine and feminine qualities.

---

[1] Theological Wordbook of the Old Testament, Vol. 1, page 10.

Created to relate.

Scripture, in describing the soul and personality of God, ascribes every emotion and gender trait that has ever been observed in man or woman. It is obvious that when God "took part of the mankind" and made woman, he took what we define as the feminine characteristics, the softness, the tender side, the emotional nature, and embodied them in woman. God in essence divided *adam* in half, made his one being into two beings. Why?

If *adam* was made in God's image, then He had created perfection the first time, and contrary to the well-worn joke, God did not try to improve on His original creation by making a woman. When God looked upon *adam* the only undesirable thing he observed about his creation was his aloneness.

Aloneness is not good; even the Trinity is three rather than one. Even though God is complete within himself, the full expression of His glory is only seen in relationship to another being. God exists as a Trinity so He may enjoy and express the fulness of His being in relationship.

This is also an essential purpose in God's creation of man. God created us to live in relationship with him. The total expression of who and what God is — for instance, God is love — is not possible without someone for Him to love. The fact that God is merciful is only abstract theory until He comes face to face with someone who needs His mercy.

Every godly quality of love, mercy, joy, compassion, and long-suffering can only find expression within the context of relationship. That God is relational is not just the outworking of how he created the universe, it is the very point of all his creative work. While His glorious power and wisdom is magnificently revealed in the universe, earth, the mountains, the way of all biological life on earth, all would be too small a display of His glory if he had not made man to reveal the glory of who God is in his character.

God looked upon his creation and said to himself, *Like me, my creation needs relationship.* God provided Adam with a companion who would live in intimacy with him. God wasn't just providing another body to exist in the same space with him. He wasn't making a person to cook, clean and wash his clothes, or one to provide a living for the other.

God's purpose was to have His *adam*, the human being made in His image, be divided into two parts in order to demonstrate His glory completely, as a relational being. God's glory is revealed in relationship, and so is ours.

So he created mankind as the expression of his best fruit, or glory; then he again brought forth fruit out of man, the woman. Why did God create man and woman in this order? God could have just made two beings at the same time, and the fact that he did not is incredibly significant, as it points to the time of Jesus Christ and His Bride. God has set his son Jesus as the agenda and center of the universe[2] so that all things point to him, portraying and foretelling his kingdom, including the creation of man and woman.

Just as the first Son of God was Adam, and out of him a bride was fashioned just for him to reveal his glory in relationship, so the last Son of God, Jesus, is waiting for His bride as she is being fashioned out of him, by the Spirit. In this sense, Adam and Eve are the prototype of Christ and his Bride.

Out of this flows the purpose of God's order and the distinction of the sexes in creation. The argument that we are created equal is true in the context of our value to God, but is misapplied by the world through the deceptive lies of Satan to divert us away from the truth of God's design for us. We are certainly not created identical in function or purpose in our different genders. To understand more, let's go back to the beginning of woman's creation.

The suitable helper.

In Genesis 2:18, God tells *adam* that He will make him a "helper suitable" for him, a word that means in the original Hebrew *other self, succorer, comforter*. The woman was created to be face to face with the man, to succor, bring comfort and provide needs. While the world wants us to believe this role is demeaning, God does not think so; indeed, the Hebrew word used for "suitable helper" is the same term God frequently uses to describe His own role towards us!

This is just another example of how a fallen world distorts and re-presents the truth, which is that woman is honored by God's design in her to be as He is in this nurturing role. The Amplified Bible helps us understand more clearly what this will actually look like:

> I will make him a helper meet (suitable, adapted, complementary) for him."

---

[2] Ephesians 1:9-12

The dictionary defines complementary as "that which completes or brings to perfection." God was saying, in essence, *I'm going to provide someone for Adam that will bring out the best in him, so that as he relates to her his full glory will be seen.* While woman was taken out of man and has his DNA, she is obviously a very different creature. (So different, in fact, that modern writers have hinted that woman is actually from a different planet than man!) She doesn't look like a man or act like a man; in fact, she doesn't even think like a man.

Differences in the feminine and masculine soul.

Because the thoughts, motivation and emotions of a person are directly affected by the gender of the body, I like to use the expressions "masculine soul" and "feminine soul" when discussing the differences in men and women. Men and women are different, and these differences do reach into the realm of the soul. The soul is deeply affected by the gender of the body it lives in. The soul is where a person really lives, where he experiences his life. His thoughts, feelings, and responses to people and circumstances determine the quality of his life more than any other factor.

Even in responding to life, the genders are different. The feminine soul reacts to life primarily on the emotional level; the masculine soul on the mental level. Women tend to experience life through how something makes us feel. Men tend to experience life on a mental, logical plane. That women benefit from the logic of men and men benefit from the emotional strength of women is clear. In fact, a person's maturity is often measured by how well one has learned to integrate their mental and emotional life. Still, these two natures, emotional and logical, will always be viewed as gender specific, because each is the state to which one reverts to the most easily under stress.

The original fruit of God embodied all His attributes in one being; for we see within our Triune God both logic and emotion, tenderness and strength, a bold leader and a submissive follower, and all the traits which we now see in the two genders.

Not only did he create them with profound differences, but in such a way that they would actually need one another, because within the strengths of each gender are the very seeds of their weaknesses or vulnerabilities.

For instance, the logical, reasoning nature of a man is a great strength. Yet, this same logic can get him into trouble — say, for instance, when he needs to find faith in a God who is invisible. A man has a tendency to reject what he cannot explain or prove; he is slower to receive the things of faith and intuition. His logical nature wants to think it over and reason out his faith and doctrine.

This is why so many churches often have a greater female population than male. The husband may take longer to receive Jesus because he is watching and waiting to see the effect this Jesus has upon others, especially his wife, which is why Peter tells women to demonstrate the character and nature of God in front of their husbands in order to win them to Christ.

But once the man becomes fully convinced of what he will believe about God, he is not easily swayed off of his faith. God uses the cautious, logical nature of the man to his advantage when he builds faith in him, because once he is convinced, a man is more likely to be stable in his faith and doctrine than a woman. Paul alluded to this fact when he said that some women are weak and easily swayed by their desires and by all kinds of teaching.[3]

The intuitive nature in women allows us to more easily trust in things we cannot see — such as God. This is a great strength because it helps us come to faith in God quickly. However, the weakness hidden in this strength is that her easy intuitiveness tends to make woman more deceivable than a man, not as discerning. We see this from the beginning, in the garden, where Eve believed what the serpent said to her, so she confessed to God, *I was deceived.* As this incident proved, by her trustful nature woman is more vulnerable to demonic influence, and more easily led or manipulated by her emotions and desires.

The same intuitive nature that has all of a woman's spiritual receptors operating full bore can make a woman easy prey to deceiving and seducing spirits. Her desire to open herself fully to the life of faith also tends to make her open to any and all things spiritual. She doesn't always test everything, but tends to grasp her inward leadings with eagerness.

These are not flaws in God's creation. Rather, we are designed to be interdependent, as 1 Corinthians 11:11 points out. God's design was perfect, because those very differences, strengths and weaknesses, were meant enhance the glory of each other. In a collection of essays on the subject of recovering Biblical manhood and womanhood, Pastor John Piper says:

---

[3] 2 Timothy 3:6-7.

"God intends for all the 'weaknesses' that are characteristically masculine to call forth and highlight women's strengths. And God intends for all the 'weaknesses' that are characteristically feminine to call forth and highlight man's strengths. God intends [man and woman] to be the perfect complement to each other, so that when life together is considered the weaknesses of manhood are not weaknesses and the weaknesses of woman are not weaknesses. They are the complements that call forth different strengths in each other."[4]

This truth is easily illustrated by magnets. Individually, the opposing ends with their differing qualities don't show much usefulness, and are terribly uninteresting. But when they are brought near to one another, something powerful happens as they madly cling to one another.

We need each other to show off our best stuff, the glory God hid in our respective DNA. Woman's nature as an intuitive, emotional thinker, is the design of God, but it needs the balance of man's reason. The men need our emotional, intuitive nature to balance their logic and take them places where their logic cannot go.

The Single Person

I believe with all of my heart that unmarried people are complete in themselves and have the same potential for joy and abundant life through Christ; just in a different way. The Apostle Paul mused about such things in 1 Corinthians Chapter 7, and observed of the unmarried woman, *"An unmarried woman or virgin is concerned about the Lord's affairs: Her aim is to be devoted to the Lord in both body and spirit."[5]* A few verses later he makes this remark concerning the widowed woman who contemplates remarriage: *"In my judgment, she is happier if she stays as she is — and I think that I too have the Spirit of God."[6]*

These comments and the balance of scripture verify that the single person does not need to be married to experience a full life. In fact, the single women I know who walk with the Holy Spirit have wonderful

---

[4] Page 49, "Recovering Biblical Manhood and Womanhood, a Response to Evangelical Feminism," a collection of essays edited by John Piper and Wayne Grudem. 1991, Crossway Books. Specifically quoting from Piper's essay, "A Vision of Biblical Complementarity."

[5] 1 Corinthians 7:34b.

[6] 1 Corinthians 7:40.

testimonies to share about what it is like to have the Lord for a husband. The Bible does not insist, and it is never appropriate to say, that a person must be married to be complete. Having said this, it remains true that woman, married or single, was designed to draw out the glory of God hidden within the men around her: whether fathers, brothers, sons or friends.

We should not define ourselves by whether we are married or single, but by the characteristics God created in our feminine souls, which the world needs from us. These include being caretakers, nurturers, comforters, and natural experts in relationship. Most men will admit that when it comes to naturally knowing what it takes to keep a relationship great, they haven't got a clue. They need us. But cluelessness is a two-sided coin in God's design: we need the natural knowledge men possess for clear-headed leadership.

In the creation story I have discovered God's design for me as a woman: to reveal and express the glory of God in His tender, submissive ways, brought forth out of man's side to live by his side as a life-giver and life nurturer, a partner in filling the earth with the fruit of God's goodness. The woman God designed lives the life He always dreamed of.

Reflecting on Chapter 11

The purpose of this chapter is to help you discover and embrace God's design and purpose for you as a woman.

❖ *Read Proverbs 31:10-31. List the qualities that you see in the woman described, paraphrasing in your own words. Do not list specific activities (such as sewing or gardening), but rather find a word to describe the character revealed by the activities, i.e, caring, prepared, strong, joyful.*

❖ *Ask the Holy Spirit to reveal any worldly patterns of womanhood you have adopted.*

❖ *If you discover you have embraced the wrong design, give the Lord permission to change your mind, and ask Him to open your eyes to the glory of your design as a woman.*

Chapter 12

The Legacy of a Fallen Relationship

When asked how he can possibly keep up with all the new ways criminals design counterfeit bills in the U.S., a Treasury agent will tell you that he never wastes time examining or memorizing the many counterfeits. His best tool to recognize a counterfeit is to be thoroughly familiar with the real thing. In that same spirit, we're going to discover the marks of a fallen relationship in this chapter by first studying the original design. The first creation story reads,

> Then God said, "Let us make man in our image, in our likeness, and let them rule over the fish of the sea and the birds of the air, over the livestock, over all the earth, and over all the creatures that move along the ground." So God created man in his own image, in the image of God he created them; male and female he created them. God blessed them and said to them, "Be fruitful and increase in number; fill the earth and subdue it. Rule over the fish of the sea and the birds of the air, and over every living creature that moves on the ground." (Genesis 1:26-28)

This account makes it clear that dominion over the earth was given to mankind, not just the male sex. Mankind is the sum of the parts that is Adam and Eve, who were given the job of ruling over the earth together as one. They were to be co-regents. God did not design them for competition, but to be a wonderful, unified, mutually gifted, mutually responsible team.

This state of co-rulership did not, however, mean that Adam and Eve were to have equal rank in headship. First Corinthians 11:3 reveals God's order for his creation in relationship to himself and to each other:

I want you to realize that the head of every man is Christ, and the head of the woman is man, and the head of Christ is God.

There is absolutely no evidence that this order was put into effect as an afterthought or response to the fall in Eden. This order has been God's design from the beginning of creation, and Jesus affirmed his place in it in the Gospel of John, where he repeatedly insisted that he came to do the Father's work, saying often, *I do not speak on my own, but say only what the Father tells me to say; I do only what the Father commands me to do.* Jesus, though equal with God, being God himself, willingly submitted to the headship of the Father. He accepted his place in God's order as revealed in the above verse.

Further proof that God had taught Adam and Eve this order is seen at the time of their rebellion. In Genesis 3:17, God scolds Adam for listening to his wife instead of Him. God had obviously taught Adam that his first obligation was to honor God's headship, under whose guidance he was to be the head of his own family, leading them rather than being led. God finds fault with Adam because in listening to Eve and doing her bidding, Adam has not just followed Eve in rebellion against God, but has actually allowed Eve to usurp God's position as head over Adam. In essence, she became Adam's head in God's place, which she could not have done without Adam's cooperation or abdication. As a result Adam actually exalted Eve over God in this instance. He gave her a higher place and priority than His creator and Lord. This is the case anytime a husband obeys the wife rather than yield to God's will as he perceives it through the Spirit and his conscience.

In the beginning, Adam and Eve must have enjoyed God's order. It was designed to bless the man and woman and cause them to deepen their knowledge of God. Eve yielded to Adam's leadership willingly, trustfully and lovingly. Adam was thrilled to have her (instead of one of the animals) for a helpmeet and he did not rule over her in a harsh, overbearing way. Surely he experienced her as God designed her to be: a most satisfying gift that healed his aloneness, who took delight in her feminine nature and offered it to him, who responded to him in such a way that the glory of his manhood was revealed in relationship to her. He knew that his place of headship required him to cherish and protect Eve. Likewise, he complemented her so that the glory of her femininity was revealed in relating to him.

Adam's headship of their family was a fact of life that was wise, natural and right, not a sexist issue or a matter of contention. But Eve's deception and Adam's rebellion changed all of that. When man broke faith with God by his disobedience and rebellion, he broke the covenant of trust between them. Man's sin now tainted the beauty of God's order for the god-man relationship and the man-woman relationship, as he had invoked the cursed life upon himself by breaking his covenant with God.

Since we are all descendants of Adam, the first son of God, the covenant-breaker, we are born not only under the curse of death, but with the DNA of his fallen nature. Jesus has saved us from the curse of death, so we are now restored to that position where God is our Father and ready to teach us how to be righteous sons and daughters. And we still have the same temptation Adam and Eve did: we are free to choose whether or not we are willing to be taught this way of being by God's design.

Apart from being taught by God, we continue to develop patterns of relationship that still look like the cursed one, handed down to us from generations of fallen people. Second, in trying to throw off this cursed life, we often discard God's righteous order for marriage and family, which still exists on this side of the cross.

Jesus has paid the price for our sin and set us free from the curse, but God's order for relationships still exists, according to the New Testament. God has not changed his mind. This chapter is to help you recognize these truths, and to recognize the effects of the curse on the current behavior and character of men and women as they relate to one another.

The seeds of rebellion: deception, doubt, and fear.

Now the serpent was more crafty than any of the wild animals the Lord God had made. He said to the woman, "Did God really say, `You must not eat from any tree in the garden'?" The woman said to the serpent, "We may eat fruit from the trees in the garden, but God did say, `You must not eat fruit from the tree that is in the middle of the garden, and you must not touch it, or you will die.'" "You will not surely die," the *serpent said to the woman. "For God knows that when you eat of it your eyes will be opened, and you will be like God, knowing good and evil."*

When the woman saw that the fruit of the tree was good for food and pleasing to the eye, and also desirable for gaining wisdom, she took some and ate it. She also gave some to her husband, who was with her, and he ate it. Then the eyes of both of them were opened, and they realized that they were naked; so they sewed fig leaves together and made coverings for themselves.

Then the man and his wife heard the sound of the Lord God as he was walking in the garden in the cool of the day, and they hid from the Lord God among the trees of the garden. But the Lord God called to the man, "Where are you?" He answered, "I heard you in the garden, and I was afraid because I was naked; so I hid." And he said, "Who told you that you were naked? Have you eaten from the tree from which I commanded you not to eat?" The man said, "The woman you put here with me - she gave me some fruit from the tree, and I ate it." Then the Lord God said to the woman, "What is this you have done?" The woman said, "The serpent deceived me, and I ate." (Genesis 3:1-13).

The first observation is that the serpent approached the one most vulnerable to deception — Eve. With the seed of doubt in God's love and goodness firmly planted in her mind, Eve falls for the lie: perhaps God did deceive them; maybe they won't die if they eat of the Tree of Knowledge of Good and Evil. She has been wanting more wisdom anyway, and besides ,how could anything that looks so good be bad for her? Whatever her reasoning is, Eve disobeys God and eats from the forbidden tree. Then she offers the fruit to Adam.

Adam's weakness.

Adam is faced with a decision: will he listen to and obey God, or will he listen to and obey his wife? He eats of the forbidden fruit, but not in ignorance. First Timothy 2:14 says that Adam was not deceived; he knew exactly what he was doing. He joins Eve in her sin apparently because he loves her and wants to please her so much. He cannot bear to be separated from her, and he, not being easily persuaded from what he knows, still knows that separation (death) will be the inevitable result of her disobedience. He chooses to "die" with her rather than live without her. By his choice, Adam revealed that he feared his aloneness or the loss of Eve more than he feared God.

This fear of being alone is mankind's greatest vulnerability. The act of dividing mankind into two separate beings left mankind haunted by the need to be connected with the other part, "the other self." Thus man has a powerful, built-in desire to please woman and cleave to her. By God's design this is meant to be a great strength which ensures the covenant bond and the fulfillment of his creation mandate for mankind to fill the earth.

Again, this strength also contains the seed of weakness, and that seed is fear of being separated, of losing that companion. The fruit of that seed is seen throughout the Bible.

In Genesis we see the first example of a woman's great influence over her man, by virtue of his great need for her, and his inherent sense of aloneness without her. Satan takes full advantage of this vulnerability in mankind and uses it to lead us into rebellion, as he did Adam. Many times God warned the men of Israel not to marry the women of heathen nations, yet we see Israel doing this, and how the wives invariably led the men into idolatry. This happened to Solomon, who married numerous foreign wives who influenced him through his desire to please them, to enter the worship of their pagan gods, causing the nation of Israel to worship idols. As a result of his weakness the seeds of destruction of his own kingdom were planted.

Eve's weakness.

While Adam's vulnerability was his desire to have and please her, Eve's vulnerability was her openness to receive and the potential for deception. Once Eve entertained doubts about God's love and his motive for withholding the Tree of Knowledge, she was vulnerable to the lies of Satan and the weakness of her own flesh. The seed of doubt in God's goodness was all that was needed to fan into flame any discontent in her heart. No longer satisfied with what God had given her in the Tree of Life, Eve was led into rebellion against God by her desire for more and the deception that she needed something other than what God had given her.

Satan used the same seed of doubt to plug into Adam's vulnerability: *Can God satisfy me without this wonderful creature? I need her, how can I give her up? If I can just please her and keep her, then my soul will be satisfied. Give me that apple!*

This is the fruit of rebellion and deception: destruction of covenant relationship between man and woman, and also between mankind and God. Satan is still at work in this. He works constantly to convince women that they need more of something else to be happy, scattering seeds of discontent. He leads men astray of God's will by the perversion of the God-designed need to have and please a woman. And the irony is that some men come to see this need for woman as a weakness in themselves, something that gives the woman a power over him that is deeply resented, giving rise to behavior that demeans and dishonors them. In fact, some men go so far as to beat their women in a violent denial of this latent power a woman has over them.

Signs of a fallen relationship.

In examining the fall of Adam and Eve, we learn more than just what happened to destroy the covenant between God and man; we see the very elements of what still destroys relationships between husband and wife. The things which destroy marriages today had their genesis in the curses that rested upon Adam and Eve because of their sin and their fallen nature.

When they rebelled against God, they suffered spiritual death (separation from the life of God). God is a spirit, and flesh cannot fellowship with him. The death Adam and Eve experienced was the death of their spirits. As noted earlier, when we receive Jesus, this is reversed as we are "born again" when a new spirit is birthed within us.

It is important to understand that when Adam and Eve betrayed their covenant of trust with God, the curses God announces in Genesis 3 are not being arbitrarily dispensed in a fit of anger; he is simply explaining the consequences of their sin, which has now separated them from God's companionship, wisdom and strength. If you study the ways of God you will find that He doesn't have to devise a punishment for us, because he knows the fruit of our own choices will do that well enough! Consider this proverb:

> *Since they hated knowledge and did not choose to fear the Lord, since they would not accept my advice, and spurned my rebuke, they will eat*

*the fruit of their ways and be filled with the fruit of their schemes.
Proverbs 1:29-31*

When a person disobeys God in pursuit of his own desires long enough, God will eventually let that person have his fill of that desired thing until the fruit of it brings its own punishment. It seems that God's logic goes like this: *If this is what you desire more than me, very well, then you shall have it. In fact, you shall have your fill of it.* This fact is revealed in God's response to the grumbling of the Israelites for meat in the wilderness. He gave them manna, but they wanted more. They wanted meat, and had their hearts set upon it. So he gave them so much quail that eventually they were neck deep in it, and sick of it. But along with that meat they got leanness of soul.[1] God never withdrew his love, but the joy of his pleasure and favor had been sacrificed to their desire to fill their bellies with rich meat. God said, *So I gave them over to their stubborn hearts to follow their own devices.*[2]

When God gives a person over to his own desire, that person begins to eat the fruit of his desire. This is how man eats from the Tree of Knowledge. It begins with acting apart from God, and thereby saying in essence, *"I know what I need better than God does."* Eventually he discovers that this fruit is rotten; but it looked so good to him that he had to taste of it himself. It is not enough that God says no to us, as if he simply wanted to withhold something from us. We still don't get it, the heart of God, that the goal of His command is to give us life. So we have to eat the fruit of that Tree of Knowledge (personal experience) ourselves. How many heartaches we could avoid if only we believed and trusted in God and his unfailing love.

Let me be quite frank: if you are determined to have what you want, forget the feast that God has planned for your soul. The most effective thing God can do to lead you to repentance is to give you over to your true desires, and let the fruit of those desires punish you, as they inevitably will. No doubt it breaks His heart, but like the perfect Father that He is, God's hope is always that when you have tasted the rotten fruit long enough, your appetite for the goodness of God will turn you back to Him. As we return to the Garden we can see this principle at work.

---

[1] Numbers Chapter 18.

[2] Psalm 81:12.

Eve, your desire shall be for your husband.

> To the woman he said, "I will greatly increase your pains in childbearing; with pain you will give birth to children.[3] Your desire will be for your husband, and he will rule over you." (Genesis 3:16)

God says to Eve, *Your desire shall be for your husband.* Many assume that this "desire" refers to the sexual or emotional desire of a wife for her husband, but such an interpretation doesn't bear out. First of all, anyone observing the average husband-wife relationship can see that the wife is usually not having to deal with her overwhelming romantic or sexual desire for her husband — she is far more likely to be dealing with her desire to fix or control her husband.

Besides, it was God's original design for the man and wife to desire one another so they could populate the earth and enjoy one another, so why would he turn this into a punishment? And this interpretation is not consistent with God's concept of punishment, as Eve was not guilty of desiring more of her husband, but of wanting something to enhance herself.

Secondly, when Moses, who recorded this story, wrote elsewhere of the desire between a man and woman, he used an entirely different Hebrew word. In Deuteronomy 5:21 when he says, *Neither shalt thou desire thy neighbor's wife...* (KJV), the Hebrew word he uses is *chamad*, which implies pleasure and literally means, *to delight in.* This is not the word Moses uses in Genesis 3:16.

Furthermore, the word he does use he employed only one other time in his writings, just a few verses later in Genesis 4:7. Here the Lord is confronting Cain over his unrighteous offering. He says to Cain, *If you do not do what is right, sin is crouching at your door; it <u>desires</u> to have you, but you must master it.* The New American Standard Version conveys the clearest sense of this word when it says, *"Sin desires to control you, but you must control it."*

"Desire" here is translated from the same word in Genesis 3:16, even the same grammatical form, thus we see that it speaks of the desire to master or control, rather than sexual or emotional desire.

---

[3] It is not clear why a woman would have more pain in childbearing because of the fall. It might have something to do with the fact that apart from God's presence, grace and strength, a woman might be overcome with tension and fear at the time of her labor, which we know affects her ability to endure pain and even the depth of the pain itself. This has been well documented by medical science.

In essence God said to Eve, *Because you usurped my authority over Adam and used your influence to control him, then you shall live with the desire to control him.* This is further reinforced by the rest of Genesis 3:16, which ends by saying, *and he will rule over you.* This confirms that the context here is not about romantic or sexual desire, but power and authority.

We are all daughters of Eve.

Again, God is not cursing Eve or punishing her by saying this, he is pointing out the result of the choice she has made. His announcement validates one of the laws of the kingdom, that one reaps what one sows. She did not want to submit to God or her husband in trustful obedience, so she is released into her desire to do it her way.

We are all descended from Eve, and as such all women are cursed with this desire in our unrenewed souls, apart from the salvation of the cross. When Jesus destroyed the curse at the cross, He destroyed the power of woman's rebellious nature to control her. She no longer lives under the same curse that still afflicts the unsaved woman.

However, this redemption, the disarming of the power of the curse over us, does not automatically overwrite the patterns of fallen relationship, which will in all likelihood still operate in believers from force of habit. After a woman is saved the desire to control no longer has power over her; it now is reduced to a habit that she can overcome by seeking out and yielding to the help of the Holy Spirit. The woman works out her process of salvation as she submits to God's ways and gives herself to faith, love and holiness.[4]

Again, when God says Adam will rule over Eve, it is not a punishment or a curse; He is reaffirming His order for the family even in their fallen state. God has created Adam with the nature to rule, lead and govern; it is part of his masculine DNA. It is still God's will for the man to lead the family, though now he will have to do it without the wisdom and strength of God's presence. And instead of being the blessing it was intended for woman, man's headship has the potential to be a source of frustration for her because she has been given over to her desire to control and have her way.

What is Adam's punishment, the fruit of his rebellion?

---

[4] 1 Timothy 2:11-15.

Adam's abandoned headship will be difficult to enforce.

God says to him in Genesis 3:17,

> *Because you listened to your wife [yielding to her instead of me — my note] and ate from the tree about which I commanded you, "You must not eat of it," cursed is the ground because of you; through painful toil you will eat of it all the days of your life. It will produce thorns and thistles for you, and you will eat the plants of the field. By the sweat of your brow you will eat your food until you return to the ground.*

Originally, God has given Adam and Eve dominion over the earth; the earth is to serve Adam and from it God will feed them and supply every need. Apparently this was going to occur without any sweat or struggle on Adam's part, because this toilsome labor is something new that is going to happen as a result of his rebellion. Before now it is likely that Adam was free to spend his life expressing all the creative power God had placed in him, rather than having to labor for food.

It seems that God is saying to Adam, *You despised the authority I gave you and allowed your wife to lead you instead of honoring me; therefore, the earth will no longer yield to your authority to rule over it. Since it will not serve you any longer, from now on you will have to wrestle with it to obtain your sustenance.*

The earth will no longer yield submissively to Adam's headship, and even his helpmeet will desire to control him and resist his authority. Adam no longer has legal authority over the earth. He basically gave it away to his wife, who then gave it away to the devil when she submitted to him.

Fallen man now has to struggle to maintain his authority, yet the desire to lead or be the head is still in his DNA, and God's plan for him to protectively rule over his home has not changed. It's just going to be much more difficult to fulfill his role. The earth, the animals and his wife no longer yield in respectful fear of him, so he will have to really be assertive to get anything done.

Apart from the influence of the Spirit of Christ, the fruit of man's fallen nature is being lived out in marriages everywhere. Men and women are not complementing one another, they are struggling with each other. In some marriages, they are even at war, a battle that is more critical on this front than any other in the spiritual realm. There are more casualties and more evil wrought in unrighteous relationships today than in any other aspect of Kingdom.

It's "second nature."

The fallen relationship is a frustrating, heartbreaking struggle over who's in charge. As a pastor's wife, privy to the private struggles of many women, I have seen that the unrenewed nature of all women is the desire to fix or control their husbands, to get them to do and be what the wife wants. I see unsaved women like this, Christian women like this, even Spirit-filled women like this — as I was. The main difference between unsaved and Christian women is that Christian women have simply found some spiritual reason to justify their desire to control the husband, usually under the guise of helping the Holy Spirit do His job.

This desire is, so to speak, second nature; it certainly isn't the first nature we were created with. Our primary nature is like God's own because we were created in His image; our "second nature" is the fallen nature. The next time a Christian tells you that they can't overcome bad behavior because it is "second nature," then remind them of their "first nature." Jesus died so that we wouldn't be a slave to the second nature anymore, and could be restored to our first nature as righteous sons and daughters of God.

Ever since Eve's deception led to her rebellion, the unredeemed or unrenewed soul of a woman surges with the strong undercurrent of discontent. When Lucy Stone vowed to lead all women to the full knowledge of their discontent, she lead them to revile everything which failed to satisfy and serve them. Sadly, she achieved her goal and our world is now full of the fruit of it. This discontent is the fuel which feeds the desire in a woman to have control of her own life, her own happiness, and thus by necessity, to control her husband.

On the other hand, the reality is that in one way or another, men have always ruled, just as God said he would. I read a newspaper article in which the leaders of women's rights organizations complained that in spite of millions of dollars spent and tremendous effort to obtain more power in the work world, men still have the majority of the power, governing positions and money in the world.

Fallen or not, there is no altering man's God-given drive to rule, though apart from God's influence this rule can be most oppressive. Indeed, the devil has done his best to pervert this nature in men. What God meant for good, the devil has turned for evil. Wherever men abandon the ways of God, their rulership easily becomes an oppression of women.

Not all men are dominating, aggressive or determined to rule. Some women complain that their passive husbands will not step up to be the head of the house. However, even in abdicating his leadership, a husband's passivity can be a subtle form of control. The passive man makes a trade-off. He will let the woman hold sway over the house, or have her way, and perhaps give her anything she wants. But in the process, he withholds himself, his very heart. He tends to give her things, but not the love, affection and access to his heart that a woman needs so much. The woman may feel like she's in charge and left with the headship of the home, but the truth is that by withholding his rulership and covering of the family, he is still the one who determines the quality of their life together.

The prevalence of abortion, homosexuality, drugs and a sex-drenched culture all stem from the battle which has been lost at home. The power struggle is dividing husbands and wives and resulting in a divorce rate that is as high in the church as it is in the world. Men and women look at each other as the enemy. Men beat their women, frustrated to the point of violence. And in the ultimate rejection of the opposite sex, men are pursuing intimate relationships with men and women with women.

Instead of seeing one another as the gift of fulfillment God intended, too many men and women now see the opposite sex as an object to be possessed, conquered, subdued and manipulated; or they are living a completely guarded existence, hiding from the other in fear being used or abused, a far cry from the delightful, life-giving relationship God created marriage to be.

Jesus has redeemed us from fallen relationship.

Clearly, righteous relationship between two people is impossible apart from God. The good news is that through Jesus Christ, we have been restored to covenant life with God, having all access to His strength, wisdom and grace. God is not only passionate about redeeming you, He wants to renew and restore your glory and calling in relating to the opposite sex.

Even Christian marriages often resemble the fallen relationship instead of the redeemed one, as people still act out the fallen relationship from habit. It is only when you completely embrace the teachings of Jesus and the

Biblical truths about marriage, that you will be able to enjoy the kind of marriage He designed.

Marriage was never meant to be a battleground. It was meant to be a refuge, a home for the heart, a place of rest, just as Naomi once said to her daughters-in-law:.

> May the Lord grant that each of you will find rest in the home of another husband." (Ruth 1:9)

Reflecting on Chapter 12

This chapter teaches you to recognize the signs of a fallen relationship so you can break habits of relating that were developed under the influence of your "second nature."

❖ *Do you see evidence of the fallen relationship in your own marriage or other personal relationships?*

❖ *Ask the Holy Spirit to open your eyes to such things and write them down as you become aware of them. One by one, ask Him to give you grace to change and embrace God's ways for relating to your husband or other men.*

Deeper Work

❖ *If appropriate, initiate dialogue with your spouse (and prayer, if he is in the faith) about the things you are learning about your relationship.*

Chapter 13

The Marriage Covenant God Designed

The word "covenant" should be clearly understood by every Christian. Jesus spoke of our relationship to Him as a covenant. In fact, the word that has come to us as "testament" (as in Old Testament and New Testament) is from the same word often translated as "covenant" in our Bibles, so our Bible might as well have been entitled "Old Covenant" and "New Covenant." And in Malachi 2:14, God speaks of the man's partner as *the wife of your marriage covenant."*

The Bible is the story of God's determination to maintain relationship with His people through a series of covenants, and is our detailed guide on how to live in covenant faithfulness to God and others. Understanding the meaning of covenant is essential to knowing God's will for marriage. The typical modern marriage tends to be relatively superficial in commitment when measured against the Biblical concept of covenant.

My husband and I got married because we were deeply in love, but like most couples, we were ignorant of the meaning of covenant at the time, so our exchange of vows seemed like more of a romantic event on our way to wedded life than a solemn ceremony of commitment. As time went by, we discovered that our love was not enough to help us weather the challenges of ministry life, and it began to suffer. Our commitment gradually weakened until it came to the point of breaking. Neither of us had the will to keep our vows and quite frankly, I had forgotten what those vows were, even though they were hanging by my bedside. In a ironic picture of reality, they had been reduced to mere ornaments rather than commitments.

Later, when we were in the process of rebuilding our love and marriage, God purposed to wipe out our ignorance, arranging for us to hear some teaching on the nature of blood covenant. A simple one-hour teaching turned my world of understanding upside down in regards to the true nature of our relationship to God and the implications it had for any covenant relationship between two people.

We embarked on a season of research, and ended up discovering a body of truth that is so powerful, so able to transform one's experience of life with God and with a spouse, that it has become our life message. We now have taught seminars entitled *Covenant: God's Principles of Relationship* countless times in the U.S. and abroad.

The practice of blood covenant was a world-wide practice in ancient days, but the practice of honoring of covenant faithfulness has practically disappeared where civilization has advanced, known today only in nations which are still fairly primitive. Most of western society's acquaintance with blood covenant is limited to what we have seen in Hollywood westerns and television shows, where two men become "blood brothers" for life. Because understanding covenant principles are so crucial to a right foundation for marriage, this chapter will you the basics.

The nature of a covenant.

Covenant was the most enduring, sacred agreement between two parties, entered into as a means of providing each party with a sense of security in what is otherwise is a matter of faith — the promise to love and stay with another person forever. The union was formed by cutting and mingling blood, and the security was provided in the form of a self-pronounced curse of death, which offered legal right to the other party, in front of witnesses, to take one's life if they ever broke their covenant promises.

So keeping a covenant was a matter of honor, enforced by the threat of death. Every primitive culture on every continent practiced a form of covenant, initiated by ceremonies that were so strikingly similar (in an age of no global communication) that some Biblical scholars conclude, and I heartily agree, that the practice and concept of covenant making and keeping was born in the heart of our creator God.

All primitive cultures viewed the covenant as means by which two parties "become one" for the rest of their lives, and the creation story reveals this to be a God-ordained reality:

> The man said, "This is now bone of my bones, and flesh of my flesh; she shall be called 'woman,' for she was taken out of man." For this reason a man will leave his father and mother and be united to his wife, and they will become one flesh. (Genesis 2:23-24.)

This is not merely a poetic euphemism for sexual intimacy. God actually knits your souls together so that you are one, as Jesus said in Matthew 19:6: "So they are no longer two, but one. Therefore what God has joined together, let man not separate." It is not that you literally become one person with no distinction between you; it is that you are so close that there is no division possible between you.

The word "united" in verse 24 means glued; two items glued together have no space between them, and are indivisible. Most importantly, you are always seen together in God's sight, which means that all of His relating to you happens in light of your faithfulness, or lack of it, in your covenant relationships. A right perspective of oneness as God sees it is the very foundation of marriage, requiring you learn the importance of relating to your husband as if he is a part of you, not a mere housemate or partner in the worldly sense.

"Oneness" is the purpose and goal of all covenants; you become as one life living in two bodies — as if, having divided mankind into two genders to enable righteous relationship that could reproduce itself, God made a way for man and woman to be one again. Oneness is at once both a spiritual reality and a process, effected with a ceremony, then fully developed over years of shared life.

In the same way that we are saved in the twinkling of an eye by putting faith in Christ, and then learn to walk in that salvation, we become one before God and then learn to walk in that oneness. This is not a matter of semantics or spiritual lingo, it is a profoundly important concept of relationship.

The rest of this chapter we will examine the ancient covenant steps as revealed in Biblical and Hebrew culture, in order to discover the deeper truths and strengths they bring to a modern marriage covenant.

Husband and wife give themselves to one another.

The first step in making a covenant was that each person took off his robe or coat and gave it to the other. An example is found in 1 Samuel 18:4 between Jonathan and David: *"Jonathan took off the robe he was wearing and gave it to David, along with his tunic, and even his sword, his bow and belt."* As in this case, often a gift was given rather than a garment, but in any case the gift symbolized the pledge of oneself to the other person, from that moment: *"I pledge myself to you. I give you all of myself, my total being, and my life."*

Today upon engagement, a ring is given. In the Hebrew culture, the moment of engagement is as binding as actually being married. For years this was quaintly called "pledging one's troth" to another. I always wondered what "troth" meant; the dictionary defines it as *good faith.* Your promise to faithfully love someone for the rest of your life is something you cannot prove, and you are asking them to place faith in you to do so. Thus all relationships are based upon faith.

We have become seduced by a worldly attitude that measures success in marriage by each one's ability to make the other happy. God does not see it this way. In his eyes, a successful marriage — the kind He designed — is one in which each one is faithful to the other, by honoring the faith that has been placed in them. So the success of marriage truly depends upon the degree of faithfulness found in each party.

The role of the witness.

A covenant ceremony, ancient or modern, is held before witnesses. The difference between then and now is that witnesses to ancient covenants were not mere spectators, as they are today. They played a crucial role in ensuring the success of the relationship, being expected to hold each covenant maker accountable for keeping his vows. It is an acknowledgement that in our human frailty, we need others to help us do what is right. In other words, it takes a community to make a great marriage. Of course, this requires accountability on our parts to such witnesses. The witness to a covenant took no sides, but acted as a defender and enforcer of the promises he had seen and heard.

Missionary David Livingstone was thoroughly exposed to covenant practice as he traversed Africa in the 1800's. He noted in his journals that if any man broke his covenant, a member of his own family would deliver him up to an appointed avenger, to enforce his self-invoked curse of death for violating his promise. I dare say that the loss of that practice has directly contributed to the rise of divorce in modern civilization!

To break the faith your covenant partner has placed in you is a hateful thing to God, who said to his people:

> So guard yourself in your spirit, and do not break faith with the wife of your youth. "I hate divorce," says the God of Israel, "and I hate a man's covering himself (or his wife) with violence as well as with his garment," says the Lord Almighty. So guard yourself in your spirit, and do not break faith. (Malachi 2:15)

God is the witness to every covenant, every marriage, watching between the two parties to enforce faithfulness in their treatment of one another. However, He isn't interested in delivering us to the avenger of death, but instead has given us the Spirit of Life to help us honor our promises.

What does God mean when he says, "do not break faith"? To answer this question is to touch the heartbeat of covenant. To break faith is to violate your promise to faithfully love the other person and give yourself to them exclusively. It can occur through adultery, abuse, withholding affection, or neglect. Breaking faith betrays or sins against the faith extended to you in an act of trust that made the other person vulnerable to your character now and in the future. The vulnerable heart offered in faith craves the security of committed love. As Proverbs 19:22 says, What a man desires is unfailing love.

God makes it clear in Malachi that he takes his role as a witness to the marriage covenant very seriously. When God sees a man or wife mistreating the other, he does not ignore it, and when they seek him in prayer or other religious activity, as the men of Israel were, he does not act as if it is business as usual. God specifically mentions divorce and physical abuse as the most extreme acts of breaking faith.[1]

Giving and taking.

A man and woman give themselves publicly at the altar, announcing before witnesses their pledge to belong to the other person forever. Each one

---

[1] Divorce and abusiveness seem equally abhorrent to God as a violation of covenant.

is asked: *Do you take this man…this woman?* In other words, do you receive them — unconditionally, completely?

Only time will tell if this is a solemn commitment of your heart or just another romantic tradition. Either way, the outcome usually depends upon the level of satisfaction you find in being married to the one you chose.

The Bible verifies that it is God's will for us to satisfy one another in relationship, both physically and emotionally:

> *The husband should fulfill his marital duty to his wife, and likewise the wife to her husband. The wife's body does not belong to her alone, but also to her husband. In the same way, the husband's body does not belong to him alone, but also to his wife. Do not deprive each other except by mutual consent and for a time, so that you may devote yourselves to prayer. Then come together again so that Satan will not tempt you because of your lack of self-control.* (1 Corinthians 7:2-5)

The Holy Spirit who inspired these words acknowledges the powerful sexual drive that God created in mankind and reminds us that the bodies of a couple joined in covenant belong to one another. God approves of a healthy sexual relationship between husband and wife, and is surely pleased when they give themselves to one another completely. Yet there is more to this scripture than meets the eye.

When Proverbs 31:11 describes the godly wife, it says the heart of her husband *"trusts in her confidently and relies on and believes in her safely, so that he has no lack of honest gain or need of dishonest spoil."* (The Amplified Bible). The Hebrew expression actually refers to the "rightful spoils" or valuables which a conquering king deserves because of his position as conqueror.

Before you throw slam this book shut, let me assure you that the Bible is not saying you are a "conquered valuable" for your husband. The emphasis is not upon "spoils" but upon the rightful gain, or the due blessings inherently available or to be expected from the kind of wife God designed.

This idea is carried forward in 1 Corinthians 7, which refers to far more than than sexual fulfillment. The Amplified Bible Version of verse three says, *The husband should give to his wife her conjugal rights — goodwill, kindness and what is due her as his wife; and likewise the wife to her husband.* Why is it that we breeze past this verse as being all about the sex, and neglect the concept that in a covenant, you owe them kindness and good will?

In fact, the original Greek carries the idea of being "well-minded" towards another — what I call being kind in the mind. In other words, giving your spouse the benefit of the doubt, not harboring mean or resentful thoughts, neither reviling them nor judging them. As a counselor I meet a lot of Christians who have the nerve to congratulate themselves on staying married because it supposedly pleases God, even though they have have developed a chronically negative and unkind attitude towards the spouse — as if God would approve of such an absurd mockery of righteous relationship, just for the sake of two people continuing to share a house!

Do not misunderstand: I'm not advocating divorce, I'm advocating absolute faithfulness of heart in marriage.

Jesus upheld this same standard when he told his disciples, *"…anyone who looks at a woman lustfully has already committed adultery with her in his heart…"* in Matthew 5:28. Clearly, after resetting the standard for faithfulness to being faithful even with one's eyes — we cannot allow ourselves to believe that Jesus would approve any mental exercise in which we imagine ourselves in intimacy with another person other than the spouse, admiring, lusting, giving them the benefit of our meditative, loving or kind thoughts, especially while withholding the same from our covenant partner.

In faith we must believe with David the facts about our exposure before God:

> *O Lord, you have searched me and you know me. You know when I sit and when I rise; you perceive my thoughts from afar. You discern my going out and my lying down; you are familiar with all my ways. Before a word is on my tongue you know it completely, O Lord. (Psalms 139:1-4)*

Covenant eyes are faithful eyes, and a true covenant heart is faithful in their private thoughts. This is the greater meaning of the passage in First Corinthians chapter seven.

Face to face.

Let's return briefly to Genesis 2:18, where we've already learned that *"helpmeet"* means "other self." You see, we only grasp the full meaning of the word used here if we add the word *"reflection,"* evoking the idea of gazing at one's own image.

Understanding these shades of meaning all together, we see that to a Hebrew mind the concept of a helpmeet included the thought of being face-to-face with one who is like himself. There is a humorous side to this when you consider that God was likely employing this term with Adam to reassure him that the partner he would provide for him would look like him, standing toe to toe, eye to eye, not being in the form or shape of an elephant or a monkey or a giraffe.

In fact, the face-to-face concept was familiar to the Hebrews, and was used in the ten commandments when God said, *"You shall have no other gods before me."* The word "before" there literally means "face;" the Hebrews used it as a preposition to indicate "being in front of." The reality underlying God's use of this word was, *I want to be face to face with you. I don't want anything separating us or coming between us. I don't want to look for you and find your back turned to me. I don't want to find you face to face with some other god. You and me kid, face-to-face.*

So we see that the idea of being face-to-face is a euphemism for exclusive relationship, or a state of unity in relationship. It has even filtered down to modern society; when we cannot agree on something we say that we *"don't see eye-to-eye."* The idea of being face-to-face perfectly illustrates God's design for man and woman in relationship and is even pictured in the sexual posture of a man and woman, which is unique among all creation. Most creatures reproduce without facing one another, but typically man and woman do not. They usually like to face one another while making love.

A reflection serves an important purpose; as I gaze at it, things are revealed to me about myself. This is how Adam and Eve, *iysh* and *ishshah*, existed together in the Garden of Eden. Before the fall, man and woman were naked before one another and were not ashamed. In order to be totally exposed and unashamed, one must feel totally accepted and safe with another. This provides for true intimacy with another person.

A marriage that lacks this intimacy and oneness has not become mature in the sense of reaching its fullest potential to heal us of alienation. One of the greatest ailments of mankind is his alienation and loneliness, an affliction that is the inevitable result of sin. As soon as man broke his covenant with God, his first reaction was to run away from God and hide.[2] Adam said, *I was afraid. I was naked (and ashamed). I hid myself.* Though he

---

[2] Genesis 3:10.

felt shame for his sin, it was bearable until he had to come face to face with God again, when the full brunt of his shame would wash over his soul.

And the unspoken fear that accompanies shame is: *You might reject me, and take your love away.* So hiding is what we do because it feels safer to hide than face the shame I will feel in being honest with you about what I have done, what I am thinking, what I want. We become pretenders, going into self-protect mode to ward off judgment, loss of face, loss of relationship, loss of love. Self-protect mode requires me to shut you out in some way.

This is why there is often an avoidance of complete emotional transparency between husband and wife to some degree. If you see me as I really am, you might not love me anymore or you might use your knowledge of my weaknesses to hurt me or judge me. Most husbands and wives would not want all of their thoughts towards one another revealed. Yet if we have the courage to give this transparency as a gift to one another, the pain and shame of being authentic with one another, the accountability of that, actually becomes a tool in the hands of the Holy Spirit to build the character of Christ in us.

It takes courage to be completely accountable, and this can only come through a genuine and fearless desire to become all we can be. Transparency before one another that refuses all hiding is a precious gift, a continued offering of the vulnerability freely entrusted to a covenant partner, given in a display of continuing faith in the other person.

Even God said when he knew he would have to destroy Sodom and Gomorrah, *"Shall I hide from Abraham what I am about to do?"* The answer was no, he would reveal his full intentions to the one he has sworn to as a covenant friend, and the result was an incredible encounter between Abraham and God in which Abraham boldly challenged God to be sure he was doing the absolutely righteous thing — challenging God to be the best he was capable of being. God humbly responded to that challenge, and did not mind. Let us be the person that is worthy of the faith placed in us, able to be trusted with the vulnerability of our covenant marriage partners.

How do I give me? Let me count the ways...

God intends for you to richly satisfy one another's needs, both for your joy and as a visible sign of the blessing attached to being united with a person under the influence of God.

It is easy to give ourselves to one another at the beginning, but every married person encounters times when you really don't want to give yourself to the other person — or receive them. Giving of yourself is a mark of faithful character on behalf of the giver, not a reward for good behavior on behalf of the recipient. Whether it is love, respect, sex, or private thoughts, the truth is that if we only give to others as a reward for pleasing us, then we are not authentic givers, we are in danger of becoming manipulators.

It would be wonderful if every husband treated his wife in such a way as to actually deserve all the good things God asks her to give him. The truth is that this doesn't always happen; and even in great marriages, it doesn't happen all the time. The temptation is to dole out the blessings as a reward for good behavior. But from God's point of view, a wife should bless her husband because God designed her to be a blessing, period.

When people get really unhappy with each other, they cease to give themselves to one another and ceasing receiving (accepting) one another. During one counseling session a wife complained that she derived no pleasure from sex with her husband. She felt she did all the giving, and sex was a duty to her.

At length she admitted she had become deeply disappointed in her husband. She didn't approve of him and he didn't meet her needs. She had actually closed her heart to him and shut him out; there was no benevolent goodness left in her minds towards him. In this frame of mind she could not receive him emotionally or physically. The physical relationship reflected what was going on at the emotional level. The man was terribly frustrated because he loved his wife and the knowledge of her deep disappointment with him made him feel awful about himself. He was not abusive, addicted or dysfunctional, just a flawed human being.

The path to renewed intimacy for them began with the woman forgiving her husband for not meeting her needs. Then she had to see that she had become equally guilty of not meeting his. She finally made the commitment to again *take this man* to be her husband. The decision to fully receive another is the most important step towards true oneness. Those in an average relationship (not rendered dysfunctional by serious physical abuse or debilitating addictions to drugs or alcohol) must sometimes push past the soul's weakness in order to continue giving and receiving as an act of covenant faithfulness.

Love and respect.

What else is due to a husband or a wife? God tells us clearly in the Bible, (the greatest marriage manual in the world). Ephesians 5:33 says *Husbands, love your wives. Wives, respect your husbands.* Have you ever wondered why he gives different instructions to men and women? Why doesn't he just say, "love and respect each other?" I think the answer lies with the differences in our gender.

The Lord commands a woman to respect her husband because this is one of his greatest needs. God created man to be the leader of the home, and it is respect that enables his leadership. He needs to know that others have confidence in him. This call to lead is also what gives men the tendency to always think in terms of their status in relation to those around them, and is the reason why they are very sensitive and easily react to any hint that someone is belittling them — especially a wife. A woman who just blows this sensitivity off to "too much pride" is in danger of misjudging him.

While a woman also needs respect, her need for it pales in comparison to her need to be loved and feel emotionally connected, since she was created by God to nurture relationships. The man also needs love, but the experience of being loved is almost wasted upon a man who feels disrespected.

Love and respect are vital to both, but in differing measures, similar to our hormonal makeup. Testosterone predominates in a man to give him manly characteristics, but he also requires some estrogen. The woman requires large amounts of estrogen to function in her femininity, but also requires some amount of testosterone for good health. This generally mirrors the balance that love and respect fill for the woman and the man.

A man who believes he is not respected by his wife is likely to be a deeply wounded or angry man. A man cannot bear to "lose face" in front of others. This shouldn't surprise us, because God, in whose image man is made, insists that He will not be mocked. He teaches his children to treat Him with the proper awe and respect and despises any behavior which brings reproach and shame to His Name.

The feminine soul needs to feel loved, even cherished. She is easily unsettled by any perceived loss of emotional connection. Her ability to follow to her husband is easily undermined if she does not feel securely loved and protected by him to whom she has given her vulnerability. Without these, a woman is likely to be unfulfilled and restless. She may go from one hobby to another, immerse herself in child-rearing or throw herself into a career. But these things will never satisfy her soul as much as being cherished and desired by her man. She is like the God in whose image she is made, for the Lord reveals His own need for tender and faithful love in many places in the scriptures.

People often marry with a "wait and see" attitude: they are waiting to see if the spouse will make them happy or fulfill them. We cannot demand fulfillment from one another, any more than one can beat a tree into producing fruit. Just as a tree yields its best fruit through being faithfully tended and watered, our own fulfillment is the fruit of giving ourselves to another in faithful attention.

And we have a bonus: God's promise that if we give ourselves to serve others, he will bless us in every way. Righteous relationship to your spouse in the sight of God means giving yourself to them completely in every way, especially giving what they need to thrive, being a life-giver, not a life-sapper. This is the way of covenant.

The husband and wife will protect one another.

In ancient covenant ceremonies each man took off his belt, which held his weapons, and gave it to the other person, as seen in 1 Samuel 18:4: *Jonathan [gave David] ... even his sword, his bow and his belt.* This act symbolizes the pledge of all one's strength to help the other person when needed: *"I give you all my strength and support. Your battles are my battles. I will always fight by your side, uniting with you against your enemies. I will never allow myself to be in a position to be against you."*

In today's wedding ceremony we vow to stand by one another through the adversities of life such as sickness and poverty. Make no mistake; these are real enemies that can severely test the love of two people. It is a sad fact that a high percentage of spouses diagnosed with diseases such as multiple sclerosis are eventually abandoned by their mates.

In any case, the strength of a covenant depends upon the commitment of each party to stand with the partner against every enemy, an enemy being defined as someone or something that threatens the security of the partner or the very covenant itself.

While most of us don't live in danger of marauding tribes, we have no lack of enemies threatening to steal or destroy our well-being, our health or abundant life, our dreams; and we easily overlook the most common enemies: the little foxes that would come and spoil our love.

The relationship itself is always guarded from anything or anyone who seriously threatens to weaken the bond, and that includes other relationships. When Genesis 2:24 says, "*... a man will leave his father and mother and be united to his wife,*" it reveals God's intention for the husband-wife relationship to take precedence over all others, including those to parents.

Many marriages get in trouble because one spouse brings a parent into the relationship by giving them a place or part that should only belong to the spouse. I am not referring to caring for aging or ill parents, or even having them live with you; there is nothing inherently wrong with these things and it pleases God for us to look after and honor our parents.

What is unacceptable is for the husband or wife to give to anyone else that which belongs to the spouse first: full attention, intimate trust, friendship, and loyalty. We counsel couples all the time where a husband is deeply angry that his children come before him in his wife's concerns, or a wife deeply resentful that her husband consults his mother about issues concerning their life more he than does her — extending an honor to the mother being withheld from the wife.

Watch out for anything like this in your life — giving of your trust, time, attention or devotion to a boss, a friend, a pastor, a sibling, parent or child — to a degree that robs the spouse of that same thing. When even a good thing or a good relationship chips away at the strength and potential beauty of our covenant, it becomes a bad thing or an unhealthy relationship.

Covenant love promises that the partner will never suffer at our hands or feel like we are the enemy. Your husband should suffer no harm from you or have to wonder if you will stand by him. (This doesn't mean you never disagree with each other; it means that you publicly support each other and then with grace and patience work out your differences privately.)

Protecting your partner includes helping him against any enemy, even if that enemy is himself. It includes praying for him, interceding for him when he is under physical, emotional or spiritual attack.

A faithful covenant partner has his eyes open to the state of his loved one, perceptive to any threat to their peace or joy or calling or dreams or....you get the picture. This requires paying attention, taking steps to inquire of the heart. When your mate becomes snarly, don't just rebuff or pick a fight or throw up protective walls, identify the enemy, go for understanding: *Why are you behaving this way? What can I do to help?*

A husband and wife will stay together until death.

In the primitive covenant ceremony the two parties killed an animal and split it in half, laying the two halves slightly apart on the ground. Then they walked between the pieces while pointing to the animal and making a declaration something like this: "This animal represents me and my life before this day, which is now dead. And if I ever break this covenant with you, may this be my fate." They invoked a death curse on themselves in the event of unfaithfulness.

Today we simply say, "till death do us part," or "as long as we both shall live," but make no mistake about it, these simple statements are not just romantic verbiage, but remnants of those primitive ceremonies and the commitment for life that God required of man from the first wedding in Eden. God's Word says, *A woman is bound to her husband as long as he lives.*[3]

Marriage was meant to be broken honorably only by death; not so long ago everyone entering marriage viewed divorce as unthinkable and dishonorable. People now enter and exit relationships almost like jobs. This permeates a relationship with insecurity, the very thing covenant commitment was meant to destroy.

We need understand that the potential of the human spirit/soul to grow, and thrive is only realized in an atmosphere of secure connection to others. Insecurity and isolation cripple the spirit, causing us to spend our days in self-protect mode instead of creative mode, for which we were made.

It's like the difference in having to be occupied with defending the fort or being free to plant your garden, build your castle and explore your domain. You can't live life fully while holding up and hiding behind a shield and brandishing a spear.

---

[3] 1 Corinthians 7:39.

What of those married to unbelievers?

Those married to unbelievers are just as much "one flesh" with a husband in God's sight. The Apostle Paul expresses his conviction that it is wrong for people who become born again to divorce an unsaved spouse in his first letter to the Corinthian church:

> To the married I give this command (not I, but the Lord): A wife must not separate from her husband. But if she does, she must remain unmarried or else be reconciled to her husband. And a husband must not divorce his wife. To the rest I say this (I, not the Lord): If any brother has a wife who is not a believer and she is willing to live with him, he must not divorce her. And if a woman has a husband who is not a believer and he is willing to live with her, she must not divorce him. For the unbelieving husband has been sanctified through his wife, and the unbelieving wife has been sanctified through her believing husband. Otherwise your children would be unclean, but as it is, they are holy. (Chapter 7:10-14)

> Each one should remain in the situation which he was in when God called him. (Chapter 7:20)

God clearly hopes to bring salvation to the unbelieving mate through the believing one. Again, we are one with our mates in God's sight whether the spouse is saved, unsaved, very spiritual or very worldly. God always relates to you as part of a one-flesh being with your husband, and there is no ignoring the "other part" of you. This is also why we are known by God today, because we are one with Christ, and God cannot ignore the "other part" of His Son. Because of covenant, we are indivisible in God's sight, and He honors this by treating us the same way He does His Son Jesus.

The modern culture of marriage today makes a mockery of covenant oneness when couples want all the benefits of covenant relationship without accepting the responsibilities of being permanently connected. As long as you have permission to escape in troubled times, you will. Divorce is a sin because it is covenant breaking in the sight of God.

Covenant requires dying to oneself.

Just as primitive covenant makers symbolically forsook the old life through the slaying of an animal, modern covenant keepers must be willing to die to self(ishness) when necessary in order to effectively love the other. You cannot honor married life while expecting to live like you did when you were single, yet some enter a relationship today determined to cling to their old habits, lifestyles, and attitudes. One way or another, with their mouth or with their attitudes, they say: *Don't make me change! Don't expect me to give up _____!* The person who does this is already turning away from the partner and saying, in essence, *If I have to choose between you and this old life, I choose the old life. You don't mean as much to me as having my way.* One might as well write on the bathroom mirror, "I love myself more than you."

The fallen nature in man will always move towards serving himself over honoring his commitments to others. So much strife enters a marriage when one or both insist on trying to hold onto the life they had before. You cannot join your life intimately with another person and expect little to change. You can no longer live for yourself alone because there is someone else to consider in all situations.

Once covenant was established, the parties then called each other "friend." This term was not used of casual acquaintances, but specially reserved for those committed to one another in faithful relationship. Jesus acknowledged this covenant tradition when he said to his disciples, *"I no longer call you servants…I have called you friends."*[4]

A husband and wife should be each other's best friend, a term Jesus further revealed in its covenant beauty when he said: *"Greater love has no one than this, that one lay down his life for his friends."*[5]

A real friend gives whatever he must in order to be faithful — even if it costs him everything, even if it means giving up a favorite habit or a personal desire, as pointed out in Chapter Eight. A real friend doesn't preserve his own life at the expense of the other; he always puts the other person first. A friend gives his all, withholding nothing. A friend can be counted on to be by one's side no matter what is happening. A friend may disapprove of something you do, but does not reject you. A friend loves at all times.

The opposite of love is hate, a term we use to describe someone or something we despise. But God, in His written Word, employs a wider use of the word, showing that hate not only reveals itself in strong animosity

---

[4] John 15:14-15. God called Abraham "friend" after their covenant was made. See Isaiah 41:8 and James 2:23.

[5] John 15:13.

towards someone, but also in the less dramatic behavior of rejecting or ignoring them. In other words, in God's mind hatred includes turning away from a person or thing in such a way that gives them lowest place of value and importance to us. A good example of this is in Psalm 50:17 when God complains, *"You hate my instruction and cast my words behind you."* God is not accusing them of deep animosity to his instruction, but of having zero value for it, as evidenced by their turning their back on it.

Jesus used the word "hate" in this way when he said that in order to love him faithfully we would have to hate parents, spouse, children. He was not calling us to truly despise them, but to give Him our highest loyalty in comparison. When a spouse ceases to value their mate to the degree that they tune them out, ignore them and choose almost anything over being them with, such as hanging out with friends, going to sporting events or — dare I include religious meetings? — then by God's definition, they are guilty of hatred for their covenant partner.

The covenant is sealed in blood.

In a typical covenant rite the two parties would make a cut on the right arm and bring the cuts together to mingle their blood. Those who have studied covenant among all civilizations found that even when there are significant differences in the ceremony, one thing remains universal: the shedding and mingling of blood (or a representative thereof). This is the seal and guarantee of the covenant, without which a covenant was not considered ratified or binding. The fact that Jesus poured out all of his lifeblood for us speaks of the totality of the commitment he made to us in creating the New Covenant.

Blood mingling symbolizes the creation of the one new life, as even those who had no Bible understood that the life of a creature is in the blood.[6] When the blood is mingled, we can no longer distinguish whose blood is whose. When two liquids are mixed, you cannot separate them again. To share blood is to share life.

The culmination of a wedding ceremony is the private moment when the man and wife join their bodies for the first time, and the hymen breaks, causing blood to be spilled. It seems likely that the Lord put the hymen in a woman just for this purpose, and if so, verifies that God intended us to enter

---

[6] Leviticus 17:11.

such a covenant only once. The blood letting as part of covenant was so ingrained in the Jewish culture that the father and mother of the groom were entitled to receive a marriage cloth upon which the virgin's blood was spilled. If such proof could not be produced, the marriage covenant was not considered to be valid.

Medical science tells us that the blood of two people is mingled on a microscopic level anytime there is sexual union (a fact verified in the spread of the blood disease AIDS among sexual partners). This means that every time a couple is intimate, covenant is again confirmed through the mingling of blood.

The husband and wife join names.

Two people entering a covenant exchange names. In Hebrew tradition, the last name of the covenant partner was added to the name. God honored this when he made covenant with Abraham. Every time God introduced himself to someone after this covenant, he didn't just say *"Hello, this is God;"* he would say, *"I AM the God of Abraham,"*[7] publicly acknowledging his covenant partner. Of course in our Western culture the woman normally takes the name of the man, but the greater point to see here is that now in the eyes of the community your names are forever linked. Two people in covenant take upon themselves the obligation to bring only honor, and never shame, to the name of their covenant partner.

A person's name always carries their reputation, the public perception of their character. When God chose Abraham for the covenant through which he would bring forth a nation and the Savior of mankind, he surely considered the issue of whether Abraham would bring honor or shame to His name. As it became known that He was Abraham's God, He would be judged and measured in some degree according to the character that people witnessed in Abraham.[8]

Hebrews 11:16, listing people of great faith, says: *"God is not ashamed to be called their God...."* The kind of person you are reflects on your spouse; your behavior either adding or detracting from their name in the community. The honor of your husband's name is in your keeping.

---

[7] Exodus 3:6.

[8] This is true of every Christian. The unsaved world especially judges God by what kind of people we are. How amazing that Jesus has entrusted us with His Name!

The public mark of the covenant.

Covenant-makers would rub dirt into those cuts or rub them together to make a scar on that right arm, as a visible mark that they were in covenant with another. If the covenant partner found himself threatened, he raised his right arm to his attacker to show the mark, revealing that he has a covenant partner who will come with all his strength (weapons, army, etc.) to fight for him, or avenge his death if necessary.

In heaven, Jesus retains five scars from his crucifixion, even on his glorified body, as marks of the covenant he created for us. Scripture says we are marked spiritually to show the spiritual world we belong to God.[9] We cannot see this mark, but beings in the spirit realm can.

The modern mark of our marriage covenants are wedding rings. When we see someone wearing a wedding ring, we know they belong to someone else. A single person attracted to another who sees a wedding ring knows they belong to another. Unfortunately this mark is not permanent like a scar, for when someone wants to be unfaithful to their spouse today, they can simply slip that ring off.

Covenant partners are expected to share everything.

In covenant making each party reveals and offers all assets and liabilities to the new covenant partner. They likewise now expect to share full responsibility for all debts owed. Everything is now ours, not yours or mine. The person who possesses a true covenant heart gladly shares, delights to meet the partner's need, and feels completely free to help themselves to what the partner has. No division, no fear, no pre-nups needed here. Ah, but we don't live in that world anymore.

Still, it is the healthiest expression of covenant oneness, this free sharing of blessings and problems. The most common violation we see of this principle is when one spouse makes an error in judgment, incurs a debt or an obligation that becomes a burden, and in turning to other spouse for help is told something like, "You got yourself into this mess, now get yourself out." This is not a covenant attitude. People in covenant give grace to one another, and they consider one another in all decisions, as a matter of honor. Covenant brings two people into mutual accountability.

---

[9] Ephesians 1:13-14.

The special sacrament of marriage.

A covenant ceremony was typically sealed and celebrated by the sharing of a meal. The Hebrews used bread and wine. Wine symbolized their blood,[10] while the bread symbolized the body, because bread eaten today becomes tomorrow's flesh. The ancient covenant-makers would break bread in two and feed it to one another while saying, *"This is my body."* Then they serve one another wine and say, *"This is my blood."* Then they affirm, *"I am in you and you are in me."*

Jesus used these words as he shared the final Passover meal with his disciples before his death, and commanded them to celebrate this meal as a reminder of their covenant with him until he returned. We now call the Lord's Supper or communion *a sacrament*, which is a visible symbol of an invisible reality; in this case the reality that Jesus is in us, and we are in him.

The only remnants of this covenant meal in today's ceremony is the feeding of wedding cake and punch to one another, often with playful young couples stuffing cake into each other's mouths or smearing it on their faces. They are simply ignorant of the deep and beautiful symbolism of the act of feeding one another this "meal." Please now enlighten them where you find them, of the beautiful symbolism of this meal.

This meal is a public celebration of their new oneness, and just as the sacrament of communion visibly enacts and celebrates our covenant oneness with the Lord, the sexual union of husband and wife physically celebrates their covenant. This is why the sexual union of husband and wife is pure in the sight of God.[11]

This is also why pre-marital and extra-marital sex is so abhorrent to God; for intimate union of husband and wife is far more to God than merely an act of passion or procreation. It is a celebration of the invisible truth of their oneness and is a complete giving of each to the other. I think God likes that a lot.

Married people joke about how fun "making up" is after a rift; but it's more than pleasant, it is necessary. When a couple become divided the covenant bond may suffer, sometimes on a deep level. After a serious argument it's not unusual for Ron and I to feel drawn towards making love, even though there may be little actual sexual desire. After we learned about

---

[10] Wine is called "the blood of grapes" in Genesis 49:11.

[11] Hebrews 13:4.

covenant we understood why: we instinctively needed to reaffirm our oneness, to give ourselves to each other once again. So it is with marital intimacy. Even after making up you may still feel emotionally distant; perhaps you stopped giving yourself freely to some degree, an instinctive response to the one who caused you pain. If you have genuinely forgiven your spouse, you should be able to give yourself to them again.

This same need — to keep reaffirming our union — is seen in relationship to Christ and the sacrament of communion. It is very difficult, if not impossible, to partake of communion when one knows there is some offense between oneself and the Lord, but after repentance and forgiveness, the Christian looks forward to the next celebration of the Lord's Supper and the joyful peace of that meal.

Being a celebration of their covenant, the sexual union of a husband and wife is beautiful in the sight of God. Therefore a wife should feel free sexually with her husband, not hindered by any sense of shame. In fact, I think it pleases to the Lord when I put effort into being a good lover to my husband.

The permanent memorial.

Most covenant makers devised a public memorial to their union. often the planting of a tree that had been sprinkled with the blood of the sacrificed animal, or have some marks carved into it. That little tree will grow strong and stand for decades as a witness of the covenant two people made. Perhaps our penchant for carving hearts with our initials into trees is also a remnant of this tradition.

We have such a memorial in our New Covenant, which is the cross of Christ, the blood stained "tree" upon which he gave his life. We remember his sacrifice every time we see one, and it is so public that people the world over know what it stands for, even if they themselves do not love that cross.

The memorial to a marriage covenant is created when the sperm of the man is "planted" inside the woman, and a child comes forth in "sprinkled in blood." Children are lasting memorials to the covenant between these two people, long after the lovers have passed on; that is, unless the child is destroyed in the womb. Society's worship of self and lack of commitment to relationship is more tragically revealed in the act of abortion than any other way.

What kind of marriage relationship did God design? Before the rebellion, husband and wife were naked and without shame, transparent to one another, clothed only in God's glory. They had no fear of one another, for they needed no protection from one another. They could share without fear their thoughts, feelings, plans and desires. They met one another's needs. They didn't compete; they were on the same team.

God's design for the marriage covenant is not a fairy tale or an impossible dream, but achieving it requires total faith in God's Word and his grace. No one can achieve God's purposes without God's power. God's design for marriage cannot be achieved without His Spirit at work in us.

Reflecting on Chapter 13

This chapter explains how marriage is a covenant and what that means in the sight of God.

❖ *If you are not still freely giving yourself to your husband, discover why.*

❖ *Ask the Lord to help you give yourself anew to your husband. Ask Him help you forgive him for failing to love you as you needed.*

❖ *Identify any issues or people that may be dividing you and your mate or weakening your covenant bond. Be honest with yourself: are you giving anything to another person that belongs to your husband?*

❖ *Ask the Lord to reveal any hindrances to intimacy.*

❖ *Can you think of any ways you may be hiding from your spouse? If so discover why, and do something about it.*

❖ *Learn to be a good sexual partner as well as a homemaker or mother. Find ways to be romantic and playful with your husband. Be fully present when making love; don't plan supper, worry about the kids or think about how your body looks. Focus on your spouse and your mutual pleasure.*

❖ *If you have serious problems in your marriage, consider seeing a good Christian counselor together to help you apply the principles taught in the Bible.*

The Wife God Designed

In this chapter we will explore any Scriptures revealing God's design for a wife that have not found their home elsewhere in this book.

The wife God designed is a priceless treasure.

Proverbs 31:10 says of the wife God designed, *She is worth far more than rubies.* Lovely, but what does that really mean? Cross-referencing Proverbs 8:11, it says that wisdom is more precious than rubies. If wisdom is more precious than rubies, and a godly wife is more precious than rubies, then such a woman is in a category right up there with wisdom in her value to man. Remember, wisdom is that thing which the author of Proverbs says, whatever you do, get it at all cost, because it is supreme — more valuable than anything. He also wrote:

> *Houses and wealth are inherited from parents, but a prudent wife is from the Lord. (Proverbs 19:14)*

Eve was not created by God as an afterthought; she was a carefully planned expression of God's love to Adam — the greatest gift he could give man besides Himself. Parents can give you money, homes or other things; but only God can give a man the gift of a really good wife, a woman of prudent character, and that only happens as she lives her life under the influence of God.

What does "prudent" mean? This word comes to us from an old French word *prude* which means "excellent." Oddly enough we use the word prude today as an insult, but it originally referred to someone of unswerving virtue.

Prudence shows itself in using discretion and wisdom in making choices and in behavior. It is considerate of consequences and understands not just what needs to be done, but when and how.

Scripture carries this idea even further when describes the wife God designed as a crown:

> A *wife of noble character is her husband's crown, but a disgraceful wife is like decay.* (Proverbs 12:4)

This draws quite a contrast between two kinds of wives. One is a crown to her husband, while the other is compared to decay — something in the process of dying. It will be really helpful to understand the meaning of both.

What does it mean to be a crown?

We think of a crown as just an ornament, and quite frankly no woman wants to be that. In Biblical days a crown was a symbol of one's glory or strength, and we need to see how God himself uses the word *crown* in the Bible.

The Hebrew word in Proverbs 12:4 is *atarah* and comes from a root word which means "to encircle," which is what gives rise to the picture of a crown. As we look at the many uses of *atarah* in the Bible we gain tremendous insight into the beauty of its meaning. For instance, it is used to describe how the Lord encircles his child in a protective way, surrounding him with his lovingkindness and tender mercies,[1] or in a beautifying way, with glory and honor.[2] And this very same word is used in Psalm 5:12 when it says that *the Lord will surround the righteous with his favor like a shield.*

Atarah is also used generally to describe *that which is a blessing, brings honor, or makes glorious:* Jesus is described as a crown of glory in the hand of his father[3]; wisdom crowns those who love her with glory and riches[4]; grandchildren are the crown of old men[5] and the Lord calls himself a crown of glory for his people.[6]

---

[1] Psalm 103:4.
[2] Psalm 8:5.
[3] Isaiah 62:3.
[4] Proverbs 4:9 and 14:24.
[5] Proverbs 17:6.
[6] Isaiah 28:5.

The crown is a universal symbol of honor. Long before athletes received olympic medals, their goal was to be crowned with a laurel wreath, an honor awarded only to those who had used their strength to become victorious champions. A crown is the supreme outward sign of status, testifying to the world the blessedness of the one who wears it. When a crown is on a man's head, he is given more respect and honor. He is looked up to and admired as a blessed man.

God is pleased when as a wife, your appearance and behavior cause other people to respect your husband and to think of him as one blessed. He is pleased when your behavior causes others to treat your husband with honor.

I know there are women reading this who feel they are married to men who do not deserve to be treated with honor. But I remind you that this is not about who he is, it is about what kind of woman you will be. God treats us with honor even though we don't deserve it, as an expression of his goodness and love. He honored us by creating us in His image, then by giving the priceless life of his Son in exchange for ours, and finally by sending His Spirit to live in us.

If the God who deserves all honor can bestow such honor on us who deserved none of it, then we can honor others like He does. Being like Christ isn't about treating people the way they deserve, but as an expression of who we are. It's called character, as in "a woman of noble character."

You, as a woman of God, were designed to add to — not subtract from — a man's honor and dignity. You should enhance him, not detract from who him. God does not want you to be an ornament; but He does want your presence at your husband's side to speak to the world of the Lord's glory and goodness. Does your husband feel blessed and favored by God because you are his wife? Does he get a glimpse of God's glory and goodness because he is married to you?

Stealing his grace, favor and strength.

The second half of Proverbs 12:4 says, *but a disgraceful wife is like decay.* The author could have used many expressions to convey how a disgraceful wife hinders her husband. But to say she is like decay, something moving from life to death, underscores the degree to which a wife can undermine her husband's strength. The Living Bible puts it in terms we can easily relate to: *A worthy wife is her husband's joy and crown. The other kind corrodes his strength and tears down everything he does*. A wife can erode her husband's strength more quickly and effectively than anyone else in the world.

The word *"disgraceful"* comes to us from a combination of two Latin phrases which together mean *to deprive of favor*. To disgrace someone is to literally separate them from the grace and favor others are willing to give them. A woman can disgrace her husband in many ways. She can be careless of her appearance, go about sloppily dressed, poorly groomed or with unkempt hair. This sends the message, *I don't think enough of myself, or you, to fix myself up*. She can interrupt her husband often while he talks and send the message to others that what he has to say is probably unimportant (and obviously unimportant to her). She can tell friends and relatives all about his faults or make fun of him at Bible study. If she really wants to disgrace him then she should bone up on correcting or pointing out his faults in front of others, or keep a real messy house for him to bring guests home to.

The grand prize for robbing a husband of his strength goes to the wife who makes sure that the husband knows what a failure he is in her eyes. She makes an issue of his flaws, tells him he is no good, or even that she wishes she had married the other guy. If she admires some other man she lets her husband know, even suggesting that he ought to be like the other guy, the one who does such-and-such for his wife.

When a wife is disrespectful to her husband, the children will follow her in that attitude. One of reason children are so rebellious today is because they have watched their mothers treat their fathers with too little respect. A disrespectful wife disgraces her husband, removing favor from him in his own children's eyes.

A wife who corrects her husband's behavior in public or apologizes for his behavior often does so because she is embarrassed by him and wants to make sure that whatever people are thinking of him — which she assumes is the same thing she is thinking of him — won't be associated with her. Correcting another adult publicly is a way of separating yourself from their behavior and is very belittling to them, especially to men who come out of the box already wired with radar to detect depreciation. Men usually feel that you are announcing to all present that in your opinion he is too stupid or inept to handle himself. He will sense you are trying to fix him, and he will be right.

Don't fix him, en-courage him.

Women are not charged by God to perfect their husbands, to teach them how to live. Yet this seems to be a surging desire in women, sometimes even more so in those who are filled with the Spirit. We should all follow the example of Ruth Graham, wife of Billy Graham, who said, "*It's my job to love Billy. It's God's job to keep him humble.*"

God did not design a wife to fix her husband, but to en-courage him (fill him with courage) in his calling as the leader of the home, gently, respectfully, lovingly. A woman who lives by faith will try to see her husband through God's eyes, living with him according to her faith in what he can be, looking for the seeds of nobility hidden in his heart and watering them with confidence and patience rather than going at him with a verbal weed wacker all the time.

Over the course of married life both husband and wife will be used by God to correct one another; there is a proper time and procedure. But if your husband senses consistent disapproval from you, he will feel too insecure to risk leadership. It is very difficult to make a decision when you expect those around you to disapprove. A man is sensitive to his status in the eyes of others, and a wife's approval or disapproval of him can potentially make or break his feelings about himself.

Learn to watch for and reinforce his strengths. It is easy to fall into the habit of majoring on your husband's faults so much that you cease to see or appreciate his strengths, yet every man has strengths and assets which make him praiseworthy. Praising his strengths will only bring them out more. Nothing boosts a man's confidence in himself like knowing that his woman believes in him, and admiration is a far more effective motivator than shame.

Be his safe place.

Proverbs 31:11 says of the noble woman, "*Her husband has full confidence in her.*" I like the way the Amplified Bible says it best:

> *The heart of her husband trusts in her confidently and relies on and believes in her safely...*

Hmm, sounds like a refuge to me. The wife God designed is a safe place for her husband. In fact, the Lord intends for the husband and wife to be a safe haven for one another. Unfortunately for too many husbands and wives, their greatest enemy (by definition, the one causing the most hurt) is the spouse. When this is the case, there is no where to hide at home, so one goes looking elsewhere.

When a husband experiences his wife as an adversary he is likely to close up his heart and withdraw from his wife emotionally as he seeks safety. A man can love a woman deeply and still hate or resent her just as deeply because he cannot trust in her with his heart, his name or his dreams. The degree to which a man feels safe with a woman is the degree to which he will entrust himself to her.

A man will avoid a woman who makes him feel less of a man, and will be attracted to the one who enhances his manhood. It is the protective woman that God designed; a man is naturally drawn to the woman who looks up to him and believes in him. If you feel shut out of your husband's heart, find out why, and help him open the door again.

A husband should be able to count on his wife to stand by him and with him against every enemy to his life and well-being, whether physical, emotional or spiritual. Just like her, the man needs her to help cover his weakness from exposure to the world — not in the sense of hiding from a healthy transparency with others, but in the way of all protective love to shield the beloved while they heal, grow, or deal with a handicap. He should be able to trust her completely in his heart. A husband who does not have this kind of confidence in his wife, who lives in fear of her disapproval, in fear of having his faults exposed to ridicule before family or community, will probably not feel as if he is married to the woman God designed.

Proverbs 31:11 in The Living Bible says, *"Her husband can trust her, and she will richly satisfy his needs."* The husband of such a wife has an abiding confidence that she is on his side. He can tell her anything without fear of rejection. He can come home knowing his wife is a refuge. He's not perfect, but he probably wants to be because his wife treats him in a way he wants to live worthy of. The wife designed by God strengthens her husband, not weakens him.

Making or breaking his strength.

Proverbs 31:12 says of the noble wife, *"She brings him good, not harm, all the days of her life."* The word "harm" is the Hebrew word *rah* and means "to spoil by breaking to pieces." To break something into pieces is to shatter it as one would a stoneware pitcher, so that it is unable to serve its purpose. You can shatter a man's ability to fulfill the purpose God designed him for if you are not careful. Not only does a noble wife refuse to tear him down to others, she is his biggest defender, especially to himself. When he confides his fears, she encourages him rather than belittling him.

I knew a woman who complained that she was very lonely because he seemed to live his life separate from her. He kept to himself, rarely spending time with her. Even when they were together he never showed interest what was going on in her heart and mind, nor would he ever open up to share his.

While this wife was mystified as to why her husband shut her out so completely, I was not. Every time I was with her, she wanted to tell me what was wrong with her husband, displaying an attitude of superiority to him, perhaps because of her relationship with the Lord. She often boasted of how she corrected him to help him be a better father and husband. She had little respect for his management of their financial affairs, and reinforced this by trying to handle them for him. She would reveal his latest failures or faults to whatever group she was praying with so that they could pray for the Lord to help him.

The husband didn't like to come to church, no doubt because he feared the truth, that she was exposing him to her friends there. She was praying that he would come to church, but she didn't see the effect her own attitude and actions were having, that she was providing the biggest deterrent to her prayer being answered.

I wanted to respect this man, but frankly, in view of all the negative things his wife had told us, it was difficult. I certainly had no personal feelings against him. But every time I came into his presence, my mind automatically reviewed for me what his wife had told me. My respect for him was diminished, and I pitied him. This is what it looks like to have one's favor removed in the sight of others.

This should never happen because a wife has exposed her husband, in essence made him "naked" to others. When a wife dishonors her husband in this way he loses all desire to share himself with her, to open himself up to her in any way that will only increases his exposure to her ridicule. One of the reasons that the husband in Proverbs 31:23 is "respected at the city gate" is because the noble wife acts as a covering and protection for his weaknesses. I make it a point to keep my husband's weaknesses to myself; I never make fun of or put him down behind his back. I try to set the example with others that I think he is to be treated with respect.

The word *rah* (harm) is often translated elsewhere in Scripture as affliction, adversity or calamity, so we could say of the noble wife, *She brings him no affliction. adversity or calamity.* There will be people and things in life that will afflict her husband, but she should not be one of them. She stands by him in affliction, even if his own mistake is what caused the affliction. After all, that's how the Lord treats us.

Rah is often translated as "misery", so we could say, *She brings him no misery.* She doesn't make him miserable with nagging or complaining. And yet another translation of *rah* is "distress," so we could say, *She brings him no distress.* She doesn't run up the charge cards and put him in debt, or make him repeatedly late for work. You get the idea.

The gift only a wife can give.

A Christian wife has the opportunity to provide an important type of protection for her husband that no one else can. In Hebrew history books, the word used to refer to the outer surrounding wall of the Temple (now called "The Wailing Wall") is *azara*, directly related to the word God used to describe woman: *ezer*, or *"helpmeet."* *Azara* refers to an enclosure that surrounds and protects. As the *azara* wall once surrounded the temple and protected it, so woman, the *ezer* helpmeet, was designed in her own way to surround and protect her husband, through the same kind of activity we see at the Wailing Wall today: prayer and intercession.

Of all the things you can do for a husband, none is more important than standing for him before the throne of grace, calling for God's will for this man to be done on the earth as it is in heaven. Intercede for him, fight for him, ask God how to bless him in the name of Jesus. As his intimate partner you are more privy to his needs than anyone else on earth, and that privileged information should be used to obtain blessing for him, not afflict him. There are many wonderful books on how to pray for a husband, and I will not attempt to teach here what they do so well already. I simply leave you with this instruction: surround your husband with your prayers.

The wife must respect her husband.

To a man, the world is a place full of challenges to his manhood and his status, so he never escapes the need to prove himself, to himself and others. A man's need to be respected and admired is generic to his God-given DNA for leadership, but it is also what makes him vulnerable. Many a woman has enticed a man away from his wife because she showed him admiration when his wife did not.

Everyone notices how a woman treats her husband. They can easily perceive what her attitude is towards him. When she's respectful, they follow suit. And when she's disrespectful, they follow suit. This is why Queen Vashti was cast away from her position by the King's side in favor of Esther, a woman who knew how to treat a husband with proper respect. The noble wife was designed by God to be a respecter of her husband. The Amplified Bible gives us Ephesians 5:33 in a way that nails it for us, that "gets" God's intentions very well:

...let the wife see that she respects and reverences her husband — that she notices him, regards him, honors him, prefers him, venerates and esteems him; and that she defers to him, praises him, and loves and admires him exceedingly.

This is what it truly means to treat someone with honor. In expanding the meaning of the word *reverence*, the Amplified Bible goes to the heart of the matter, helping us to understand that God is asking us for more than the mere outward demonstration of respect. Words like revere, esteem, admire speak of deep and sincere feelings. The husband needs to be esteemed and admired by his wife. While it is true that not all men are worthy of respect, it is also true that God calls all women to be respectful, as a matter of character and disposition. The wife should aim higher than an outward show of respect and seek the help of the Holy Spirit to deeply love and admire her husband.

You have a unique position in your husband's life. You can build him up or tear him down in a way that no one else can. You should be his loudest cheerleader, the one he can run to for encouragement when he feels like a failure. Everyone needs someone who looks for the best in them, and when they fail, encourages them to get up and try again.

This sort of respect creates the atmosphere in which a man can best fulfill his role as head of the home. A leader cannot effectively lead without the sincere respect and esteem of those he leads. When any leader is treated with dishonor, his leadership ability is undermined, a fact that Hebrews 13:17 address when it tells us that God's wants us to show honor and respect to every authority over us, so that they will have the courage to do their best.

A noble wife gives her firstfruits to her husband.

Solomon's poetry beautifully describes a groom's expectations for his new bride, the one who gives herself exclusively to him:

> You are a garden locked up, my sister, my bride; you are a spring enclosed, a sealed fountain. Your plants are an orchard of pomegranates with choice fruits, with henna and nard, nard and saffron, calamus and cinnamon, with every kind of incense tree, with myrrh and aloes and all the finest spices. You are a garden fountain, a well of flowing water streaming down from Lebanon. (Song of Songs 4:12-15)

And the bride's (appropriate) response in verse 16: Let my lover come into his garden and taste its choice fruits.

Everything created by God has potential for fruitfulness, and in the case of us who are made in his image, our potential is to bear fruit out of who God is. The Holy Spirit's task is to bring God's children into their full strength and glory so that, like Himself, they may satisfy and bless those who relate to them. You are meant to be God's fruit, and taste like something that fell from His tree.

Have you ever picked up a delicious looking peach and bit into it, only to find it tasteless? Sadly enough, some Christians are like that. They look great on the outside, but those live with them, who get to "taste" of them most intimately are disappointed every time they go for a bite. The noble wife doesn't just look fruitful, she is full of flavor. To "taste" of her is to be satisfied. She does not disappoint the one who comes to sample her love, kindness, reassurance, or support.

The kind of wife you are reflects your true relationship to Christ. A real relationship with the Lord always produces sweet, juicy fruit. If you cooperate with the Holy Spirit he will always lead you in the ways of love, patience, kindness, goodness, faithfulness and gentleness towards others. If this "fruit" is on your "tree," who should have the right to pluck the best of it? Your husband, of course, and along with the rest of your family. If your relationship with Christ produces patience, yet you offer that fruit only to those at church or your neighbors, then you are robbing your husband of his right to your choice firstfruits, his rightful due as your husband.

She adapts herself to her husband.

The Amplified Version of Titus 2:5 says of godly wives, they should: *be adapting and subordinating themselves to their husbands...* This echoes the very moment of woman's creation in Genesis 2:18:

> *Now the Lord God said, It is not good [sufficient, satisfactory] that the man should be alone; I will make him a helper meet (suitable, adapted, complementary) for him.* (Amplified Version)

The Amplified Bible rightly brings out the fact that the woman God designed should learn how to adapt herself to her husband. But there is a right way and a wrong way to do this. The wrong way is to become a doormat or a non-person, which husbands actually hate. The right way is found in moments of choice, doing what is best for the loved one even at cost to self, when clearly necessary for their well-being or calling in life.

One of the most familiar expressions in the Bible of adapting to a covenant partner is made by Ruth in her vows to Naomi:

> *Where you go I will go, and where you stay I will stay. Your people will be my people, and your God my God.* (Ruth 1:16)

These words beautifully express Ruth's commitment to love and faithfulness to Naomi, and a willingness to adapt to her need at that time of her life. Ruth was wise enough to know she could not effectively love and serve Naomi without a total commitment to fit into her way of life.

By the time a betrothed couple comes to the altar, they should have been instructed as to the true and permanent nature of the covenant they are entering, and the Biblical concept of sacrificial love, for this is the true nature of marriage. Adapting to another always requires a measure of sacrifice.

Obviously, change will be needed on both sides, but the amplification of Genesis 2:18 says adapting is especially important for the bride, the helpmeet. Why might this be true?

I suggest it would be that the call to lead which is given to every man comes with the responsibility to provide for his family. Therefore, it is essential that the wife be willing to live wherever it is necessary for the husband to practice his chosen career or trade, or where he is able to find work, or to follow him in the calling of God, which can be really inconvenient at times. There also may be certain aspects of a man's work which affect the lifestyle of the family, such as an unusual shift at his job. If this is the case, the wife should try to be available to her husband whenever possible for the same companionship, meal provision, etc. that he would have if he worked normal hours.

Some men's careers require them to entertain business associates, sometimes on short notice. The wife of such a man honors him by keeping the house and herself presentable and her pantry in a state of readiness for entertaining on short-notice, although it is certainly a appropriate for a wife to ask the husband's help in making this a team effort, helping her to help him by his thoughtfulness in any way.

I met a woman once who separated from her husband just because she didn't want to move to a new town with him when he changed jobs. There were no health or other issues; just her preference. They had young children, and the family was torn apart because the wife was unwilling to adapt to her husband. She obviously cared more for herself than either her husband or her children. When this attitude prevails in either spouse, the marriage is headed for trouble.

Loving your husband includes working at adapting to his strengths and weaknesses, his career, goals and calling. Don't force him to fit into your mold, or that of your parents. When you embrace the attitude of being adaptable you are saying to him, *I believe in you. You and your work for us are valuable to me. I'm your helper. I'm your friend. We are in this together, and I want to do my share.*

How she may please her husband.

> *...but the married woman has her cares centered on earthly affairs, how she may please her husband. (First Corinthians 7:34)*

The wife who is a gift from God looks for ways to please her husband, considering his preferences and tastes as well as her own in choosing decor, food, clothing. Apparently it is easy for a woman to assume this is her domain alone, because I meet too many of them who act and feel this way. Invariably every woman has some area they think the husband should stay out of, such as how they wear their hair, how they dress, or how the house should be decorated. I've seen women keep a house so frilly that a man feels out of place and hangs out in the garage as often as possible. I've seen wives make sure every single meal is good for the guy regardless of whether he likes the taste of it or not.

When a wife has this attitude, it says to the husband, *Your opinion is unimportant to me in this area. I don't care what you want.* It can be a subtle way of putting him in his place as a price for not having control in other areas, an expression of a woman's deep resentment over being asked to submit to his headship. Watch out for that.

But the more common problem in this area is that it is easy for a wife to do exactly what she wants and please herself, while thoroughly convinced it is really the husband she is trying to please! Ron and I went to a marriage counselor several times during the rough season of our relationship. One day the counselor turned to Ron and said, *"Ron, what do you need from Tonia to feel loved?"* I was eager to hear his answers, ready for some big discovery. But Ron's answer surprised me: *"I would feel more loved if she would spend more time with me."* I should have known this was important to him because he had openly said so over the years.

I thought, *Why didn't I pay more attention?* After pondering this a while I realized the reason was that I was so focused on what kind of wife I thought I should be, that I hadn't listened when he tried to tell me what kind of wife he really wanted. My concept of the ideal wife in those days was still a hodgepodge of what my mother modeled for me, what my friends were doing, what the ladies' magazines said I should be and a little of what I saw on television. If Martha Stewart had been around in those days Ron would have never seen me since I would have been busy hand painting our china. I was certain that no one could find a woman trying harder to be the perfect wife than I, but I realized in the counselor's office that what I had been striving for had little to do with what Ron really wanted and needed from me.

For example, I used to spend enormous amounts of time baking bread from scratch, preparing gourmet meals because I convinced myself that this would please Ron and show him what a good wife I was. He never seemed quite as pleased as I thought he should be, and I frankly felt very unappreciated. In fact, for a time we argued about this more often than anything else. Baking took lots of time, and what Ron wanted most was for me to spend time with him — how many wives wish their husbands felt that way?

I finally had to admit that what I was doing I did for me, not Ron. Gourmet cooking and being a super wife made me feel great about myself, gave me a deep sense of satisfaction and value. I had deceived myself in thinking I did it for him, which merely helped me to justify my desire to do it all just how I wanted.

I began to find ways to spend more time with Ron and less in the kitchen and on my creative housekeeping efforts. Indeed, he did take pride in my efforts, I later learned; but I had indulged in them to the point of neglecting him. I learned the importance of balance, and by the way, one of our favorite things to do now is cook great meals together.

Forget everybody's advice, even mine if you must, to focus on one thing: the only accurate way to know how to please your husband is to ask him what he likes, really pay attention, and do something about it.

Nagging — no torture allowed.

Like many proverbs, Proverbs 19:13-14 draws a contrast:

> … *the contentions of a wife are as a continual dripping of water through a chink in the roof. House and riches are the inheritance from fathers, but a wise, understanding and prudent wife is from the Lord.* (The Amplified Bible)

We have two pictures here: one of a prudent, understanding wife, stood up against a nagging, contentious wife. The author uses the annoying drip of a leaky roof to evoke the feeling of what it's really like to live with a nag.

Anyone who has lived even a short time with a dripping faucet, knows how irritating, how positively maddening it is to live with. In fact, the Chinese employ it as a means of torture. Not only is a dripping faucet relentlessly annoying, it seems to grow louder with each drip, although the volume never actually changes.

This verse implies that a wife is one or the other, either prudent, or a nag, inferring that you cannot be both at the same time. As mentioned earlier, prudence refers to living in wisdom — not just possessing it, but knowing how and when to use it. One might think that the opposite of prudence would be foolishness, but the opposite of prudence is presented here as contentiousness, nagging and being quarrelsome. A quarrelsome wife is not the one God designed.

I wondered what God's definition of nagging was, so I asked him one day. His response was, *Ask your husband what he thinks nagging is. It is him you have to live with, and him I designed you to bless!* God frequently amazes me with this kind of obvious-but-I-never-would-have-thought-of-it insight.

If there is anything men have in common, it is their contempt for and aversion to being nagged by a woman. They often talk as if all women are prone to nag, yet most women don't honestly see themselves this way. Why this gap in perception?

To answer this question, I asked a woman first — me. To me, nagging means to repeatedly and relentlessly bug someone about something — like that dripping faucet. Then I did what God suggested, and asked my husband. His definition of being a nag? *"If you mention it more than once, you're nagging."* Uh-oh.

I thought perhaps I was married to a particularly intolerant man; but when my friends polled their husbands, virtually the same response came from all of them! What do you know: God understands men! The truth is, if we women want something, we usually mention it in some form or fashion until we get it. We may try to disguise it, but our men are not fooled.

When you tell a man two, three or four times that you want something done, you can tell him just as quietly and sweetly as you know how, maybe even using that little trick where you don't actually say it to him but in some sideways fashion like telling the kids in front of him, *"When your father does so-and-so then we can do such-and-such,"* but he will hear it just like that repetitive, annoying drip: louder and more annoying with every mention.

Why do men hate nagging so much? Men feel that nagging is an insult to their management. They interpret it as something like this: *"You're not handling this right; you're too stupid to remember this yourself; you can't do this without my help."* Regardless of how you mean it, the average man takes your nagging comments as a put-down or inference that he is incompetent, or worse, as an effort to control him, to take over the leadership of the home.

Now I know you are never trying to do that when you want him to take out the trash, but hey, it's in that leadership DNA of his, always alert to the threat of someone trying to lead him about. (I realize at this point I've said an awful lot about that DNA, as if it is sacrosanct and can't be touched or corrected. I don't feel that way — I only hope you will realize that trying to fight it is rubbing against the grain in a man, and it will give you a nasty splinter if you don't live with him wisely.)

A prudent woman finds effective ways to communicate with her husband about the things that really matter. She can say, *"Honey, one of the ways I feel loved is when you take care of the house. I know you really do care about me and the house, and I don't want to be a nag. Do you have some ideas for how we can work on this together?"* I have had my husband apologize and make a commitment to try harder. When I refrain from nagging my husband about things, his attitude often changes, so that he wants to be more attentive to the things I do ask of him. And on certain occasions he has actually given me permission to nag him until he got something done.

God created the woman to be the maker of the home.

Titus 2:4-5 says, *train the younger women…to be busy at home.* It is generally God's plan for a wife to give herself to the making of a home, seeing her husband and children as her highest priorities, not to be sacrificed to careers, soap operas, hobbies, social clubs or even ministries. The woman has been uniquely gifted by God to create a nurturing environment for the whole family. A woman who claims to love and worship God should embrace His priorities for her life.

Today families are often in a financial position where the woman must work outside the home. I believe that while the children are young, this should be a last resort, especially when there are many ways to earn money at home. But if the husband insists that his wife work, then she must honor his wishes. If she believes this is not God's will, then she should pray and ask the Lord to change the husband's heart. If the husband and wife both want her to work and the family can still be managed well, and the children properly loved, supervised and taught as they should be, then there is nothing wrong with it. But the woman who can balance all of these things while maintaining her strength and fulfilling her call at home is rare. It is a very tough balancing act and usually everyone suffers, especially the woman.

We see the sad results every day of women's exodus from the home. Children are being raised on television and spending more time with friends, video games and computers than with their parents. These things are not going to teach your children character, nor will they notice when your child needs special help through the growing pains of life. Some of the greatest tragedies in our time (such as killing rampages in schools) have been committed by young people who came from nice homes with parents who were good people, but uninvolved with their children. When interviewed later and asked why they didn't see the problems developing in their children the parents often said, "I guess I just didn't notice."

It's not wrong for women to enter the work force; they have a lot to offer and a lot to gain. A good job or career can be very fulfilling and a great blessing from the Lord. The Lord himself has given me jobs and the ability to do them well. But He usually did this only when my children were in school, my home in order, my marriage strong. In other words, according to the plan and timing of his priorities for my life. The wife God designed recognizes and gives herself fully to the respective seasons of her life.

A season to train my daughter.

I distinctly remember a time when I was full of zeal for the Lord and absolutely certain He was ready for me to begin a ministry of teaching and speaking publicly. One day I was praying and fasting about this very thing, waiting on the Lord for vision, wisdom, instruction, guidance. As I sat quietly with the Lord, a vision of my mother formed in my mind or spirit.[7] She was holding her arms out to me, as if trying to give me something, yet her hands were empty. The Lord then said to me, *"Your mother's hands were empty, but yours are not. You have so much to give to your daughter."*

---

[7] As Hebrews 4:12 says, it's hard to know where one begins and the other ends, so closely intertwined are these two parts of us.

My daughter was eight years old at the time. She had been a playful tomboy for a long time, riding her bike, playing league t-ball, soccer and anything she could talk her big brother into. We had a big tree in our front yard, and anytime I couldn't locate her right away, I knew I could find her up in that tree. But not lately.

Lately, she had abandoned the tree, and I rarely had to go looking outside for her because she was always underfoot. When I was baking in the kitchen, she wanted to help. When I was dressing, she watched me intently and showed an interest in dressing like a young lady. When I cleaned house, she wanted to help. She had wanted to learn to sew one night when I was working on a project, but I brushed her off because I didn't have time.

Until the Lord brought this to my attention, I had barely noticed it. I was too preoccupied with the ministry I thought the Lord was preparing me for. The Lord showed me that my daughter was at the age when she was eager to learn, submissive and trusting, her focus making the natural shift from play to wanting to be taught how to be a woman. It was time to begin. The student had already started taking lessons; the teacher was lagging behind.

I knew clearly what my ministry was in that moment, and it was private, not public. Lots of women could teach other women, but no one was going to come and teach my daughter how to be a lady. As I accepted this the Lord graced me with the knowledge of how important it was, and again assured me I did not have empty hands offered to my daughter. My mother was a wonderful and unique woman, but she had empty hands in the vision because she divorced our Dad when I was six and raised us as a single Mom, working full time and often overtime. She was a good mother, raised in a Christian home, but one in which she had never been taught to know the Lord intimately, so she had never taught these things to me.

I gave myself completely to our daughter's training and had the time of my life. It was a great joy, to both of us, a season I am so glad I did not miss, which, when it passed, would never be available to me again. Up to the age of ten or eleven her world centered around Mom, Dad and home. She was a sponge, eager to learn. But this season ended quickly enough; just a couple of years later it was hard to get her undivided attention, because her world expanded rapidly in junior high with after-school jobs, summer camps, music lessons and friends. When I realized her world had expanded irrevocably past our influence I was so pleased that I had not missed my once-in-a-lifetime opportunity to teach her the things that no one else could.

Gabriele is an adult now, a lovely woman who loves the Lord. She can cook and sew her own clothes. She has a strong sense of identity and the well-adjusted nature of one who knows she is loved. I am so pleased to say she is not repeating the mistakes I made at her age; while I spent my early adult years looking for love, she is spending hers out on grand adventures and education. She has lots of womanly wisdom stored up in her heart, the result of numerous spur-of-the-moment mother-daughter discussions which might never have occurred if I had been absent from home and too busy with my own ministry.

There is a reason we call them "seasons" of our lives: seasons do not last forever, and if we try to cram everything into one season, we cannot possibly enjoy it for all its worth. This is especially true of the tender years when our children grow from infancy to their teens. It is a time that goes all too fast and will never come again.

The fact is that if you do not possess the heart of your child before they come to the age of personal accountability, you may never possess it. By this I mean you will never be able to influence them for God, for excellence, for integrity. A Christian mother who truly loves her children will teach them how to read the Bible and how to know and worship God. Though it is the job of both parents, typically a mother has much more opportunity for this kind of instruction. Parents mistakenly assume this is the job of the church, which is not true.

We often counsel women seeking solutions for stress. God did not create us to live such overstuffed lives. We all function best in a life of balance, with recreation and rest built in between work. We live far more effectively if we are able to give ourselves fully to a few things than try to do everything. When the season of child raising is over, the average woman still has 35-40 productive years in which to pursue careers, hobbies and have other grand adventures. I have often heard a woman express regret that she did not give herself fully to being a mother; but I have never once heard a woman wish she had given up raising her children personally to do other things.

The Bible says that our daughters are not the only ones we are called to teach:

> Bid the older women…to give good counsel and be teachers of what is right and noble, so that they will wisely train the young women to be sane and sober-minded — temperate, disciplined…self-controlled, chaste, homemakers, goodnatured… (excerpts from Titus 2:5, The Amplified Bible).

The fact is that older women are always teaching the younger women something, whether they do it intentionally or not, because the younger women tend to imitate them. What are you teaching other women by your example? Are you a teacher of what is right and noble?

The wife God designed reveals His heart to an unbelieving husband.

First Peter 3 reveals that God wants to express himself, his love and character, to the unsaved husband through the behavior and attitudes of his wife:

> Wives, in the same way be submissive to your husbands, so that if any of them do not believe the word, they may be won over without talk by the behavior of their wives, when they see the purity and reverence of your lives. (1 Peter 3:1-2)

God's plan for winning unsaved husbands is not for the wife to preach him into the kingdom, or shame him into the kingdom. The plan is this: the woman who follows Christ is to be such a great wife, and treat her husband so righteously, that the man will want to taste of Christ for himself. She is, after all, his most personal taste of God.

God wants to live and move and have his being in every Christian, and when he is allowed to express himself freely in his goodness, grace, wisdom and love, an unsaved spouse will have their best glimpse of the invisible God. It should be the aim of a wife to know the heart of her God and portray it truly to the husband, so that she can say, as Jesus did, If you have seen me, you have seen the good Father, because I act just like him.

A story from my own marriage will help to illustrate the importance of this, even though it deals with a husband who is saved. One day Ron treated me in a way that wasn't wonderful and hurt my feelings pretty badly. I just knew God wasn't any more pleased about it than I was, but since I had been learning about overlooking offenses, I decided not to make an issue about the way Ron was acting. I felt real good about my decision to be so forgiving and I promptly marched into my prayer place and got on my knees to intercede for my errant man. *"Lord,"* I prayed, *"please do not hold this against Ron on my account. Please have mercy on him."* The Lord shot back this reply: *"Why don't YOU have mercy on him?"*

I wasn't expecting this. *"What do you mean, Lord?"*

"You are the main vessel through which I want show my mercy to Ron. If you don't give him mercy, mine won't mean much to him."

That one hit me like a ton of bricks, reminding me that when we judge others we often become guilty of the same things we judge. We tend to treat others the way we think God is going to treat them, which would be fine if we all had the same loving and gracious heart toward people that God does. I repented of my arrogance and determined to give my husband the mercy that God wanted to show him.

I realized later that what the Lord had shown me was just as true of patience, kindness and every other virtue. After all, God has chosen to live in me; I am the vessel through which He wants to express himself to the other people in my life. Just think what would happen if every Christian wife treated her husband the way Jesus would.

Reflecting on Chapter 14

This chapter explores scriptural truths about the wife God designed.

❖ *Ponder your life in relation to the season you are in. Think about whether you are fully present in this season, accepting it and enjoying it, or whether you have too much going on.*

❖ *Ask the Holy Spirit to reveal anything the Lord wants you to know about your season, and whether he might want to re-order your life in any way. If you are married, discuss these things with your husband.*

The True Spirit and Purpose of Submission

I often work with women who are hungry to know God and his ways. Because I teach the whole counsel of the Bible concerning women, submission is a topic that always comes up. Inevitably challenging to women, submission is a subject fraught with dread and misunderstanding and too often associated with abuse. But it is a subject that will not go away, and not just for women. Submission is an issue for every person who would seriously respond to God. An honest reading of the Bible reveals that in God's kingdom, everyone must submit to someone.

Far from being limited to the home front, we find that all Christians are commanded to submit to their spiritual leaders,[1] that all citizens are told to submit to the governing authorities in their lives,[2] and finally, all believers are called to submit to one another as an outward display of their reverence (worship) for Christ.[3]

Christians are reminded to be submissive to their bosses, serving them as if they were working for the Lord himself, in a respectful and obedient manner.[4] Everyone must submit to someone, and even though God wants no one to be a slave, if one is a slave God asks him to serve his master submissively, even if the master is harsh.[5]

---

[1] Hebrews 13:17.

[2] Romans 13:1-2.

[3] Ephesians 5:21.

[4] Clearly implied in Colossians 3:23.

[5] 1 Peter 2:18-20.

This is no arbitrary requirement of relationship that God dreamed up; like everything else created through his vast wisdom, submission serves a vital purpose in the process of growth, a fact we find reflected in man and nature at every level. The seed must yield to the soil in order to fulfill its potential for new life. Everything and everyone yields to something or someone as a means to achieve full potential.

This is the principle of growth and fulfillment Jesus was referring to when he said that a seed cannot become what it was meant to be unless it first dies by being buried in the soil and letting that soil destroy the outer covering of the seed to expose the living germ inside, the spark of new life. Just as the soil does with the seed, submission requires a little death to things which protect our treasure from harm, but also prevent it from blossoming.

Though we equate submission with weakness or a place of being diminished, in God's kingdom it is just the opposite. Jesus' submission to those who tortured him appeared to be the ultimate expression of weakness, but in reality was the path to the greatest power and authority ever given to a man by God.

Submission is that willingness to yield which is necessary for all things to fulfill their created glory as they share the world together.

Even the Godhead is submissive.

God the Father, God the Son, and God the Holy Spirit are all equal, but they do not function equally in rank. They do not all lead or act as the head. Only God the Father does this. It is also clear from scripture that the Holy Spirit serves the Father and the Son, submitting to both of them while dwelling within the believer.

Incredibly, even God the Father put himself in a type of submissive relationship to mankind when he gave man a free will, and then gave him dominion over his creation![6] Even though God did this in order to further his own sovereign purposes, it reveals a profound ability within the Almighty to bend down and submit to those lower than himself.

The submissive nature of the Godhead enables the glory, power and wisdom of each one to be fully revealed and even more, gives man the opportunity to be like the God who made him.

---

[6] Psalm 8:4-6.

Women will show the world how the bride submits to her bridegroom.

The Godhead is looking for a fourth party to make their joy complete, and that is the Bride for the Son. In order for her to be a worthy addition to the family, she must develop the same nature and character as they, including the submissive spirit.

Although Jesus is called to lead the world in righteousness, he will not do it alone. In the Father's wisdom he has ordained that the Bride will be at Jesus' side, ruling with him. This is the true calling of every bride. By her respectful and submissive response to Jesus, the Bride/Church will enhance and even enable the full expression of his rulership and his glory. Even the glorious goodness that is in Jesus will not be fully revealed through his solitary rule, but only as he relates to his bride.

Likewise, man and wife were created from the beginning to co-rule in a way that would reveal the unique strengths God built into each of them. Marriage is a prophetic picture of Christ and his Bride, and even more: it is a school to help every believer learn how to relate rightly to Jesus Christ. The demands of marriage create the perfect practice field for drawing out the strengths and covering the weaknesses of the man and woman, who learn to work together in a way that brings out the highest potential of each. God intended for the husband and wife to live together in a relationship that would spur one another on to godliness and would produce godly offspring for God's kingdom, children with the character of Christ.[7]

God asks the Christian wife to develop that disposition towards her husband which is submissive and respectful. While there is much yet to be said on this subject, for now let us focus on the lovely truth that such a wife can help a husband be all that he was created to be. She will enhance and encourage his leadership and draw out of him the best that God has hidden within his soul. For a man was created to be a leader, a worthy and loving and protective shelter to the woman, the child, the helpless. How a woman responds to her man will bring out either the worst or the best in him. God has called wives to show both the Church and the world how a bride responds rightly to her bridegroom.

As yet, the church does not look much like a bride because she is still struggling against and hurting her own body. She still does not understand

---

[7] Malachi 2:14-15.

her oneness with her own members. The Bride has yet to come into the submissive relationship with the Holy Spirit that would transform her and teach her how to love deeply, sincerely and faithfully. When the Bride comes to the place of true submission to the Lord Jesus Christ that naturally flows from true and passionate love, then all that Jesus is privately in the hearts of individual believers will be revealed to the world in united glory.

Using the language of covenant, God calls this bride the very body of Christ and asks her to live with her husband in covenant oneness. That oneness is an expression of God's highest will for marriage and for the church in her relationship to Christ:

> "For this reason a man will leave his father and mother and be united to his wife, and the two will become one flesh. This is a profound mystery - but I am talking about Christ and the church." (Ephesians 5:31-32).

Oneness is a big topic in the heart of God. It is the goal of covenant relationship, and it is absolutely impossible where there is no yieldedness between two people. Oneness can be a synonym for unity, that thing which Jesus so passionately prayed for:

> "I pray also for those who will believe in me through their message, that all of them may be one, Father, just as you are in me and I am in you. May they also be in us so that the world may believe that you have sent me. I have given them the glory that you gave me, that they may be one as we are one: I in them and you in me. May they be brought to complete unity to let the world know that you sent me and have loved them even as you have loved me." (John 17:20-23).

True unity has been the most elusive goal of mankind. The parting of a sea is an awesome miracle, but to see men truly love each other would be a miracle of unparalleled proportions. Such a miracle would be the greatest display of God's glory as it reveals his effect upon the hearts of men, and the only one which will truly show the world that God exists and loves them so much that He sent his Son to die for them.

But God had to give us a free will if we were to have the potential to share in His glory, and only in surrendering that free will back to him will we do so. One saved heart is a joy to God; many saved hearts are a great delight; but only in the unity of a multitude of saved hearts does a true kingdom exist. And only in such a kingdom is God fully glorified through the unhindered expression of his goodness in his creation.

Unity cannot exist in an atmosphere of competition; it is a fruit of cooperation. It begins in the home between a man and his wife, the smallest building block of our society, and then multiplies in the church and community. In this context I join wholeheartedly in the cry of my feminist sisters, "Never underestimate the power of a woman!"[8]

The devil would convince a woman that submission is a burden from God, something she must wrestle with just between her and her husband. The good Lord wants us to know that it is much more, that her personal honoring of God's ways makes a difference not only in her home but in her community, her church, her extended family, and in the world itself.

Like most Bible doctrines, submission can be carried too far and applied inappropriately, in an abusive way that destroys the very thing it was meant to accomplish. Always, we must set our hearts upon understanding and obeying the <u>spirit</u> of the law, rather than become legalistic.

Defining submission.

The Amplified Bible translation of 1 Peter 3:1-2 reveals the underlying attitudes that honor God's intent in the command:

> *In like manner, you married women, be submissive to your own husbands - subordinate yourselves as being secondary to and dependent on them, and adapt yourselves to them, so that even if any do not obey the Word of God, they may be won over not by discussion, but by the godly lives of their wives, when they observe the pure and modest way in which you conduct yourselves, together with your reverence for your husband; you are to feel for him all that reverence includes - to respect, defer to, revere him - to honor, esteem appreciate, prize, and in the human sense to adore him; that is, to admire, praise, be devoted to, deeply love and enjoy your husband.*

The expanded meanings of the key words "submissive" and "reverence" point us to the true spirit of submission: the inward attitude of a woman's

---

[8] There is an equally important call upon the men to reveal to the church and the world what godly leadership looks like; but this book is not written to them.

heart towards her husband. Submission is far more than outward obedience: it is a respectful nature and an expression of devotion. It is voluntary. It is an act of love and trust, and when it is taken out of the realm of willingness, it loses its beauty and becomes ugly, an oppressive enemy of love.

John Piper, Christian pastor and author, has defined submission in a way that captures its true spirit:

> *"Submission refers to a wife's divine calling to honor and affirm her husband's leadership and help carry it through according to her gifts. It is not an absolute surrender of her will. Rather, we speak here of her **disposition to yield** to her husband's guidance and her **inclination** to follow his leadership."*[9]

The word submission in the New Testament is translated from the Greek word *hupotasso*, a combination of *hupo* (to place under) and *tasso* (to arrange in an orderly manner, to appoint to a certain position). It refers to the orderly placement of one person under another. It is important to note that it does not refer to the superiority or inferiority of those so placed. It is about order, not value. In God's economy, being under someone does not assume inferiority in any way.

Just as the strength of the military is achieved by order, so is the kingdom of God. The military is made up of vast numbers of men and women. Some soldiers have to lead, some have to follow. The rank of a person in the military has no bearing on his or her worth as a person. The order does not assign value, but responsibility for leading others and the authority that must go with such responsibility. The higher ranking officer has authority to make decisions which affect those under him, but he is also held responsible for their well-being and performance.

This system is necessary for the military body to function to its greatest potential. So it is with the kingdom of God: someone has to lead; someone has to follow. Rank is a function of unity. Unity cannot exist as long as there is a struggle over who is leading whom. Rebellion divides people; submission unites them. God revealed his ordained "rank" for mankind in 1 Corinthians 11:3:

---

[9] From Piper's essay, "A Vision of Biblical Complementarity," page 61 of "Recovering Biblical Manhood and Womanhood, a Response to Evangelical Feminism," a collection of essays edited by John Piper and Wayne Grudem, 1991, Crossway Books .

> *Now I want you to realize that the head of every man is Christ, and the head of the woman is man, and the head of Christ is God.*

The whole concept of submission deals with who is the master. And frankly, though we call Jesus "Lord," most of us would have to admit that self is still the master most of the time, not the Lord. Furthermore, most of our conflicts with other people arise because there is a struggle over whose will is going to prevail.

Submission is how Christ is made head of the home.

It is not unusual to hear a woman say she can submit to God but can't bring herself to submit to her very human husband. The irony is, of course, that if you won't submit to your husband, then you are not actually submitting to the Lord either, who gave this command! And if this is the case, then Christ isn't ruling over your home and family, you are. But in this case you rule only as a usurper, without the blessing and strength of God.

There is a surging spirit in mankind that is eager to assert ourselves over against others. Self-assertion is the way of the world, the flesh and the devil. The devil became God's enemy because he served himself instead of God. The desire to serve self is the very spirit of Satan. He is full of self-will, self-exaltation, self-satisfaction, self-centeredness. His chief characteristic is preoccupation with self.[10]

Satan's disguise is smart. He usually can't get you to serve him in obvious sin, but if he can get you to serve yourself, then you end up serving his purposes. In serving ourselves, we hurt others. Most people do not honestly want to hurt others. But I have observed that when I protect and serve myself, others around me often get hurt. I don't want to hurt the people I love, but when I do, it is invariably because I have been selfish, and have loved myself more than them.

Submission is a disposition, like being sunny or sullen. It's an inward graciousness that ignores self and status in order to honor the other person. It is a willingness to bend in order to help or lift up the other. It is part of the very nature of God, of whom David said, *"...you stoop down to make me great."*[11]

---

[10] His description is in Isaiah 14:13-14.

[11] 2 Samuel 22:36.

God, the Almighty Creator of the universe, is profoundly gracious to us. He has removed every barrier to intimate knowledge of him, even though he is God and we are humans who have no basis for deserving his awesome love and company. His actions towards us reveal that a submissive disposition approaches others with a will to serve and bless them, rather than assert their own will, even when they have the right and power to do so.

God could use his power to make us do right, but in doing so he would rob us of the joy and glory that comes when we finally learn what is right and exercise our freedom to do it. He submits his great power to our wills for a season to allow us room to grow into true sons and daughters.

Some of those most gifted in the church have the greatest difficulty with submission, because it is easy to slide into an attitude of superiority. It takes grace to develop a submissive spirit while leading and excelling in spiritual gifts. But any casual witness to the way Jesus related to people must acknowledge that He who was the most superior to us all, treated the lowly with graciousness and honor. The only people Jesus criticized were the Pharisees who treated others with condescension, contempt and even cruelty in the name of godliness.

Submission prepares us to rule and reign with Christ.

Many Christians long to see the power of God operate through them and in their lives. They read the Bible, pray fervently and make demands on heaven. It is right to believe in his power, but it is wrong to think God's power is ours for the taking regardless of our walk with God and other people. We are too presumptuous with God. Even though we are God's children, it is obvious we do not have indiscriminate access to his power.

It is only as we set our hearts fully upon his ways — including submitting to those he tells us to — that we will prove ourselves to be trustworthy recipients of this power. We must learn first to submit to God and then demonstrate that if entrusted with God's power, we will use it for His will, His purposes and with His wisdom, not our own.

Jesus, the very Son of God, was reverently submissive to the Father, and Hebrews 5:7 implies that this is the reason his prayers were heard — not just because he was God's son. He repeatedly states in the gospel of John that he only did and said what he saw the Father doing. He announced in the beginning, "For I have come down from heaven not to do my will but to do the will of him who sent me." (John 6:38).

Life on earth is practice for reigning with Christ. I thank God that we don't all have to drink the same cup he did, but we do have to go through the same school that taught Jesus to live worthy of the calling: the school of submissive obedience. Developing the submissive spirit is not just a nice trait for a Christian woman to have, it is the kingdom way for all.

The building blocks of a kingdom: relationships.

Submission is not just a command to women, it is a part of the character of God himself. It was never meant to be a burden laid upon a weaker sex, but one of the "ways of God" for all who would enjoy the best his kingdom has to offer. And until that kingdom is well established, submission is a high calling upon women, a strategic part of God's plan to reveal his heart to the world.

We must never forget that God is building a glorious community of those whose hearts and relationships are governed by righteousness. Countless men shall be found in it, husbands overcome by the goodness of God revealed in the gracious disposition of believing wives who consistently honored them, who learned from the Holy Spirit how to draw out of their man the noble dignity and tender protectiveness God built into their masculine DNA.

Women are meant to inspire in their men proper servant leadership rather than authoritarian abuse of power. In *Recovering Biblical Manhood and Womanhood*, Pastor John Piper describes the mature woman of God as one who has developed a disposition "to affirm, receive and nurture strength and leadership from worthy men..."[12]

Submission produces the fruit of the Spirit.

Have you ever wondered why submission is not listed as a fruit of the Spirit? Perhaps if it were, it would be more easily recognized as part of God's character rather than being viewed as a wife's burden. I believe the reason submission is not found among lists of the fruit of the Spirit, is because it is

---

[12] From Piper's essay, "A Vision of Biblical Complementarity" Page 36, ibid.

more appropriately classified as the soil in which the seed of the fruit is grown. Allow me to explain.

The fruit of the Spirit is a metaphor for the character of God. Contrary to popular misconception, we do not develop the character of the Spirit just because we are spirit-filled, or because we read the Bible every day, or attend church at every opportunity. These things help us understand what the character of God looks like; but we are only able to consistently walk in the character of God through yielding our will to the Holy Spirit. He is all of these things, and he is our mentor, teaching us how to act in any given situation, until God's character becomes our character — or as the Word of God says, until Christ is formed in us.[13]

Only as we allow ourselves to be controlled by the Holy Spirit will we develop love, gentleness, or the ability to suffer long with the flaws of others. The fruit of self-control only operates in us as we yield to God regarding our desires. Patience grows through bending to trying circumstances or people when we would rather demand that they change. Joy flows out of resting in God's goodness and sovereignty, and out of feeling His joy in us.

So it is not being filled with the Spirit but being controlled by the Spirit that God's character is grown in us. The Amplified Bible aptly renders "spirit-filled" as *"filled with and controlled by"* the Holy Spirit.[14] It is safe to say that our ability to experience the life promised by and through Christ rests entirely upon developing a submissive spirit towards God and by extension, the people he tells us to yield to in our lives.

Real submission requires great strength.

The world would have you think submission is a sign of weakness. Nothing could be further from the truth. Only a person of strong character can graciously bend his own will to another without resentment. It is the weak person who cannot cope unless he has his way most of the time. The longer I work at developing the submissive spirit the easier it seems to remain in self-control, love, and faithfulness to God.

This is why the meek will inherit the earth: they know how to endure and remain faithful, not giving in to unrighteous behavior and rebellion because of the unfairness of life and the offenses of others. It has been well

---

[13] Galatians 4:19.

[14] For example, this is said of Barnabas in Acts 11:24.

said that meekness is not weakness, it is strength under control — in our case, the control of the Holy Spirit.

A submissive disposition is a mark of fellowship with the Spirit of God.

Paul implies in his letter to the Philippian church that one evidence of being in true fellowship with the Spirit is that we display the same submissive attitude Jesus did:

> If you have any encouragement from being united with Christ, if any comfort from his love, <u>if any fellowship with the Spirit</u>, if any tenderness and compassion, then make my joy complete by being like-minded, having the same love, being one in spirit and purpose. Do nothing out of selfish ambition or vain conceit, but in humility consider others better than yourselves. Each of you should look not only to your own interests, but also to the interests of others. Your attitude should be the same as that of Christ Jesus: Who, being in very nature God, did not consider equality with God something to be grasped, but made himself nothing, taking the very nature of a servant, being made in human likeness. And being found in appearance as a man, he humbled himself and became obedient to death...even death on a cross! (Philippians 2:1-8)

Colossians 3:18 plugs into the same idea when it says that a submissive disposition is especially fitting for the woman who claims to live "in Christ:" *Wives, submit to your husbands, as is fitting in the Lord.*

The Greek word for "fitting" means to be present in or arrive at. We could therefore say with a smile, *Wives, if you want to show that you are present in the Lord, that you have really 'arrived' in the matter of being a Christian, then support your husband in his leadership of the family!*

The woman God designed has a disposition that is trusting and respectful, willing to yield to and wanting to enhance the leadership of the men in her life. That's just the way she is.

Reflecting on Chapter 15

This chapter establishes that submission is a special calling for women who want to take their place in building Christ's kingdom.

❖ *Read Ephesians 1:9-10. Consider the purpose of a wife's submission in light of this scripture.*

❖ *Take notice of your own attitude about submission this week: do you resent it, or do you accept it wholeheartedly? Are you willing to submit in some areas and not in others?*

❖ *Ask the Holy Spirit to renew your heart and mind regarding submission. In other words, ask him to help you see it from God's perspective and to understand the fruit it will bear. Ask him to give you the grace to embrace it fully.*

For Further Study

❖ *Read the book of Esther.*

Chapter 16

The Blessings of Submission

Wives in difficult relationships are afraid that if they literally take God's Word to heart, they will become miserable doormats. It doesn't help that most men have not become the kind of servant leaders in their homes that God created them to be. But never forget that this is not really about the husband, it's all about the God who asks this of us.

It is easier to accept submission if we look to the nature of the One who gave us this command. He is the same one who loves us beyond our ability to comprehend. Would the God who loves us so passionately give us a command that is would lead us into a terrible existence? I think not.

The task of living by faith is impossible apart from understanding the character of God. If we truly know what God is like and what his motives are, we can fearlessly accept what He gives us and asks of us, accepting by faith that it will be good, and right, and lead us to life. Submission will always be a problem for the one who has not come to full faith and trust in the goodness of God.

Submission is not part of the curse.

Some believe that man's headship over woman is actually a part of the curse which came upon Adam and Eve after their fall from grace, and the logic that goes with that goes on to conclude that this "curse" was done away with at the cross.

But submission is not a curse and it is not Eve's punishment for her rebellion. We have already seen that God's original plan was for the husband to lead and the wife to follow. Submission is not Plan B, it is Plan A, and it was created by God for the obvious reason that he thought it was a good plan.

God's pattern for relationship was meant to thrive in every culture and every age; it was, and is, and always will be God's wisdom for the building of a family and a kingdom. The fact that man in his sinful nature perverts God's way does not negate its wisdom and rightness.

Regardless of the fact that submission has been too often perverted by fallen man, we should, under the guidance of the Holy Spirit, become the kind of men and women God created us to be. I defer again to Pastor John Piper:

"Biblical headship for the husband is the divine calling to take primary responsibility for Christlike, servant leadership, protection and provision in the home. Biblical submission for the wife is the divine calling to honor and affirm her husband's leadership and help carry it through according to her gifts. This is the way of joy. For God loves his people and he loves his glory. And therefore when we follow his idea of marriage we are most satisfied and he is most glorified." [1]

Knowing the goodness of God, there is no doubt that He gave the man leadership with the intention and motive of blessing the woman. Scripture instructs the husband to treat his wife with consideration and respect, never forgetting that wives are co-heirs with them of God's inheritance in all its aspects. First Peter 3:7 underscores the equality that men and women have in the sight of God.:

> *Husbands, in the same way be considerate as you live with your wives, and treat them with respect as the weaker partner and as heirs with you of the gracious gift of life....*

However, notice that woman is called the *"weaker partner."* Why is this? Is it simply referring to the lesser physical strength of women? Not likely, considering the context of this remark is the way wives and husbands relate to one another. I believe the label "weaker partner" actually refers to the uniquely tender nature God created in a woman.

When God made woman, he made her soft and vulnerable, trusting and receptive. She is the receiver in the physical male-female relationship, and this physical reality mirrors the emotional reality of her feminine soul. The

---

[1] Page 52, Recovering Biblical Manhood and Womanhood, ed. John Piper & Wayne Grudem, 1991, Crossway Books.

qualities of openness and receptivity are necessary to make woman a perfect and complementary companion for the man. Vulnerability is just a natural and potentially weak aspect of this characteristic.

Submission is actually for the protection of a woman.

Being the weaker partner does not lessen our dignity or value in the sight of God. If anything, it only increases his protective care over us. However, this vulnerability is also what opens a woman up to being easily deceived. Thus it is clear that one reason God wants a woman to submit to the leadership of a husband is for her own protection.

The woman's tendency to be deceived is obvious from the beginning, when Eve confesses: *"The serpent deceived me, and I ate."*[2] The Apostle Paul refers to the deceiveability of woman in voicing his fear that the church will also be deceived and accept teachings other than the true gospel of Christ:

> But I am afraid that just as Eve was deceived by the serpent's cunning, your minds may somehow be led astray from your sincere and pure devotion to Christ. (2 Corinthians 11:3)

Paul is not putting women down, he is merely pointing out that in the devil's cunning plan to get man to betray God, he approached the more vulnerable one in Eden. Scripture clearly says that Eve was deceived by the serpent, but implies that Adam willfully, knowingly sinned: *And Adam was not the one deceived, it was the woman who was deceived and became a sinner.*[3]

The dictionary defines "deceivable" as "capable of being misled or entrapped." The problem with being deceived is that we don't know we are! We can be very wrong while being certain that we are very right. As created by God, woman's vulnerability and openness is a good thing, but it requires the strength and protection of a wise and loving leader.

Is a Spirit-filled woman above being deceived?

Spirit-filled women may reject this idea because they assume the anointing of the Spirit automatically delivers them from this vulnerability,

---

[2] Genesis 3:13.
[3] 1 Timothy 2:14.

putting them on the same level with men. That may well be true if the woman walks in continual fellowship and complete surrender to the Holy Spirit. However, while that is our ultimate goal as Christians, few of us actually live there.

I have certainly known men who were deceived and women who were much more discerning than the men around them. Even so, to assume that a Spirit-filled woman's vulnerability to deception has been rendered a non-issue is foolish.

A person filled with the Spirit of Christ does not instantly become perfect in judgment and perception. It does not automatically make a woman safe from deception, anymore than it automatically makes a man a wise and godly leader. In fact, I have observed this paradox: when a woman accepts the fact that she is vulnerable to deception, her ability to be deceived actually diminishes. This is because awareness of a weakness causes us to make allowances for it. The woman who denies the truth is already easy prey to more deception. Being deceived on this issue only produces the fruit of more deception.

Some women try to excuse themselves from submission by quoting the verse which says that in Christ we are neither male nor female.[4] When I hear this I always fight the urge to say, "If you really believe this wipes out all the gender issues that God created for your earthly life, then I invite you to stroll the mall naked!"

It is foolish to assume gender is irrelevant in God's sight since he is the one who made you what you are. It would also make the Apostle Paul a man of two minds since he wrote this verse AND all the other words describing a woman's earthly relationship to a man.

The verse in Galatians is clearly, by its context, letting women know that all the blessings of being "sons of God" refer to men and women. The Jewish culture and society out of which Jesus came was clearly a patriarchal one which, in its tendency towards legalism about the Mosaic law, had become one which excluded women from the deeper things of knowing God. Paul is speaking here against that prejudice, but he is not in one sentence wiping out all of the other instructions he has so prayerfully given in his other letters as inspired by the Holy Spirit.

---

[4] Galatians 3:28.

The Bible does not support the attitude that gender is unimportant. Rather, it carefully teaches us how to live our earthly lives before God on the very basis of our gender. When we accept the truth of our created nature, we can willingly receive God's provision for our potential vulnerability: the balance and protection provided by the logical and more cautious man.

This protection was meant to be experienced as what the Bible calls coming *"under the shadow of his wing."* In fact, the concept of submission in the original Bible languages carries the very idea of "coming under," in a sheltering, protective manner.

God holds men accountable for their leadership and protection of women.

We must admit that God's call of leadership upon men should look very different than it often does today, and you can be sure that whether he is saved or not, God will hold your husband accountable for your welfare and that of your children. Those who are given the right to lead us carry the responsibility to watch over us protectively.

> *Obey your leaders and submit to their authority. They keep watch over you as men who must give an account. (Hebrews 13:17.)*

When God gives one person authority over another it is an expression of his goodness, and comes with responsibility for the welfare of those under them. They are held accountable by God (and ideally by the community of faith) for how they use that authority on behalf of those weaker, more tender ones under their care.

Where responsibility is shirked or abused, authority is diminished and can be made invalid. No person has the right to exercise authority over someone when they refuse to be held accountable for that person's welfare. To the degree that a husband is incapable of or refuses to use his position of leadership to love and care for his family, his authority over them will be diminished.

Even so, God's call upon a believing wife to do her best to honor the husband as the leader is not laid aside unless criminal neglect and abuse is involved. God holds you accountable to do all you can to encourage and help your husband to carry out his role as leader. Knowing God's nature, I cannot imagine that he would be pleased with a wife who sits back in scornful judgment of a poor, ignorant or untrained husband rather trying to help him.

Submission is also meant to bless the woman married to an unbeliever.

The Bible does not give a different set of instructions regarding submission to the woman married to an unbeliever. Still, it is reasonable to wonder if a wife is expected to similarly respond to the headship of an unsaved husband. I believe the answer is generally yes, for two reasons.

Number one, by the responsibility test, the husband has authority. Saved or unsaved, God holds your husband responsible for your welfare, and unless his lifestyle is a complete denial of that responsibility (through things like drug addiction, mental or physical abuse or endangering neglect) God still expects you to look to him as a protector and guide.

Secondly, the Bible makes it clear that if one spouse is in the Lord, then the unsaved spouse has a measure of a type of sanctification. This is made clear in 1 Corinthians 7:14:

> For the unbelieving husband has been sanctified through his wife, and the unbelieving wife has been sanctified through her believing husband. Otherwise your children would be unclean, but as it is, they are holy.

Your unsaved husband has a measure of sanctification through your relationship to God. This is not equal to salvation, by any means. Every person must come to God through the atoning sacrifice of Christ for his or her own sin.

Remember that sanctified means "set apart for." Paul is explaining that your unsaved husband is not walking around totally void of the influence of God, because you are in a covenant which makes you as one in God's sight. Because you are "one flesh,"[5] your husband is given wisdom and a type of grace (assistance) from the Lord for your sake and the sake of your tender-aged children.

Through your submission to your husband, God will use his power to influence your husband to lead you both in the direction of his will in order to bless you. It remains true that your husband has his free will, and unsaved

---

[5] Mark 10:6-8

people are in different states of resistance to God. (To be perfectly frank, this is true of many saved people!) One unsaved husband may be quite responsive to the leadings of God while another may be so hard of heart that he resists God totally. However, you can definitely help to change this through prayer and your demeanor. Your intercession for your husband can help to make the powers of darkness ineffective in their work to control your husband and blind him to God.

The Bible tells us that God responds to you according to your faith.[6] When you believe God will provide leadership for you through your husband because you are obeying His commands, God will answer your faith. I have seen this proven many times in the lives of women married to unbelievers and immature or backslidden believers.

God is bigger than your husband. The issue really isn't your husband; the issue is always Jesus. After all, it is his character and his promises that are on the line.

Submission demands utter reliance upon Jesus and brings us into greater intimacy.

When you commit to submit to God and to others whom God asks you to, you'll find that it takes much more strength than you have. You can't do it, and you'll realize you need Jesus every step of the way.

When I determined to embrace submission I did so because I knew it was right, but I was unprepared for the blessing that came with it: the demands of submission drove me to my knees often and actually thrust me into a wonderful dependence upon the Lord. In that place I experienced a degree of the Father's love and faithfulness that no amount of study and prayer had ever brought me into before.

When we commit wholeheartedly to practice what Jesus preaches, his intimate presence and power flow to us. Bible reading, tithing and church are important, but what builds intimacy with the Lord is a determination to obey His Word without excuse, discovering his will and turning to him repeatedly for strength, grace, and wisdom to carry it out. We are assured that God is ever watchful to help us in our commitment to honor him and his ways:

---

[6] Matthew 21:21.

For the eyes of the Lord range throughout the earth to strengthen those whose hearts are fully committed to him." (2 Chronicles 16:9, NIV).

Submission produces true co-rulership and unity.

Rather than being an instrument of suppression, God intended for submission to be the means through which a woman would co-rule with her husband. Before I understood the principle of submission, I saw myself as an equal leader with my husband, presuming the right to exercise the same power to make decisions for the family that he had. I wasn't willing to trust his leadership and I often questioned his decisions. Anytime I thought something should be handled a certain way — which was quite often — I told him how I thought he ought to do it. What this meant to him was that I didn't have confidence in him to lead the family. My attitude undermined whatever confidence he had in himself.

Ron's instinctive reaction was to resist me. A woman who robs her husband of his opportunity to lead will usually face his strong resistance to her, regardless of the wisdom of her input. Men have very sensitive "radar" for disrespect and manipulation, no matter how subtle. No doubt this radar was installed by God at the factory.

Even when Ron did accept my input he often resented it. This caused a terrible friction between us that made decision-making a constant battleground. He resented my lack of trust in his leadership, and I resented his not putting value in what I had to offer. At other times he even went against his better judgment and took my advice about something just to please me.

Men have such a strong desire to please their wives, and many a wife has learned to manipulate her husband just by casually hinting at what she wants. I was no exception. Eventually the Holy Spirit convicted me of interfering with Ron's leadership in our family and helped me realize I needed to support his leadership rather than try to direct it.

In the beginning I decided to keep all my opinions to myself unless asked. Making this choice caused me to come face-to-face with the depth of my lack of trust in both Ron and God — not to mention my pride and desire to control. Up until then I would have sworn I didn't have a real problem with either of those things. It's kind of like insisting you don't have a problem with sweets and then finding the truth when you are not allowed to eat any!

Taking my hands off of things was not easy. It probably amused the Lord because I would often mutter prayers under my breath like, *"Let him ask my opinion, Lord!"* To be very honest, in the beginning I actually grieved at what seemed a profound loss of self in giving up the freedom to express my opinions. This was such a drastic change from how I had always related to my husband and quite frankly, did not seem a bit fair. But I was in for a surprise.

Ron began to notice the change in me. At first he did not trust in my new attitude, but once he realized it was going to last, his own attitude began to change. I must add that in this process I also asked Jesus to help me sincerely respect and trust Ron. Not only did Jesus faithfully answer this prayer, I also sensed deep within my spirit that he was very pleased that I asked. In the familiarity of married life, we can become blind to the great qualities we admired in our mates that attracted us to them in the first place.

As I found new ways to express respect and trust in Ron's leadership, he began to blossom. In addition, I have to admit that when I let the responsibility for leading our family fully rest upon Ron, I became a lot less stressed and more carefree. It takes a lot of emotional energy to make sure a husband is doing it right!

It turned out that God was a lot better equipped to help a husband become a good leader than I was. Inevitably Ron began to feel the true weight of responsibility for making right decisions since it now fully rested upon him. As a result he began to turn to Jesus a lot more often for help, especially since he didn't have me to deal with. As I saw him seek the Lord more, I in turn began to feel much more secure. But that's not all. Ron began to actually feel a need for my help. For the first time in our marriage, he realized he needed a helper. To my amazement and delight, Ron began to ask for my input on decisions. He now wanted to share the leadership of the family with me. How different it was when Ron came and asked my opinion instead of having it forced on him! Not only did he feel and act more like a responsible leader, my input also became increasingly valuable to him.

As we settled into God's order we saw great change. Instead of two people struggling over issues and fighting for power, we began to yield to one another, and sought the will of God more often together. We were both awed by the new power and peace that began to flow in our lives. The constant undercurrent of fear and strife was gone. The very things that divided us before — major decisions on how to spend money or time, the discipline of our children — became the things that united us.

The difference in our marriage is profound. The whole atmosphere of power struggle has been removed. Ron is now free to be the leader he was called to be, rather than wrestling with me for control of the family. By obeying his Word, Jesus has transformed me from being a competitor and a usurper into a complementary partner, and transformed a divided home into a unified one. One day it occurred to me that I actually had more real power and influence in the submitted position than I ever had before.

This truth is vividly illustrated in the story of Esther, whose deeply respectful behavior towards her husband the King won her so much favor that when she came with a request of him, he announced before he even heard what it was that he would give her anything she asked, up to half of his kingdom! In other words, the answer was yes before she made her request. I suspect this truth also finds expression in our total submission to God and his response to our cries. He is, after all, our king.

The resistance that a husband may feel towards us can be melted by God's influence when we please Him. The Bible says, *When a man's ways are pleasing to the Lord, he makes even his enemies live at peace with him.*[7] Of course, your husband is not an enemy, but in the midst of a huge disagreement he may sometimes feel like one. The point of course is that if God can make even an enemy be at peace with you, then he can bring your husband to that same place, and will put his considerable power into the job when you are committed to doing things His way.

In a paradox typical of God's kingdom, when I gave up what I wanted, then I actually received it in abundance. When I forced my opinions upon Ron, I was trying to possess an authority over our lives that I did not rightfully have. It was a stolen authority which did not have God's approval, and it was not motivated by faith but by my fear that Ron wouldn't do it right, or my selfish desire to have it my way.

Changing my motivation to love and serve both the Lord and my husband changed all that. The resulting authority that subsequently flowed to me from Ron was genuine and right. From this position I became very

---

[7] Proverbs 16:7

conscious that as a godly woman I should be careful to influence my husband only in the direction of God's will, not away from it.

As we follow the Holy Spirit, submission will bless us.

Like every other religious law, when submission is applied apart from the influence and guidance of the Living Spirit of Christ, it can be abused and horribly perverted. Because we live in a fallen world we face a continual challenge in that the very thing that God intended to be a blessing, the devil continually tries to use for evil. But that fact does not change God's plan to use submission to bring you to your fullest created potential as a woman and to bring the blessings of his kingdom into your home. Your abundant life will never come through adopting the world's ways and the world's attitudes.

As children who have been set free from the law, we must follow the spirit of God's commands, rather than the letter, by seeking to understand his heart in the matter at all times. How far does a woman submit to an ungodly man? Who is the worthy man a woman should affirm by her submission? When I first began to teach on this subject I felt obliged to answer these questions for women, but now I understand that I serve the Lord and women far better to teach them to seek God's personal guidance in these matters.

In the chapters that follow I have given guidelines on these matters, but I cannot emphasize enough how important it is for each woman to personally seek the Lord and hear from him as to how to respond to her own husband.

Setting her heart upon reverent submission to the Lord, every woman must follow her own conscience before the Lord in how to honor his Word. If necessary, she should seek the counsel of a mature, godly pastor who knows her and her husband personally, to resolve any difficult issues.

Reflecting on Chapter 16

This chapter reveals the blessings that God provides for a woman through honoring the headship of a husband.

❖ *Read Job 22:21-30. Can you see any way in which the principles and benefits of submitting to God might apply also to your relationship with your husband?*

For Further Study

❖ *Read the story of Sarah in Genesis Chapters 12-23.*

Chapter 17

Sarah, the Fearless Woman

Our course in submission would not be complete without a study of Sarah, who is held up to us as an example of the woman who has pleased God in her submission.

Speaking of the holy women in ancient days, Peter wrote:

> *They were submissive to their own husbands, like Sarah, who obeyed Abraham and called him her master. You are her daughters if you do what is right and do not give way to fear. (First Peter 3:6)*

Of all the women in the Bible, Sarah is a most interesting choice. Why not pick Esther, whose story illustrates the power of submission so well? We have to take Peter's word that Sarah used submissive language with Abraham, because when you read her story[1] you will not find a single example of Sarah saying, "Yes, master" to Abraham. What you will find is a woman married to a man who sometimes blew it and sometimes did it right. My hunch is that Peter chose Sarah because like the rest of us, she was married to an imperfect man who was just trying to do the best he could.

We all think of Abraham as a great man of faith, and this he was; but the road to becoming such a man was filled with ups and downs, good decisions and bad. You will find in Sarah's life unsettled times, crises, an abundance of life-changing, stressful events, and ample opportunity to doubt her husband's leadership.

But Peter implies in verse six that the reason Sarah triumphed and is our greatest example, is that she overcame her fears:

---

[1] Sarah's life is told in Genesis Chapters 12 through 23.

"It was thus that Sarah obeyed Abraham [following his guidance and acknowledging his headship over her by] calling him lord (master, leader, authority). And you are now her true daughters if you do right and let nothing terrify you [not giving way to hysterical fears or letting anxieties unnerve you]." (1 Peter 3:6, The Amplified Bible)

This verse hits the nail on the head when it identifies the biggest hindrance for any woman trying to submit to her husband: fear.

Women are notorious fretters and worriers. What kind of fear does the average wife usually face? The fear that the husband is going to make a mistake, get the finances in a mess, fail to protect the family, open us to harm, mishandle relationships, or crush the spirits of the children — just to name a few. Let's review Sarah's life and see if we can relate.

Sarah's story.

When her story begins her name is Sarai and she is 66 years old. She lives in Ur, one of the most advanced and prosperous societies of her time. Sometime after she marries Abram, her father-in-law leads the clan in a move to Canaan. However, on the way they come to an incredibly lovely country called Haran and settle there instead. It is a paradise in the Middle East, having been described by travelers as fruitful plains surrounded by pastures and mountain forests. It would be hard to leave, but when her father-in-law dies, Abram is summoned out by an invisible God named Yahweh, who commands him to go to Canaan with the promise that he will become a great nation.

Keep in mind that Abram is childless at this point, which is a huge issue for a man in his culture. What man could resist the promise that not only will he father children at last, but that they will endure to become a nation. God is offering Abram nothing less than dynasty, but it will cost Sarai much.

If she is going to follow Abram she must trust him as he leads her on a difficult, tiresome and even dangerous journey of hundreds of miles on foot or donkey, and leave her comfortable home behind. And has he really heard God, or is he having a grand case of male wanderlust for glory? Opportunity number one for Sarai to question her husband's leadership, to give in to fear. The distress of it would only add to the wrinkles she would get from multiplied sun exposure traveling across a vast land. We know Sarai follows

Abram, and though it doesn't say so here, we can assume from Peter's insight that she does so submissively, and not in a fearful or angry spirit.

Once they arrive in Canaan, Abram doesn't settle down in one place, but continues to move Sarai and their household. They even spend time in what has been called "the great and terrible Negev," a rocky desert region which is almost impossible to live in. Nothing grows there; no bushes, no grass, no shade trees, no place to plant petunias in the spring (is there even a spring?) and hardly enough water to take a spit bath with. How many women would be willing to follow a husband into that kind of neighborhood? Sarai's second opportunity to give in to fears regarding the cost of following her husband. It would be enough to make a woman eat everything in sight.

But Sarai won't have that problem, because a famine develops in the land and they are faced with starvation. What wife wouldn't be tempted to say at this point, *Look at the mess you've gotten us into!*

Opportunity number three to give in to fear, which by now, added to malnutrition, would probably cause her hair and nails to become brittle and her skin to lose whatever youthful glow she hadn't already sacrificed to the journey.

Famine

To escape the famine, Abram takes them to Egypt on a journey filled with the greatest danger imaginable from bandits and the elements. When they arrive, Abram instructs Sarai to tell everyone they meet that she is his sister. (Now this is true in that they shared the same mother, so he is actually her half-brother. Such marriages were not uncommon, but it is clearly a deception to hide the fact that they are married.)

Our "man of faith" doesn't seem to have much faith at this moment, apparently motivated in his decision by fear for their lives. Sarai was beautiful, and the world could be a dangerous place for the husband of such a woman. Abram feared he would be murdered by any man who wanted his wife and it was apparently well known in the region that a king had once murdered a husband for his wife.

He reasoned that this little deception would keep them safe, since as a brother, Abram would be the one through whom all potential husbands would barter for Sarai's hand in marriage. He would be in a position of control and probably assumed that the usual bride negotiations would give them time to escape. Still, quite not the way of integrity or wisdom.

His plan might have worked, except for one thing: the one who wanted Sarai was Pharaoh, king of Egypt, and Pharaoh doesn't negotiate for brides!

Opportunity number four for Sarai to doubt her husband's judgment and be terrorized by the fear that another man would take her against her will. Could the potential for anxiety get any higher?

Many women in her position would probably vow by now to never trust the husband again. The average woman would be strongly tempted to expose her husband's foolishness, but apparently Sarai honors her "master" even in this deception. As a result she is taken to live in Pharaoh's palace, and spends some days being made ready to be his bride.

Meanwhile, Pharaoh is honoring Abram, his brother-in-law-to-be, by making him rich with livestock and servants (and no doubt including a handmaiden named Hagar). I can only imagine how this situation must have tempted Sarai to feel towards Abram. Making a decision based in fear, Abram has not only put Sarai at great risk but threatens the entire plan of God to bring forth a great nation from their union.

By submitting to her husband's wishes, Sarai has allowed herself to be put in a position where no one has the power to rescue her, except God himself. Of course, he does just that! God directly intervenes by speaking in some way to Pharaoh, who is not a "believer," before he ever actually touches Sarai. Not only is Sarai rescued without any true harm coming to her, but at the end of this episode it is clear that the Lord has turned Abram's mistake into a blessing. (Still, we don't recommend you try this at home.)

It seems obvious by his actions that Abram made his plan in the face of a decided lack of faith and trust in God to keep them safe! Regardless of his listing in the "faith hall of fame" in Hebrews Chapter 11, at this moment in his life Abram resembles every husband who has no confidence in God and makes his decisions out of fear rather than being led by the Lord. Are you beginning to relate to Sarai a little more?

The message of this episode is unmistakably clear: God can handle even the biggest mistakes a husband might make, and will protect the wife who submits to her husband's leadership. Obeying God's ways will always throw us into God's arms, and He is absolutely committed to keep us wherever our obedience takes us.

"Honey, I think we should move again."

Now Abram moves Sarai again; it seems they have become nomads. From the beginning of their journey Sarai's life has dramatically changed from stability to almost constant change. What will happen next? Where will she be tomorrow? Any woman knows this can be awfully hard on the feminine soul, which instinctively craves a cozy nest to call her own.

At long last they arrive in Canaan and settle down in lovely Bethel. Having watched Sarai apparently stay in possession of her quiet spirit through all that has happened so far, we now watch her face new challenges to her serenity. It becomes necessary for Abram's household and flocks to separate from Lot's because the land will not support them both, giving rise to discord. Abram solves this problem by taking Lot to a high place where they can survey the land. On one side is the plain of Jordan, a land so lush and fertile that it is compared to Eden, the garden of the Lord. The other side is far less desirable, more desert-like. Abram allows Lot to take his pick, and naturally he picks the best land.

Sarai is presented with yet another opportunity to fret over her husband's judgment: he has given the best land away to an undeserving relative. Watching such potential wealth slip through your fingers, especially when you have been through so much to get there, would tempt any woman to doubt her husband's leadership. But Peter would have us believe that she did not give in to any anxiety and the manipulative nature it can bring out in a woman.

Life settles down, except for the incredible moment when God appears to Abram and promises this elderly, childless man that he will some day have as many descendants as there are stars in the sky.

Eleven years pass. Sarai is 76, and probably not even ovulating any more. She has given up hoping that she can conceive a child, and decides that God's promise has become her problem. Resorting to a common practice of their culture, Sarai gives her Egyptian maidservant Hagar to Abram to produce an offspring. Hagar does conceive a child, but her relationship with Sarai is ruined, and she now despises her mistress.

"I only wanted to help God out."

In our one vivid glimpse of Sarai actually giving into her fears, we see her at her worst. Overcome with jealousy, she loses control and mistreats Hagar severely. In fact, God has to rescue Hagar from Sarai's bad temper. At this moment in her life, it is safe to say that Sarai is not possessed of the gentle and quiet spirit. Sarai has given into her fear that unless she takes control, things will not turn out as they should.

The fruit of Sarai's fear affects our world to this day. We watch the Arab nation which was birthed in Hagar's womb struggle with the nation later born of God's promise in Sarah's womb. This incident should speak volumes to women who feel justified in taking the lead in the home when they think it is in the furtherance of some purpose of God. It is never okay to behave unrighteously in order to make God right. God does not need your help; He needs your trust and your obedience.

Thirteen years pass. One day when Abram is 99 and Sarai is 90, God tells Abram to take in his body the covenant mark of circumcision and change his name to Abraham. Abram means *exalted father,* while Abraham means *father of a multitude*.

By now Abraham, being older and wiser, is probably a joy to submit to. At his age surely he can be trusted not to make stupid mistakes. Or can he?

Abraham and Sarah go on the road again. Apparently all these years of having a mostly quiet spirit has preserved Sarah's beauty so well that she is still incredibly attractive at the age of 90. During their travels, Abraham's old fears resurface and he falls back into a familiar pattern. He tells Sarah to join him in the same deception as before in hopes that it will keep him safe: *"Tell people you're my sister and hide the fact that we're married."*

Every woman who has watched her husband make the same mistake twice can relate to this. Incredibly, another powerful king by the name of Abimelech decides to take Sarah for his wife! Again, Sarah submits to her husband under the most trying of circumstances. Another prime opportunity for Sarah to turn on her husband out of fear for her safety. But the good part of going through the same thing is that now Sarah has this history of watching God rescue her from her husband's failure.

Sure enough, God comes through as good the second time around as the first, and rescues her completely without harm.

What a life Sarah had! I don't think any woman could claim that her life has more ups and downs, more tests to her serenity, or more challenges to her commitment to trust God and a husband. Sarah is an example for us today because she made a choice to trust her husband in the face of inevitable fears that her husband's leadership might interfere with her abundant life. Fear is usually what motivates a woman to take over.

I believe Sarah was like all women born into this fallen world: with an instinctive nature to dominate and master the husband as a result of the curse upon Eve, needing to be saved/redeemed from that curse. In fact, the name Sarai means "dominator"; when God changed her name to Sarah, the meaning changed to "princess." This speaks of the fact that when God's influence comes upon us we can leave behind our old nature and possess the life and character befitting children of a king.

Like the rest of us Sarah had to learn to live God's way. It seems God used every trial in her life to teach her to trust him more. Her fearless submission allowed Him grow Abraham into a man of God. If Abraham was a great man of faith, Sarah's support of his leadership was surely one reason why.

God's faithfulness doesn't depend upon a man.

We have seen it proven again and again: God is bigger than any mistakes the husband may make. When a woman puts her faith in God to work things out while she obeys the husband wholeheartedly, God will work it all out. God's ability to keep his promises to you doesn't depend upon any man. Romans 3:3 says, *"What if some did not have faith? Will their lack of faith nullify God's faithfulness?"* The answer of course is certainly not.

We don't know the day-to-day workings of Sarah's relationship to Abraham, nor do we know the details of Abraham's temperament. But we don't have to because the issue here is <u>not</u> the husband's temperament, personality or ability; the issue is God's faithfulness. That is always the issue for a woman of God. Either she believes God is faithful, or she doesn't. God is faithful to those who follow his ways.

A certain story from my personal history comes to mind that illustrates this truth. A woman in our church was married to a man who claimed to be a Christian but never went to church or read his Bible. She wasn't sure if he was really saved, but in any case he certainly did not understand the will of

God. Furthermore, he was addicted to gambling and often put the family in a financial bind because of his losses. So he did not lead or manage the family in a responsible way. The wife worked, sometimes two jobs, to make sure that they and their young son had their needs met. Yet this very thing caused a conflict when she realized that God wanted her to submit to her husband, because oddly enough, he didn't want her to work outside the home. He wanted her to quit her job.

Jane[2] wanted to be at home but felt that she couldn't submit to her husband in this because of the money he lost gambling. She feared that if she submitted to Larry[3] and quit work, they would run out of money. She was certain on the one hand that this couldn't be God's will because their son might go hungry or lack for clothes or medicine; on the other hand, she had this scriptural command to submit to her husband, and a desire to honor God's ways.

The Holy Spirit began to show Jane that by bringing in an income she was actually enabling Larry to continue in his addiction, protecting him from facing the consequences of his gambling. Once she saw the situation in this light, she realized she had to choose between her fears and continuing to save them all from Larry's problem, or trust God to take care of them while she honored His ways.

Jane had testified often in church about how much Jesus could be trusted; now she was asked to prove it. Jane decided to quit work. She also determined not to nag Larry but to gently and respectfully look to him for the family's provision. They had a few skinny weeks and did without a few things while God worked on her husband's heart, but no one actually went hungry or suffered any serious lack.

Before it reached such a point Larry finally saw how his gambling was robbing the family. He gradually stopped throwing their money away at the gambling table and took his role of provider more seriously. Jane was relieved of the burden of providing for her family, and she rejoiced in her new freedom to be at home for their child. The best part is the end to the story: Larry was eventually so drawn to Christ by the changes in his wife that he became a disciple of Jesus Christ!

---

[2] Not her real name.

[3] Not his real name.

Jane discovered firsthand how God moves to help the wife whose heart is set upon obedience to Him. The fact that Jane sincerely tried to honor her husband was no small part of the improvement in their life. Any man will appreciate and want to serve a wife who gives him this honor and brings out the best in him.

This story also illustrates another very important point: our world is full of women carrying burdens they were not meant to. God did not give us the job of turning a husband into what God wants him to be. Women will find it a great relief to turn this job over to the Lord. A lot of the emotional energy we expend probably goes into getting a husband to do what we think is right.

However, be prepared for the fact that just because you submit to your husband doesn't mean everything will turn out perfectly. At times it will seem as if your submission even causes problems. Be patient; God will show himself in every situation if you wait for him. Remember what the Lord has told us: *Be joyful in hope, patient in affliction, faithful in prayer.*[4] Or as we have also been told, be still and know that He is God.

If you lack trust in any area you can be sure your fears will surface when you commit to submit to God and your husband. The cure for this fear is faith in the fact that if you are submitted to God then He is in control of your life. Psalm 91 teaches us that the Lord is the refuge of those who totally place their trust in Him.

The righteous shall live by faith.

Look to your husband with faith. Not just faith in him, but faith that God is standing behind this man to fulfill his plan for you and back up your obedience. One day in prayer the Lord gave me a picture or vision showing me that as I face Ron, the Lord is standing right behind Ron, facing me. This picture taught me more than a thousand words, because I realized that in reality I am not being asked to trust in Ron so much as I am being asked to trust in Jesus, who is always working to help my husband in response to my trust.

That same vision also made me realize that in a very real sense, when I dishonor Ron, I dishonor the Lord. Jesus confirmed this when he announced, *"As you do it to the least of these, you have done it to me."*[5]

---

[4] Romans 12:12.
[5] Matthew 25:40

Most husbands can be trusted as far as their intentions and motives, even if they don't have a great track record in managing things. No man wants to intentionally mess things up. A husband's responsibilities and position are not easy, and can seem overwhelming to him at times. He doesn't want to handle it poorly. He wants to do it right, wants to care for you, wants to be a good man. As a general rule, the man who feels that his wife trusts him will work even harder to be worthy of that trust.

If God's will is for you to trust your husband as you would the Lord, then know that he himself will back up your trust. I have seen this proven many times in my own marriage. Whenever I commit to trustfully follow my husband's lead, God makes everything work out, regardless of any individual decision Ron makes. To trust in the husband because the Lord calls you to do so, is to trust in the Lord himself.

Sarah's life reflects these truths. She had a beauty even in old age that was legendary, in spite of the fact that the Bible tells every woman that her beauty lasts only for a brief season of life.[6]

The greatest beauty secret of all: a quiet spirit.

> Your beauty should not come from outward adornment such as braided hair and the wearing of gold jewelry and fine clothes. Instead, it should be that of your inner self, the unfading beauty of a gentle and quiet spirit, which is of great worth in God's sight. For this is the way the holy women of the past who put their hope in God used to make themselves beautiful. They were submissive to their own husbands, like Sarah... (1 Peter 3:3-5)

Peter is not telling women it is wrong to wear jewelry and nice clothes; he is saying they should not depend upon such things to give them their beauty.

Real beauty begins on the inside and radiates outward, and if the inside is in turmoil, the skin will tell. Any physician or psychologist will tell you today that what goes on inside a person eventually shows on the outside. Every time I made trips to the dermatologist with a bad complexion, I was always asked: "Are you under stress?" A dermatologist once told me that

---

[6] Proverbs 31:30 says, "...beauty is fleeting..."

because of stress, women in their 30's and older had passed up teenagers in acne problems.

Peter implies that Sarah's beauty had its source in her quiet and submissive disposition. A gentle, unmanipulative spirit and a restful soul reveal the true nature and blessing of submission, along with one of its greatest rewards: the unfading beauty that all women long to possess.

A woman who has this kind of spirit possesses a special beauty, whether she is classically beautiful or not. We have all encountered women who were not beautiful by society's standards, yet possessed a loveliness that we envied. A woman who is peaceful and happy inside is radiant with a beauty that is much more than skin deep.

Likewise, a woman who is miserable, bitter or depressed will reveal such things in her countenance. Naomi, mother-in-law of Ruth the Moabitess, is a good example of this. Naomi goes through famine and her family relocates to find food. In the strange land they move to her husband dies, and then both of her sons. She blames God for her misfortunes, and such a bitterness takes hold in her soul that it completely changes her appearance. Upon returning to her hometown, all of her relatives and friends barely recognize her, exclaiming *"Can this be Naomi?"* Naomi (whose name in Hebrew means "pleasant") snaps back at them, *"Don't call me Naomi any longer! Instead, call me Mara!"* (which in Hebrew means 'bitter"). Obviously her outward appearance had changed dramatically because of her bitter spirit.

So what is the quiet spirit, and how do I have one?

The word "quiet" in 1 Peter 3:4 does not refer to a person's outward behavior, but to an inward state of the soul. The Greek word is *hesuchios*. It is combination of two words, the first meaning *immovable*, and the other meaning *possession or condition*. Put together, it means *immovable condition*. The word picture is one of a person keeping their seat in an undisturbed manner in spite of what is going on around them. The idea is that nothing can knock them off of their "chair" or secure position.

Jesus demonstrated this state of soul often when faced with adverse circumstances, such as when he slept soundly in a boat during a fierce storm. That moment perfectly demonstrates the security which flows out of a conviction that Father is in charge and has the will and power to keep one safe.

The word *hesuchios* is the same word used in First Timothy 2:2, where Paul says to pray that we can live peaceful lives. It indicates a tranquility arising from within, a state of being undisturbed. It is a matter of attitude, not personality. A woman can be talkative or quite lively and still have this inner quiet and gentle spirit.

The woman who possesses this spirit isn't exercising will power to make herself calm. She's not gutting it out for the sake of standing in faith, she has real peace. She has simply learned how to rely on Jesus and lives by faith in his love for her. Apparently such a spirit in a woman brings great delight to the Lord:

> Let not yours be ... the inward adorning and beauty of the hidden
> person of the heart, with the incorruptible and unfading charm of a gentle
> and peaceful spirit, which is not anxious or wrought up, but is very
> precious in the sight of God. (1 Peter 3:3-4, The Amplified Bible)

Why is this quiet spirit so precious to God? Because it is the ultimate evidence that this woman is resting in His love. No matter how many promises God has made or how awesome his love is for you, if you are fearful, anxious or miserable, then you are not enjoying his love and goodness. It is as if they are wasted, which surely grieves God.

The quiet spirit shows God that you really do trust him with all your heart. The woman who belongs to God should be "sitting down on the inside" at all times. The storms of life can come and go, but such peace should abide in her soul that fear cannot penetrate. The woman who gets knocked off of her seat constantly probably doesn't know Jesus very well. She needs to do as Peter did in the storm: get her eyes on Jesus, and off of the circumstances.

The evidence of faith is not in how many scriptures we can quote or how often we testify of our confidence in God; but the state of the heart. Faith is revealed in the way we respond to problems. The quiet spirit is not obtained simply by confessing scripture, it is the fruit and reward of real trust in Jesus.

Jesus says, *Peace I leave with you; my peace I give you. ... Do not let your hearts be troubled and do not be afraid.*[7] In this verse the word "troubled" in Greek refers to something that is constantly in motion, like the agitations of a washing machine tub spinning back and forth. Jesus said we should not

---

[7] John 14:27.

allow our hearts to be in this state but to receive the peace He offers. But the price of that peace is trust.

The gentle spirit.

God wants us to be overcomers, but we often try to overcome the wrong thing. We tend to spend a lot of emotional energy trying to conquer the problem, when what God often wants is for us to overcome our response to the problem, to overcome the temptation to be fearful, angry or bitter.

The word "gentle" in 1 Peter 3:4 means "mild, gentle or humble." It speaks of meekness, as it is translated in the King James. Jesus described himself as meek and revealed by his actions that meekness is not weakness, but strength under control. A woman of gentle spirit knows she doesn't have to fix something just because she has the power to do so. Not only are her fears at rest, so is her power. In other words, her "power" is at rest in God's will, the same place Jesus parked his power.

Hannah Hurnard pictures gentleness beautifully in her book *Mountains of Spices*. Gentleness is developed, she writes, *"by the daily practice of bending submissively to life's hard and difficult experiences without bitterness, or resentful resistance, or self-pity."* No storm of life can break the gentle spirit that has learned to bend rather than break.

I grew up on the Texas Gulf Coast, and I have seen hurricane winds of 150 miles per hour ravage steel structures or proud, 100-year old oaks while the lanky palm trees, almost fragile looking, remained standing when the storm was over. This is because they were pliable, able to bend with the wind. The trees that resisted the wind were easily uprooted in these ferocious storms, but not the relaxed palm trees.

God delights in the woman who trusts him.

The message of First Peter 3 is clear: God finds precious the woman who has overcome her fears and is at rest in her spirit. It is God's goal to bring us to rest. Rest is one of the greatest rewards of submission. God delights in such a woman because her demeanor proves to Him that He is no longer on trial with her. Her trust in God enables her to submit to an imperfect husband and retire from running the world. In fact, the subject of trust is so important that it needs its own chapter.

Reflecting on Chapter 17

The goal of this chapter is to understand the inner workings and the outer expression of Sarah's quiet spirit.

❖ *The author says that fear is usually what motivates a wife to take over the leadership of the family. Can you think of other reasons? (I.e., a desire for control.)*

❖ *Read Psalm 91 and ponder its truths in relation to this chapter.*

❖ *What kind of fears get you up from your "undisturbed place of rest"?*

❖ *Ask the Lord to minister to you in your fears, and help you to come to rest in Him in those specific areas.*

Deeper work

❖ *Ask the Holy Spirit to alert you when you are about to help God out. Note these times in your journal and talk to the Lord about the reason why. Let him reveal areas in which you do not trust Him or your husband.*

Chapter 18

I Will Trust In My God

The wise woman builds her house, but with her own hands the foolish one tears hers down. (Proverbs 14:1).

Wisdom has built her house; she has hewn out its seven pillars. (Proverbs 9:1).

In the first half of this book we discussed the foundation of our house — the place where we share life with God — and explored the pillars which make it strong. It remains for us to put "walls" on this house, without which we remain vulnerable to the enemies of our new life. You would not live in a real house without walls, no matter how strong the foundation and the framing pillars.

What forms the walls in our house of life with God? I believe it is trust.

I came to this understanding through this verse penned by King David:

Many are the woes of the wicked, but the Lord's unfailing love surrounds the man who trusts in him. (Psalm 32:10)

David is eminently qualified to teach us about trust in God, because he has, as we are fond of saying today, "been there and done that." David faced the entire gamut of things that test trust in God: being betrayed by loved ones, battles with adversaries stronger than he, the threat of being murdered in his sleep. Perhaps most crucial, David had to face the consequences of his own moral failings. If you read the whole of David's story in scripture, you see that through all things, David's heart consistently trusts in God's love and promises. This surely was one of the secrets of his great exploits, and undoubtedly one of the primary reasons that God called him a man after His own heart.

The Lord's unfailing love surrounds the one who trusts him.

The word picture David paints for us in Psalm 32:10 is of a wall that completely surrounds one, a wall constructed of God's faithful love. David also implies, however, that if there is a gap in one's trust in God, there will be a corresponding gap in the experience of His unfailing love. Notice that the gap is not in God's faithful love but in the ability to experience that love. Nothing can separate us from the love of God that comes to us through Christ. So while your lack of trust may create a gap in your experience of God's love, it never diminishes that love.

Christ loved and died for us all; having made a way for us to enter heaven and experience life with God, the expression of his love is complete. However, millions still do not experience this love, because they still do not fully trust the Lord. God is still on trial with them.

The terms "faith" and "trust" are synonyms in most Bible usages. In fact, the Amplified Version of the New Testament translates the word "believe" as *"adhere to, trust in and rely on."* The Greek word translated for us as "believe" does not refer to simple mental acknowledgment, but a deep belief which causes a person to entrust oneself to the object of belief.

Here is a revealing story about trust: a daredevil attracted a great crowd on top of a skyscraper by promising to cross over to the next skyscraper, balancing on nothing more than a wire. He asked the crowd, *"Who believes I can do this?"* The crowd enthusiastically raised their hands and shouted their affirmation. The daredevil then asked, *"In that case, which one of you will climb into this wheelbarrow and let me take you across?"* That is what we call "a reality check." My reality check came the day God told me to return to my marriage with Ron.

Toni, do you trust me?

The day I ran away from Ron and the Lord told me to go back to him and our marriage, I was certain that to obey Him would be to sacrifice all my hope of joy in that relationship. It didn't occur to me at first that it was the best thing for me; I assumed God was simply motivated to make me "do the right thing." I ultimately decided to obey Him and went back to Ron because of the desire to prove my love for God. I honestly did not believe that God could make anything different, only that somehow he would carry me through with His love and grace. Yes, I was going to slog it out by faith, do the right thing.

When the Lord brought Ron and I back together, he had to teach us many things in order to keep us from falling into the same old pattern of relating to each other. As I prayed that first night, thinking the Lord would talk to me about our problems, I was surprised when he asked instead how I felt about Him: *Toni, do you trust me?*

I thought about that a long time, sitting on the edge of my bed. I was exhausted from the tears I had cried and the emotional strain of our fight. I wanted to blurt out the correct Christian answer, *"Yes, of course!"* But there is something about complete failure that undermines your ability to lie to yourself any longer. I knew in my heart that the answer was *No, Lord, I don't trust you.* I trusted who God is, but I did not trust His personal will for me. There is a difference, as I hope to explain shortly.

This realization was something of a shock. I had studied God's Word diligently for years, prayed faithfully, and taught others to have faith in God. I had earnestly praised God for his goodness and love. I had assured others countless times with complete confidence that God could and would meet their every need. Now, in my greatest personal test, I discovered that I did not really believe my best life would occur if I obeyed God.

I trust you, Lord (when you do it my way).

It began to dawn on me that what I thought of as a marriage problem was much bigger; it was a faith problem. I was not really living a surrendered life. Among other things, because I did not like submission I was resenting both Ron and the Lord over it. The Lord showed me this and a few other attitudes in my heart that had been undermining my life. The good part of being totally broken, as I was in that moment, is that usually the things you have built your life on get broken too.

As I began to honestly face the deep beliefs in my heart I saw that my trust in God stayed in place only when things happened that lined up with my understanding and maintained my comfort level. If we got away from those parameters, I quit trusting. What I had been calling trust had not been trust at all, but mere expectation. Real trust is resting in God's will with a satisfied heart. I certainly wasn't doing that.

I gradually realized that not only was I failing to actually trust the Lord, but deep in my heart lived this unspoken but sincere dread that if I lived exactly like God asked me to (i.e., submissively), I would not enjoy life; I would lose all control; and I might even be hurt. Without actually saying the words, the Lord and I had been living out this dialogue for several years: *Toni, trust me completely.*

Oh God, I can't! I'm afraid to. It might hurt!

Or, *But I might not get to do what I want!*

Regardless of the biblical truths I professed and taught, these were the truths I actually lived from. The Holy Spirit showed me that in daily life I only trusted God and let him have complete control until I got hurt, disappointed or frightened, then I would take control back again. My lack of trust translated quickly into lack of surrender — disobedience — which led to rebellion.

Both rebellion and idolatry begin with lack of trust.[1] Disobedience at its root is a trust issue.

What we really believe is revealed in the choices we make. Our actions are motivated by the beliefs that live deep in our hearts, where words do not even exist, only a visual, audio and emotional history of our lives. I call these the ruts in my soul, deepened by being traveled again and again, taking me to the same place I've always gone when certain things happen. The fear of being hurt in love or the expectation of joy in a certain activity, all these things live there.

It is these things that dictate our responses to everyone and everything in life, whether it is the truth that God loves me or the "truth" that I am of no value to anyone, or the "truth" that God does not hear me when I pray. These deeply rooted beliefs are what God wants to change in you. He wants to renew your whole being through one encounter with him after another, until new ruts are formed in your soul that always take you back to His love and goodness.

---

[1] Most admit to some rebellion; few think of themselves as idolatrous. But scripture reveals that rebellion is trusting in oneself instead of God, and idolatry is trusting in something or someone else other than God.

Back to my crisis: as I came face to face with my lack of trust in God, the Holy Spirit again reminded me of the words of Jesus: *I have come that they might have life, and have it to the full.* (John 10:10) When he said this I saw it as if for the first time: giving me abundant life is what motivates the Lord!

In other words, whatever God commands is consistent with his will to lead me to this abundant life — even the command to submit to a husband. His will for me contains my very best life within it. I saw in that moment that if God is love, every command He gives is an expression of that love. God's will always expresses his love and goodness.

The Holy Spirit taught me that God's command to return to my painful marriage was an expression of his love, and the path to my abundant life. I couldn't see then how that could be so, but now, many years later, I can testify that the Holy Spirit was right. My faithful and loving and good Father has given me abundant life by keeping in this marriage.

Is God on trial with you?

A willingness to disobey God is a huge clue that you do not trust Him. There is only one reason not to obey God, and that is if we believe to do so would be bad for us. We all want that abundant life. So the question is, when it becomes clear that God's will for you is contrary to your desire, do you trust him enough to trade in your desires for his? Or do you think you can love yourself more effectively than he? This is the mistake man has made continually in history.

The Bible says that the events which transpired between God and the Hebrews trekking in the wilderness have much to teach us about our relationship to God. The most tragic lesson is this: that in spite of witnessing God's great love and goodness displayed through awesome miracles, the Hebrews easily abandoned all trust in God when they got too hungry or thirsty or uncomfortable; when He did not respond to those needs to their liking or their timing.

These Hebrews experienced the greatest wall of God's protective love, at times literally, ever known to man. Their lack of trust sealed their destiny when it was time to go into the promised land, for the Hebrews refused to go, afraid that God was sending them not to their abundant life, but to their death. This is Moses' record of that day:

But you were unwilling to go up; you rebelled against the command of the Lord your God. You grumbled in your tents and said, "The Lord hates us; so he brought us out of Egypt to deliver us into the hands of the Amorites to destroy us. (Deuteronomy 1:26-28)

In their fear, the people actually chose to believe that God's motive was to lead them to their harm! Moses pleaded with them, to no avail:

Then I said to you, "Do not be terrified; do not be afraid of them. The Lord your God, who is going before you, will fight for you, as he did for you in Egypt, before your very eyes, and in the desert. There you saw how the Lord your God carried you, as a father carries his son, all the way you went until you reached this place." In spite of this, you did not trust in the Lord your God, who went ahead of you on your journey, in fire by night and in a cloud by day, to search out places for you to camp and to show you the way you should go." (Deuteronomy 1:29-33, emphasis mine).

Their lack of trust led to rebellion, and their rebellion kept them out of the promised land. God had given them his best and was trying to give even more. But to whom much is given, much is expected; God expected and deserved their trust, and they refused it. Their suspicion of God's motives and slanderous assault on his character angered him so much that he withdrew their opportunity to go into the promised land. Instead of receiving God's best, they got to wander in the wilderness until they died; not because God did not love them, but because God ever remained on trial with them.

And here is the most tragic part of it all: they totally misunderstood the heart of God. When we read the record of the Hebrews' wanderings in the book of Numbers, including all of their grumbling about wanting meat instead of manna, we find this stunning glimpse into the private conversations between Moses and God:

He asked the Lord, "Why have you brought this trouble on your servant? What have I done to displease you that you put the burden of all these people on me? Did I conceive all these people? Did I give them birth? Why do you tell me to carry them in my arms, as a nurse carries an infant, to the land you promised on oath to their forefathers? (Numbers 11:11-12)

Not only did God not want to harm these people; he had instructed Moses to lead them as tenderly and lovingly as a nurse with an infant. Is this the heart of a heartless God? Is this the way of a cold, impersonal deity?

We make the same mistake today when we fail to really know our God. Their grumbling and rebellion came out of ignorance, and it cost them the experience of the fullness of God's love and provision in the promised land.

The lesson to be learned is that while fear, disobedience and rebellion cannot separate us from God's love, it can keep us from entering the promised land God has for us, where we experience the best his love has to give. God still loved the Hebrews faithfully even in their rebellion by continually providing food, water and shoes that did not wear out during forty years of desert wandering. The Bible says that he even kept their feet from swelling.[2] Now that's love.

How do you begin to really trust God?

The answer is terrifying: get in the wheelbarrow. Throw yourself in God's arms, leap even though you can't swim, abandon yourself completely to his love. Make up your mind to obey Him no matter what, even when it seems difficult or hurts your heart to do so. This will thrust you into having to trust him as a continual occupation, to get to know him in ways that are impossible from the safe side of faith. Each time you trust, he will answer. Each time he answers, you will experience anew the impenetrable wall of His love around you.

To do this you must overcome your fear of temporary loss, suffering or discomfort. Trusting and obeying God can mean you experience initial loss, suffering, or discomfort. We powerfully dread these things, especially suffering — even when we know it is temporary. Wholehearted trust in the Lord is impossible as long as we dwell on our fears more than his goodness. When you exchange your will for God's you are always trading up, always getting more than what you gave up.

Going back to Ron was difficult for me because I was deeply hurt and knew I was likely to be hurt again as long as the faulty dynamics of our relationship existed. My failure to trust God in submission was based in two things: the fear of being hurt and the fear of losing myself.

---

[2] Deuteronomy 8:4.

The fear of being emotionally hurt is great, and the devil — the real thief of our abundant life — uses this fear to manipulate and rob us. We will go to great lengths to protect ourselves from those who might hurt us, even to the point of disobeying God. Man's determination to avoid emotional pain is a major cause of drug, alcohol, nicotine and even food addictions. We will do almost anything to insulate ourselves from emotional discomfort.

Yet the human soul and spirit is remarkably resilient and readily heals if allowed. We have all been hurt in the course of life, but we survive. Not only do we survive, but we usually get stronger when we have gone through a painful situation. Most of the time the fear of being hurt is often worse than the actual experience of it. No one likes to be hurt, but the truth is, we can recover from most emotional pain without permanent damage to our souls, especially if we belong to the One who can heal our hearts.

We are stronger than we think. And any therapist will tell you that the unpleasant feelings we must face in this life — grief, rejection, disappointment — will pass away more quickly if we allow ourselves to face them than if we stuff or hide from them. When we are motivated by the desire to avoid discomfort, we tend to shut others out, even those who love us. We easily become emotionally handicapped because the same wall that keeps out pain also protects us from the things and people and experiences that give us deep joy.

This is the hardened heart; one that is walled in, insulated from pain, but also from joy. Unfortunately, if you avoid every discomfort or uncertainty, then you also shut out God. This in turn keeps you from experiencing his power and love in the troublesome areas of your life. Your own wall of self-protection prevents you from ever experiencing the wall of God's love.

Is God really Sovereign?

For the purpose of our study, we will assume this question means, is God really in control of everything that concerns me? The answer is yes, but only for those who have come under the shadow of his wing by their obedience.

God's sovereignty is often doubted by those who think that if God were truly all-powerful, he would prevent anything bad from happening to people. Bad things do happen to good people, even Christians. What does God have to say about this subject?

In a biblical nutshell, we live in a world that God gave to man, whom He promised to sustain through the Tree of Life. Man chose instead to sustain himself instead through the Tree of Knowledge of Good and Evil, thereby opening the door for evil to have access to his soul. By this choice man gave his authority over this world to Satan, who now rules over this world and those who are unredeemed. Jesus referred to Satan as "the prince of this world."[3] The horrors of disease, famine, poverty and war are the fruit of man's choices, not the acts or disinterest of a capricious God.

Yet we can do something about these things, and God's power can intervene. Though Jesus legally destroyed the power of the devil at the cross, he is still at work in the world. The task of literally overcoming the works and power of the devil has been given to us, the church, who has not yet reached her full strength. Today, it is through people in covenant with Jesus that the Lord exercises authority upon the earth.

God gave us the name of Jesus to use, and free access to his throne of grace, and the power of the Holy Spirit. He asks us to love men so much that we make ourselves available as conduits through which God's will is released on the earth as it is in heaven. The bottom line is that if evil is on the earth, it is because we released it by giving ourselves to it. If evil prevails upon the earth, it is because we allow it, through our passivity, our failure to pray, to love, to stand for righteousness, to stand against the schemes of the devil.

Still, the question remains: how can a sovereign God keep his promises to his born-again child, promises of safety, blessing, and deliverance from evil, when the child lives in a fallen world full of people who do not submit to Him? The answer lies in understanding that neither the exercise of man's free will nor any of Satan's works are greater than the will of God for the person who trusts in Him.

Ephesians 1:11 declares that God *works out everything in conformity with the purpose of his will.* In other words, God has the final say in all matters; he gets the last word. Neither man's will nor the devil's will can override or interfere with the will of God. The accomplishment of God's perfect will does not depend upon the specific things which man does or does not do. If our ability to receive the abundant life of God could be thwarted by the devil or the people around us, then how truly powerful would our God be?

---

3 See John 12:31, 14:30 and 16:11. The Greek word for prince here means *ruler.*

Although God gives all men free will, the free will of men cannot thwart his ability to fulfill his purposes and keep his promises to those who look to him in faith. It is, for instance, his will to bless his children. If he wants to bless you with a certain job, but the employer does not cooperate with God and hire you, then God will continue to position you for a great job until you receive it, or give you great joy in a lesser job. This conforms with His sovereign will to bless you.

When a person trusts in God enough to surrender to His will, he gives God freedom to exercise all of his power on that person's behalf. He brings himself under God's protective authority, a place of refuge where evil cannot overcome God's goodness. In such a state of surrender, this Christian is where God wants him to be, doing what he asks him to do. If a person has allowed God to order his steps, he can be sure that either his steps will lead him away from all evil, or that if God allows evil to cross his path he can rest in the fact that God will fulfill his purposes and bring him through safely. As long as it was God's will for the Apostle Paul to remain on this earth, he survived everything: stonings, beatings, shipwrecks, deprivations, betrayals, and even death itself.[4]

Furthermore, this is true for the one who actually misses God's will but does it in faith; in other words, he takes a course of action that he thinks is God's will, but has somehow not perceived God's will rightly. God's love is bigger than our mistakes. The Bible begs us to relax and trust God to cover us in our honest attempts to walk with him. When we miss it, God weaves our mistakes into his plan to bless us. When our weaknesses overtake us so that Satan tempts us away from God's will, we open the door for the devil to afflict us, and he rarely misses an opportunity. But when we turn back to God even this He will use to fulfill his purposes to ultimately bring us to our personal promised land and show us His glory. That's just the way God is.

Is your understanding an insult to the character of God?

It has been theorized that man has four basic needs which drive him, one of which is *the need to know*. It is easy to see the truth in this. We have such a need to know the truth that if we don't know, we tend to make something up just so we'll know! This is what becomes our fears, worries and

---

[4] Acts 14:19-20 records that Paul was stoned and left for dead, but when the disciples prayed over him he got up again and resumed his ministry travels the next day!

assumptions. This is what led man to decide that the world was flat and that a man could actually travel to the edge of it and fall off! In the absence of a way to discover the truth, man made up the truth so he would have something to believe. Man needed to know.

There will always be times we will not know what God is up to. Why did God let this thing happen? Why didn't he heal this person? When is he going to answer my prayer? I need to know! Underlying these questions is the issue of God's character and trustworthiness. We often decide that if this thing or that thing happens, then God loves me. We put God on trial and commit the arrogance of determining what He must do to be worthy of our trust.

The implication is that if God didn't answer a certain prayer, then maybe He just doesn't answer prayer. If He didn't heal a certain person, maybe He really isn't all powerful, or doesn't heal today, or just doesn't exist. Maybe God's Word doesn't really mean what it says.

It is imperative that you recognize this language, which is the language of doubt. It is the language the devil used when he spoke to Eve in the Garden, where he planted seeds of doubt in her mind by asking, "Did God really say…"

Proverbs 3:5 says it best: *Trust in the Lord with all your heart, and lean not on your own understanding.*

Entering God's rest.

The most crucial thing we can learn from those Hebrews under Moses is that your personal promised land will only be gained through confidently resting in God's love. We are often no different than the Hebrews, failing to really trust in God while going through some trial. Considering the magnitude of His love for us, this is both incredible and tragic.

When you trust God completely, trials of life lose their ability to torment you. By trusting Him wholeheartedly you can experience the same amazing grace the Apostle Paul rested in, as he exulted in 2 Corinthians 7:4: *"In all our troubles, my joy knows no bounds."* A member of the tribe of Benjamin, Paul ultimately walked in the prophetic blessing Moses spoke over that tribe at the end of his life:

"Let the beloved of the Lord rest secure in him, for he shields him all day long, and the one the Lord loves rests between his shoulders." (Deuteronomy 33:12).

These words paint a picture of what the New Testament calls *entering God's rest*, the subject of Hebrews chapters three and four. In fact, the author of the book begins by warning the reader against being like the pilgrims in the wilderness:

And to whom did God swear that they would never enter his rest if not to those who disobeyed? So we see that they were not able to enter, because of their unbelief. (Hebrews 3:18-19).

The footnote of the New International Version says of verse 18 that the word "disobeyed" could also be translated "disbelieved." Apparently, these are synonymous in the original language used, and no wonder; disbelief is what causes us to disobey! What is it they disbelieved? They did not believe in God's goodness and love. They did not trust God; therefore they did not obey Him. To disobey keeps us from entering God's rest and the personal promised land He has prepared for us, even in this life. As the writer concludes by begging us,

Therefore, since the promise of entering his rest still stands, let us be careful that none of you be found to have fallen short of it. For we also have had the gospel preached to us, just as they did; but the message they heard was of no value to them, because those who heard did not combine it with faith. Now we who have believed enter that rest... (Hebrews 4:1-3).

Let us, therefore, make every effort to enter that rest, so that no one will fall by following their example of disobedience. (Hebrews 4:11).

When you withhold trust from God, you only rob yourself. Trusting in God means choosing to believe that no matter what anyone else in your life does, says, or believes, God is able to bring about his will as promised to you, and that his will is to cleanse, bless, and transform you and your life into something lovely and glorious. In short, his motive is to give you life.

You must decide for yourself if God can be trusted and until you do, God will be on trial with you. Make no mistake, the issue is His character. A

Christian is called to discover who God is, and then live by faith in Him, not in having things a certain way. When you really trust God, you can bear not to know because you are trusting the One who does, and he is at work.

What kind of woman will I be? I will be a woman who trusts in her God, who rests in his love. Because God is no longer on trial with me, I can surrender to his ways and his commands with my whole heart. I will get in God's wheelbarrow and let him carry me to my personal promised land.

Reflecting on Chapter 18

This chapter teaches the importance of wholehearted trust in the character and motives of God.

* *What personal truths do you hold close and live by? Do these truths agree with God's Word?*

* *Think of areas where you are pretty certain that your will for you runs contrary to God's desires. Do you trust God enough to trade in your will for His?*

* *Is God on trial with you? In what areas do you still feel the need for him to prove himself to you? Talk to God about these, honestly expressing them. Journal about your issues and any responses you receive.*

* *Ask the Holy Spirit to reveal areas where you do not trust God. Ask Him reveal His truth about them.*

Deeper work

* *For a season continue to ask the Lord to reveal areas where you do not trust him. As these issues become clear to you, journal them, and confess them to God, asking His forgiveness and for the grace to trust Him in that area.*

* *For each issue revealed above, ask the Lord to lead you to the truth in His Word, so you may exchange his truth for your "knowing."*

As To The Lord

Wives, submit to your husbands as to the Lord. For the husband is the head of the wife as Christ is the head of the church, his body, of which he is the Savior. Now as the church submits to Christ, so also wives should submit to their husbands in everything. (Ephesians 5:22-24)

We could ignore the other scriptures on submission much easier than this one, because this one implies that submission to the husband should be approached just like submission to the Lord! Any discussion on submission must address this command, because it is the 600 pound elephant sitting in every Christian living room.

Our task is to understand what the Holy Spirit was asking of us when he inspired these words through Paul. What does it mean to submit to a husband as you would to the Lord? I believe that primarily it refers to your attitude.

It is safe to say that most women have a very different attitude towards their husbands than they do towards Jesus. To begin with, Jesus is given the presumption — rightly so — that he is a leader worthy of being followed, but rarely do we give this presumption to our flawed, very human partners.

Wisdom tells us God did not design marriage this way because He thinks your husband is as infallible as Christ. Still, it seems outlandish that God has told us to submit to him as we would submit to the perfect Lord of Lords. We want to say, *God, how on earth can you expect me to submit to my human husband as if he were Jesus?*

What was God thinking?

Wholehearted submission "as to the Lord" alarms the average woman because it is obvious to her that the man she is married to is not exactly like Jesus, and it would be wrong to suggest that any wife should unquestioningly submit to any man who may be totally captive to an evil lifestyle or who would cause her to sin. This would make a mockery of God's wisdom and ways. However, it would be equally missing the mark to say that God meant for a woman to submit only to the Christlike husband.

What do we see when we look at our men? At worst, we see an unbeliever who has no regard for God, doesn't intend to have any regard for God, may be terribly irresponsible and in general, a lousy husband. (Again, if your husband is abusive, get help immediately.)

At best we may have a man pursuing meaningful relationship with God, yet still fully human, subject to making mistakes and weaknesses — far from perfect in some areas. Whereas we expect and rely on the perfection of Jesus, we have no such expectation or hope in a human husband.

Yet this command does not give conditions or exceptions; it doesn't let anyone off the hook, even the woman married to an unbeliever. Women married to unbelieving or seriously backslidden husbands tend to excuse themselves from obedience to God's word in regards to this command. The flawed logic they follow is that they are not expected to submit to a husband because he is not loving them as Christ loved the church. In other words, *"When my husband acts like Jesus Christ, then I must submit to him, but not otherwise."* There is no basis in scripture to justify this attitude.

The first problem with this is that a woman with this attitude puts herself in a position to choose when to honor her husband and when not to, which essentially removes Jesus from his position as Lord. There is no escaping the fact that when you refuse to honor your husband's headship you are essentially refusing to honor the one who gave the command to do so.

Yes, there are absolutely times when one should not submit to a husband, which we will cover later. But for the sake of this discussion, dealing with the average wife relating to the average husband, our hearts should always be set on finding ways to obey the Lord's commands, not trying to explain them away or excuse ourselves from them.

The devil is in the details.

We have a tendency to focus on specifics: Do I submit to my husband in this, do I submit in that? The answer is, of course, pray; ask the Holy Spirit to guide you.

Meanwhile, understand that God's command to submit *"as unto the Lord"* is not about specifics so much as it is about motives of the heart, about having an attitude or disposition that is appropriate for anyone under the leadership of another. It is not commanding us to do the ridiculous, which is to obey any man as if he were Jesus Christ himself. To live by such an interpretation violates God's other commands, including *"You shall have no other gods (masters) before me!"*

To say you should submit "as unto the Lord" is to say that your response to the leadership of your husband should be the same as your response to the leadership of Jesus your Lord. It's all about attitude. For example, when you think of submitting to Jesus, is it with dread and fear that he will lead you into harm? Do you presume from the outset that Jesus doesn't know what he's doing? Do you continually resent his direction and want to argue with him about it? Are you likely to assume Jesus is wrong in expressing his will? Not likely. (If you answered yes to any of these questions, please reread the chapter on trusting God again and stay there until something changes!)

But is he worthy?

God undoubtedly wants a man to be worthy of his wife's trusting submission, but nowhere in Scripture will you find him letting you off the hook if such is not the case. (Believe me, we have all looked.) So even though it is appropriate to take into account whether a man is worthy of his wife's submission, we must be very careful. The determination of whether a husband is worthy of following is highly subjective. Such a judgment would undoubtedly differ from one woman to the next and could even can change from day to day depending on the wife's mood.

How do we decide if and when a man is worthy? There is only one sure way, and that is to learn how to walk with the Holy Spirit and in His counsel, focused on understanding the Lord's thoughts and ways regarding our own situation. His personal guidance is our best protection against life-robbing legalism, and needless suffering. We would serve the Lord much better by being less concerned with a husband's worthiness and more with our own worthiness to be co-heirs.

The hope of God's design is that a woman experience the joy of relating to a man worthy of her respect. The truth is that the man of the house doesn't always do it right. He isn't perfect and may occasionally make very big mistakes. He may not act respectable all the time, much less be worthy of honor.

Still, these facts do not alter God's ways. Though it is God's perfect will that the husband handle his position with honor, his failure to do so does not automatically free the wife to deny him his position as head of the house. You will find no scriptures to support such an attitude.

Godly submission flows out of character that honors.

In her most excellent book "Honor, What Love Looks Like," Fawn Parish asks the question, "Does God expect us to honor people who are not honorable?" She prepares us for the answer by teaching us that honor as applied to men in the Bible has three levels. Quoting now[1]:

"The first level is intrinsic honor. It is honor possessed by God and given to every human being. This honor is an attribute of God and He freely bestows it on us simply by creating us in His image. The second level is honor based on character. The third level is honor based on performance."

The first level, Ms. Parish says, is that which "God gives to every person, regardless of merit, character or performance."

This is a very significant truth for us to understand. We have all been highly honored by God without deserving a bit of it. Being the first level of honor, it is the most common, being given to all mankind.

Ms. Parish adds later, "The essence of honor is found in the personality and character of God. In fact, he is honor personified. On the other hand, Satan personifies dishonor."

We always tend to make the other person's behavior and character the issue, but the primary issue for any Christian is always to be like Jesus. Your character and your behavior should be your main concern. You are called to be the kind of woman who shows respect to her husband and honors his headship because that is the way women of God behave.

---

[1] Page 29, Honor, What Love Looks Like by Fawn Parish; Renew Books, 1999

The woman God designed is always inclined to treat her husband honorably. God wants you to honor the man himself if at all possible, but in any case to honor the position which God has called him to as head of the family. A woman can give respect to her husband in the same way God gives it to us: as a gift of grace. God treats us with a dignity and respect we are rarely worthy of. Let us be women who are rich in grace, like Jesus.

God gave this command to women while fully aware they would be married to imperfect men, a fact which is apparently a non-issue with Him. Please remember these things about your Father in heaven:

He would not ask you to do something you cannot do.

Whatever He asks of you He will give you the ability to do.

He is greater than your husband's weaknesses and fully aware of them.

He is greater than *your* weaknesses, and is fully aware of them.

Attitude is everything.

Jesus condemned the attitude of the Pharisees because they performed the law perfectly, but their hearts were far from God and therefore they totally misunderstood his purposes. In their self-serving attitude they misapplied the law so that what was intended to bless the people became a burden and the thief of real abundant life.

It is the attitude underlying our submission that God cares about, the stance of a heart in relation to a leader and his will. Of one thing we can be sure: "as to the Lord" means with an attitude of sincere yieldedness. It is easy to be outwardly submissive while secretly scorning it. Such submission is really a sham!

I love the story of the little boy who was riding in the back seat of the car who insisted on standing up. His father kept telling him to sit down, and the little boy refused. Finally, the father threatened him with such severity that the little boy slid down defiantly into the seat, and announced, *"I'll sit down, but I'm standing up on the inside!"*

This story illustrates my attitude when I first tried to be submissive. I attempted to put it into practice before I accepted it wholeheartedly. I wanted to be submissive because God said I should, I wanted to be spiritually correct, but I sure didn't like it. Inwardly I resented submitting to Ron and had sort of a perpetual pout going on inside about it. I worked hard outwardly at submitting to him but threw it up to him frequently, bragging about my behavior.

However, Ron didn't seem to appreciate my efforts. He wasn't responding at all as I expected; in fact, he even seemed to resent what I was doing. I was smiling sweetly outside but inside I was thinking, *How dare you resent my great sacrifice of submission!*

One day I was complaining about this to a close friend of mine who had lived with us for several months and witnessed our lives up close. After listening to me boast about my new submissiveness one day she shocked me by declaring, "Toni, you're about as submissive as a rattlesnake!"

I didn't like hearing this at the time, but after I quit fuming at my friend, I had to admit it was true. Her words pierced my heart, and punctured my self-deception. I had to repent. I praise God for friends who are so committed to loving God and loving me that they will tell me the truth when I can't see it for myself.

The Lord later showed me that my initial attempts at submission were really just a new way to manipulate my husband. Instead of the attitude that he should do things my way, it became *I'm submitted to you now, so you should appreciate it enough to give me what I want!* I was still motivated by the need to have my way and my fear that Ron wouldn't do it right.

It is very easy to fall into this trap: "I'm being submissive now, so you have to be the kind of husband I want!" Or, a woman may simply give in and submit in small things while continuing to subtly have her way in the things that matter most. A woman who doesn't really want to submit can be very creative in finding ways to use submission itself to control and manipulate her husband. To my shame, I caught myself doing that several times, until the Lord showed me that I had not given up control to God and my husband, I was merely playing the same game, just with new rules.

"Rattlesnake submission," as it is now called (and laughed about) in my home, is easily discerned by men. You won't fool your husband long. My husband wasn't fooled, and his discernment of my real attitude was the reason he didn't appreciate my efforts.

Real submission is cloaked in sincere respect, not resentment. I have to confess that trying to live by this command challenged me more than anything else I have done. It has exposed fears and judgments and wrong attitudes in my heart I didn't know existed. Though uncomfortable at times,

I treasure the whole process because it has grown me in ways I now love and shown me things about God's heart I might never have seen otherwise.

Submission should be motivated by love.

Jesus is our greatest example of what the submissive heart looks like. Jesus' submission was motivated by love for the Father and mankind. It was entirely devoid of legalistic self-righteousness, manipulation or resentment. It was an act of love, for he said, ...*the world must learn that I love the Father and that [therefore] I do exactly what my Father has commanded me.*[2]

It is in the same spirit of love that we are asked to be submissive to a husband. A woman who resents submission will always find it a burden, not a blessing, and it may look ugly. I know from experience how very different it feels to yield to another person as a gift of gracious love rather than a begrudged duty.

It hardly needs to be said that this is as true of our submission to the Lord Jesus as it is of a husband. Your love for the Lord makes you want to honor Him. Jesus made it clear that obedience is the only way to honor Him and prove our love. Submission is an act of love, and it will fail as long as it remains nothing more than a duty.

To the woman reading this book who feels she has no love left for her husband. I want to encourage you with two things. First, I have been in your situation. I know from experience that if you want a new love for your husband and ask the Lord for it, He is willing and able to answer this prayer and help you love again. Secondly, until your heart is established in love again, you can give honor and respect (with the help of the Holy Spirit), for the sake of your love for Jesus.

Never forget that honoring the husband's headship is something you do for the Lord. The Amplified Bible version of Ephesians 5:22 says: *Wives, be subject — be submissive and adapt yourselves — to your own husbands as (a service) to the Lord.* This truth is confirmed by Colossians 3:23-24:

> *Whatever you do, work at it with all your heart, as working for the Lord, not for men, since you know that you will receive an inheritance from the Lord as a reward. It is the Lord Christ you are serving.*

---

[2] John 14:31.

Submission and co-rulership go hand-in-hand.

When God calls a woman to be the submissive half of a marriage partnership, he is not asking her to be a passive, silent partner. She was created to be a suitable helper, an equal co-heir, a partner to work alongside and share in the process of leadership. The woman was created by God with unique strengths that her man needs to carry out his leadership.

Ms. Parish also observed in her book on honor, *"I believe God is placing within women today a passion and desire to see men enjoy all that God desires for them. Honor desires God's fullness for all that God loves."*[3] The wife God designed understands her responsibility to nurture and even enable her husband's leadership.

This mirrors our relationship with Christ. We are not servile puppets to the Lord; rather he shares his own wisdom with us and invites us — even requires us — to participate in his rulership of the world. We are asked and expected to learn how to rule by his side. We have free access to the throne of grace and are invited to intercede in the Lord's affairs with men. Our submission to his leadership enables the Lord's strength and wisdom to be seen on earth as it is in heaven.

People usually try to live up to the way we treat them.

People really do want to live up to the faith we put in them and the honor we show them. I was deeply impressed with the story of a woman in a small town married to an adulterer. This woman suspected what everyone else knew about her husband, that he was unfaithful to her, but she chose to keep silent about it. Rather than give in to anger or bitterness, she always treated her husband with kindness and respect. In other words, she extended him grace instead of judgment.

After observing how well she treated her husband one day, some of her friends decided to tell her what a scoundrel he was, in case she didn't know. She astounded them when she informed them that she believed in her husband, that he was a good man and she would not tolerate them speaking about him so. She was unaware that her husband had come in the back door and overheard it all.

---

[3] Ibid, page 132

Knowing that she could not be ignorant of his indiscretions, the stunned husband was shamed by the way his wife stood up for him. Because she demonstrated such faith in him, he gave up his adulteries and determined to live up to the way she honored him in her heart. Her attitude made him want to be a better man.

I do not share this story to suggest that a woman should not confront an unfaithful husband. What was right for this woman might be very wrong for another. I only wish to illustrate what I've seen proven many times: people want to live up to how you treat them.

On the other hand, a man will usually become antagonistic towards a wife who consistently treats him with disrespect or scorn. Men are incredibly sensitive to and affected by the attitudes their wives have towards them. If a wife shows confidence in her husband's ability to lead the family, he will be encouraged and inspired. If the wife expects her husband will mess everything up, his lose his confidence and become discouraged, perhaps even bitter or resentful. He will eventually give up.

Many a husband has abdicated leadership in his home, yielding to the discouragement of a wife who continually found fault with him. A worthy wife helps a husband to discover his strength rather than attempt to be it for him. A worthy wife covers her husband's weaknesses rather than magnify them.

Pastor John Piper wisely observes: "… a wife's submission would take different forms depending on the quality of a husband's leadership. This can be seen best if we define submission not in terms of specific behaviors, but as a *disposition* to yield to the husband's authority and an *inclination* to follow his leadership. This is important to do because no submission of one human being to another is absolute. The husband does not replace Christ as the woman's supreme authority. She must never follow her husband's leadership into sin. But even where a Christian wife may have to stand with Christ against the sinful will of her husband, she can still have a spirit of submission — a disposition to yield. She can show by her attitude and behavior that she does not like resisting his will and that she longs for him to forsake sin and lead in righteousness so that her disposition to honor him as head can again produce harmony."[4]

---

[4] Page 47, "Recovering Biblical Manhood and Womanhood; a Response to Evangelical Feminism," a collection of essays edited by John Piper and Wayne Grudem. 1991, Crossway Books.

"As to the Lord... in everything."

> *Now as the church submits to Christ, so also wives should submit to their husbands in everything. Ephesians 5:24*

You cannot choose to let your husband be the head in some things, and then take over leadership in other areas. Would you do that to Jesus? (In point of fact, we do, but we know this is wrong.) Here again, if you're going to honor God's command, you have to resign from being the manager of issues, the decider of who is the boss of what.

This can be a difficult situation for spiritual women married to unspiritual men. It is tempting for such women often seek counsel about family issues from their spiritual friends rather than go to the husband. A husband may make his will known about a certain matter, yet the wife fears to trust his decision because she doesn't believe he hears from God or prays about what to do.

A woman once came to us and said, "My husband thinks we should buy this house, but I'm not sure it's God. I prayed, but I'm just getting confusion. What I should do?" In this instance we believed that the woman had probably already heard from God through her husband's decision and if so, her difficulty in hearing God's voice may have resulted from her refusal to honor him and in second-guessing his decision.

When God has already revealed his will to you through the husband's sense of direction, a continued search for God's will in another direction will usually result in confusion. Be cautious of any counsel that leads you against the will of your husband, unless he has asked you do something which violates your conscience or exposes you to danger. Remember that God created man and appointed him the leader of the family, so somewhere within that man of yours is the God-designed ability to carry out his job.

We have repeatedly seen God lead a woman through her husband even when he is unaware of God's influence. It is really not hard for God to do, and probably very common except in cases where the husband has stubbornly set his will against God, is always under the influence of drugs or alcohol or participating in occult practices.

Even so, God can make Himself and His will known to anyone, any time, anywhere. He is God! His ability to influence and direct the hearts of unsaved people is well documented in the Bible, and something we have witnessed repeatedly for the sake of believing wives.

While it is true that any man can only completely fulfill his potential as a leader when he follows Christ, I have seen ample evidence that God will help the unbelieving husband be a good leader for the sake of the believing wife and their children. We have the testimony of 1 Corinthians 7:14 that God does influence the heart of an unbelieving spouse.

Even though I am married to a godly man, I have periodically mistrusted the direction he was going or some decision he had made. I cannot tell you how many times the Lord has backed him up. There are times when Ron is right in God's will and I — woman of faith that I am — don't know it. I have also seen occasions when Ron was wrong but because he acted in faith, God honored it and made it all work out or turned it all into a blessing. God's heart is to bless and redeem. When will we get the message that God is bigger than our hearts and our mistakes?

Without a doubt there will be times when you will be in the right, you will be the one hearing from God, and if you want to make it easy for God to bring that forward, then cultivate honor between you and your husband.

The real issue is always Jesus.

A determination to honor Jesus inevitably demands sacrifice. The abundant life he promises is not an add-on, it is a trade-in. You will always have to give up something to have more of his life. When I purposed in my heart to honor the Lord by being a submissive wife, I found out for the first time what it truly means to take up one's cross (the instrument of death to self) and follow Jesus.

I assure you that there will be times when submission to another will require you to die to yourself in some way. Frankly, it is relatively easy to deny self in lots of little ways that don't require much real sacrifice even while maintaining a strong will, ready to stand up for what it wants in the important matters. God won't let you get away with that. Not because He is mean or demanding or legalistic, but because his goal is to see Christ formed in you — which is your hope of glory and beauty and being what you were created for.

Once a wife decides to submit to her husband, it won't take long for strongholds of self-will to surface, exposing areas where self is still on the throne, trying to call the shots. Women who think they don't have a rebellious bone in their body will be shocked at what they will cling to rather than let a husband have his way!

Real submission takes place in the heart first. You must first surrender to God in full trust and be willing for him to change your heart. The woman who is not submissive to her husband cannot claim to be surrendered to the Lord who gives the command. To think otherwise is to deceive oneself. Choosing to trust the husband because Jesus asks you to is choosing to trust Jesus himself.

The first step in submitting to your husband as you would to the Lord, is to acknowledge that you are incapable of doing so without His help. It's like everything else — part of the plan to grow you in complete dependence upon Jesus.

Be wholehearted in submission. Give yourself to it; relax about it. Don't sit around worrying about when to submit, but trust the Holy Spirit to guide you in all things. That's his job, and he's good at it.

Ask the Holy Spirit to help you in your day-to-day relations with your husband. You can do no better than to seek the wisdom of The Wonderful Counselor, who knows the perfect way to relate to your man and can show you how to live respectfully towards him. We can be confident that God will always give us the grace to obey his commands and honor his Word.

Reflecting on Chapter 19

This chapter helps us understand that the command to submit to a husband as to the Lord is less about specific actions than it is about a wife's attitude towards a leader that God has appointed and honoring the authority He has given them.

❖   *What attitudes do you see in yourself in regards to honoring your husband? Ask yourself, "Would I respond to the Lord like this?" Journal your answers and dialogue honestly with the Lord about them.*

❖ *As you relate to your husband from now on, ask the Holy Spirit to make you alert to wrong attitudes towards him. Ask the Holy Spirit to inspire in you the attitude that is right in the sight of God.*

Chapter 20

Issues and Answers

Your goal in submission should be to walk in wisdom and righteousness. Simply put, it should be done in a way that is fitting for the situation and the man you is married to, the right thing to do at the right time to honor God and release His goodness. Only through the personal guidance of the Holy Spirit can you carry this out, and hopefully you are developing such a relationship with Him. But while you are learning to know the Lord in this personal student/teacher way, we will attempt to answer the most commonly asked questions on issues that come up with submission.

What if my husband won't take the lead in our family?

There are actually husbands who resist or dislike a wife's new attempts at submission. There can be two reasons for this. Number one, we get comfortable with what is familiar, even if it is something we don't like. We become accustomed to and even secure in knowing how someone is likely to treat us. It's comfortable knowing how they will react to certain things. When we break an established patterns of responding to another it is hard to know how to react to them. When you change what you do, I have to figure out how to change.

Secondly, if a man has never felt the full weight of being the head of the family, it may terrify him at first. If your husband resists your new submissiveness and isn't ready to lead the family, go slowly. Don't go home and announce that everything is going to change. Be wise and considerate, giving him time to adjust to your new attitude. Don't overwhelm him by suddenly dumping all decisions in his lap. Rather, gently begin to affirm your husband's leadership, watching for opportunities to express confidence in him. Don't go to him and say, *"Tell me what to do!"* Instead, say, *"Here's the problem, what do you think we should do about it?"* If the children usually come to you for permission to do things, begin sending them to Dad. Let the children see you consulting their father.

If your husband wants you to make decisions about something, do so; this too is submission. The aim of submission is not for the husband to take care of everything, but to carry the responsibility for the welfare and moral direction of the family. In some families, the wife may have training which makes her the obvious choice for handling certain things, like the family budget. Some women are better at handling money than their husbands and if you're both comfortable with you making those decisions, fine.

Proverbs 31 paints a portrait of a wife with many skills, who is deeply involved in the business and management of the family. Submission does not ask a woman to give up using all of her gifts and talents and thrust the job upon a man who lacks them. God relates to each family member according to their unique gifts and does not expect every family to conduct their affairs exactly alike. So don't try to do submission the way your best friend does it.

If you must take responsibility for the children's spiritual guidance, do it respectfully. Don't try to force your husband to take the children to church or read the Bible with them; quietly do it yourself. Pray for God to work on his heart in this regard. If he won't go to church, don't try to pressure or shame him every Sunday. Invite him just often enough to let him know you'd enjoy his coming with you, but don't nag him about it.

Often, the best way to get an unchurched husband into church is to find social ways for him to get acquainted with the pastor or other men in the church, perhaps at a men's breakfast or a church picnic. If your husband feels that you and your church life are separate from him, he will feel left out. If he senses an attitude of superiority in you because of your faith, he will resist going to church for fear that everyone else will feel the same way about him as you do. Only a sincere interest in him as a person on the part of other church members will draw him in. He needs to develop his own relationships among your Christian friends. Find men who share your husband's interests and invite those couples to your home so that your man can get acquainted on his own "turf."

Follow the Holy Spirit in what's right for you, not someone else.

How each woman submits to her husband is a highly personal matter. I cannot look at how my friend feels she is led to respond to her husband and apply it to my life. It does not fit. The faith walk is intensely personal, because God know our hearts even better than we do. He knows what we need for growth. God has called me to a degree of submission to my husband that is not always appropriate for women married to immature or ungodly men. We must acknowledge that a woman's ability to submit to her husband will be affected by the kind of leadership he gives to the family.

We knew a woman married to an unbeliever whose irresponsible behavior made her life absolutely miserable. The woman loved Jesus with all her heart, and, wanting to live according to His Word, was determined to submit to her husband in everything. He did not abuse her physically or verbally in any traditional sense. However, he was so completely selfish and unloving, so unconcerned about her comfort and safety that submitting to him often put her in terrible situations, such as losing her home and having to live out of a car for a while. But she kept on, believing that this was honoring the Lord.

After years of emotional starvation nearly crushed her spirit, and much agonizing and counsel with her pastor, this woman finally left her husband. She waited a long time to write and tell me about her decision, fearing I would disapprove of her choice after trying to follow my example. But I felt no disapproval; my heart went out to her, and as I searched inwardly for the witness of the Holy Spirit, all I sensed from Him was compassion and mercy, not judgment. I believe the Lord in his grace and mercy actually led her away from a man possessed of a selfish and evil heart. God knew whether that man would ever change or not. We must not judge one another's experience and walk before God.

How far do I carry submission to my husband?

It is not right for me to tell you how far to submit to a husband. You must learn to seek the Holy Spirit yourself, and the counsel of godly men and women who are a witness to your life, character, strengths and weaknesses, and those of your husband. I will say that God never intended for a woman to submit absolutely in all circumstances to any man regardless of his character or behavior.

Jesus' conduct on this earth illustrates that truth very clearly. He upheld the law, but knew when not to join in the lawful stoning of a woman caught in adultery. He knew when to be quiet before the religious leaders and when to confront them. Knowing when to submit and when not to is a matter between each woman and her God. There will be occasions when it would be wrong for you to submit to the husband — such as when doing so would place your life or your children's lives in danger.

It is always wrong for you to knowingly sin. We have the negative example of Sapphira in the book of Acts to verify for us that a woman is not protected from God's judgment of her sin because she follows her husband into it. Our highest authority is God's Word, so do not obey your husband if it will cause you to sin by violating God's commands in scripture. When you become a Christian you should accept the authority of God's Word to tell you what to do and how to act.

After the authority of God's Word, the next highest authority is your own conscience as you understand His personal will for you. Your conscience before God has more authority to guide you than any human being has over you. Paul explain this thoroughly in the 14th Chapter of Romans where he acknowledges that in our personal experience of knowing God, we would not all follow Him identically. Some Christians drink wine, some don't; some consider it a sin to gamble, some don't. Paul called these issues *"disputable matters."*

Paul implies that what we believe on these issues is not as important as whether we live according to what we do believe. Each person should obey what he believes the Lord requires of him and surrender to the guidance of their own conscience before God. We must not rely on the conscience of others, because they cannot answer for us when we face the Lord. This is why we have been given the mind of Christ, so we will always be able to answer the question, *"What does God want me to do?"*

Our refuge from error is twofold: being thoroughly familiar with the Bible, and drawing close to the heart of God so we may know his intent and purposes. It is only through regular fellowship with the Holy Spirit that your conscience becomes sensitive to what God wants of you in any given situation. Just remember that as the Holy Spirit leads you in your personal walk with God, He will never contradict the Bible's truths.

Be sure, as you read your Bible, that you do not form your doctrines based upon a single verse. All of the crucial truths of God's heart are established by clear repetition in the Bible, so that everything is *"established by the testimony of two or three witnesses."* Most of the great error we have seen committed by Christians begin with making assumptions based upon a single verse in the Bible while neglecting to consider the whole counsel God gives about a subject. Divorce is a good example of this, as well as the subject following this one.

What if my husband forbids me to go to church?

This question is a good example of one of those *"disputable matters"* Paul mentions in Romans 14:1. Therefore, your conscience will have to answer this for you. I can only offer my opinion based upon my conscience before God. Sometimes a husband makes it clear that he does not want his wife to go to church. How is a believing woman to respond to this?

Some believe that it is a sin to not go to church based on Hebrews 10:25:

> *Let us not give up meeting together, as some are in the habit of doing, but let us encourage one another—and all the more as you see the Day approaching.*

There is nothing in this verse alone that justifies the assumption that not going to church is a sin. This is not a command, but an encouragement and a warning to those who would abandon church or underestimate the importance of fellowship with others who have faith in Christ. The context is that of pointing out the things which will help us to stay strong in our faith, as we see from the two verses just preceding it:

> *Let us hold unswervingly to the hope we profess, for he who promised is faithful. And let us consider how we may spur one another on towards love and good deeds. (Hebrews 10:23-24)*

Certainly, God wants you to have fellowship and be spurred on by the faith of others; but it is a big leap from this truth to asserting that it is a moral sin to be absent from church on occasion or for a season.

Church attendance is God's will for you, but so is honoring your husband. Which is the higher priority to God? I suggest that the ultimate goal of winning your husband to the Lord is the far greater purpose of God than your uninterrupted attendance in church.

Having said this, I would also point out that in line with my strong belief in personally following God, remember that only God knows your strength and what you need. Only God knows when one woman's isolation from the fellowship would spur her to greater personal study, worship and faith, and when another woman's isolation would weaken her and leave her backslidden.

Experience shows us that the devil often uses this issue to incite an unbelieving husband to test his wife. The husband may feel he is competing with God and/or the church for his wife's devotion. It is not unusual for a husband to deeply resent the church or the God who seems to have robbed him of his wife's attention.

When the wife of such a man defies her husband to go to church she may reinforce these feelings and push the husband even further away from God, which is just what the devil wants. Often when a woman yields to her husband for a while, he soon has a change of heart and even may want to go with her. By honoring her husband, the wife powerfully reinforces her love for him and destroys the devil's lie that church is robbing him.

On the other hand, a different man who resists his wife's attendance at church might be most influenced for God through her respectful assertion that she feels compelled to honor God by participating in worship and the fellowship, or strengthened by the preaching. Perhaps the joy and good disposition it brings out in her will make him jealous to have this fellowship for himself.

Only the Lord knows the heart of the husband. There is a time to submit to a husband's wishes in this, and a time not to. Our goal is to develop a wise heart that knows how to respond to the authority God has placed over us:

> Since a king's word is supreme, who can say to him, "What are you doing?" Whoever obeys his command will come to no harm, and the wise heart will know the proper time and procedure. (Ecclesiastes 8:4-5).

If your heart tells you that God would be pleased if you would forego church attendance for a season, remember that the strengthening benefits of church attendance can be found in other ways. The woman who really desires to grow strong in the Lord, to be trained in spiritual matters, and be strengthened by the fellowship of other believers can usually obtain these things through personal study and informal fellowship groups like Bible studies and cell group meetings. One can meet with a personal mentor or study partner. In the internet era one can be connected numerous ways to other believers for prayer and encouragement and enjoy worship and great preaching as well.

Should I express my opinion in making family decisions?

In a good marriage teamwork exists between husband and wife in which both partners share input on making decisions, but both know that the final responsibility for major decisions affecting the family rests upon the husband. There should be mutual respect, freedom to communicate, a sharing of wisdom and perspective. A good leader does not make all the decisions himself, but asks for and considers the input of his wife. The judgment and wisdom of a loving, trusting wife are great assets to a man. But as leader and protector of the family, God ultimately holds the husband accountable for the direction of the family.

Turning again to *Recovering Biblical Manhood and Womanhood*: *"... headship [does not consist] in a series of directives to the wife. Leadership is not synonymous with unilateral decision making. In fact, in a good marriage, leadership consists mainly in taking responsibility to establish a pattern of interaction that honors both husband and wife (and children) as a store of varied wisdom for family life. Headship bears the primary responsibility for the moral design and planning in the home, but the development of that design and plan will include the wife (who may be wiser and more intelligent)."* [1]

This describes the mature relationship, and is the goal. But when a woman first adopts the submissive stand, she may have to go through a season where she is willing to be less forward in the decision-making process. Wisdom is not found in refraining from offering advice, but being sensitive as to when and how to offer it. If your opinion isn't wanted, don't force it on your husband. I promise you that as you become a supportive wife, your opinion will be asked more than ever before.

One of the greatest tasks of growing together in intimate relationship is learning how each other communicates and finding ways to overcome

---

[1] Page 62, "Recovering Biblical Manhood and Womanhood, a Response to Evangelical Feminism," edited by John Piper and Wayne Grudem. 1991, Crossway Books.

differences. Understanding the differences in how men and women communicate can also help you avoid problems. Men and women by nature use communication to accomplish different things. A woman primarily uses words to establish intimacy or emotional connection. A man primarily uses words to establish status and preserve his independence (i.e., "I don't need help."). This is simply built into your respective male and female DNA.

The average man listening to someone is sensitive to whether that person is challenging his ability or his status. When the average woman listens she is usually sensitive to whether the other person is confirming closeness or moving away from it. Men tend to think that women talk too much about how they feel, instead of relating facts. A man communicates to simply obtain information, while a woman uses it to establish closeness. When you share your opinion with a man, try to focus on sharing facts more than feelings. This will make it easier for him to listen and consider your point of view.

Don't be surprised if your husband asks your opinion and then cuts you off after one or two sentences. Women use on average three or four times more words than a man. Men often fear women are going to get long-winded. The woman wants to really discuss things; the man wants the bottom line, so often the wife tells her husband more than he wants to know and he may accuse her of babbling. If you want your opinion to be heard, try to offer it without burying it in endless words. If a woman goes on talking a long time the man is likely to feel that she is lecturing him, which masculine DNA translates as *"You are stupid."*

When your husband does ask your opinion, be sure you give it to him with total freedom about using or not using it. Your husband needs to know you won't fall apart, feel rejected or start an argument if he doesn't follow your advice. And if you think your husband is making a wrong decision about a critical issue, talk to him respectfully. Godly submission is not realized through a woman's silence, but is an inner quality of gentleness that affirms the leadership of the husband and honors him as leader even when she disagrees with him.[2]

If he refuses to listen, talk to the Lord about the situation, listen to His counsel and trust Him for the outcome. Give God time to influence your husband about a situation.

---

[2] From essay: "Wives Like Sarah, and Husbands Who Honor Them" by Wayne Grudem; Page 196 ibid.

What if God tells me to do one thing and my husband tells me to do something else?

If you feel you have received guidance from God which results in division or a serious breakdown of the husband-wife relationship, then reconsider such guidance. It is doubtful that you are hearing from God. God's ways are generally always aimed at improving your relationship with Him and with your husband. I had an extraordinary experience with the Lord in this kind of situation which really opened my eyes about how God is motivated to lead me.

In my morning prayer time, the Lord revealed what he wanted me to do that day, so I left prayer with a certain agenda. I immediately encountered Ron, who proceeded to tell me to do some things which would prevent me from doing what God wanted. Now today I would just say to Ron, *"But the Lord told me to do something different,"* and he would simply tell me to do what the Lord said. But in those days things were tense between us; I was in the throes of learning about submission and he was wary of my trying to control things. I knew that if I disagreed with Ron that day I would seem to be uncooperative and we could easily fight.

So I went back to the Lord, and complained, *"Lord, you promised you would never put me in a position to choose between two masters! What am I supposed to do now?"*

The Lord replied ever so gently, *"Do what your husband wants you to do."*

I was flabbergasted! Although I was relieved that I did not have to force the issue, it seemed to me that the Lord was actually submitting to my husband. Surely, I thought to myself, this could not be right. I pressed in to check it out:

"Lord, it seems as if you are actually submitting to Ron."

"Yes I am," he replied, *"because it is easier for me to bend my will today than it is for Ron."*

This totally rattled my theology. My assumption was that God, being God, would always insist on his will being done. So I asked the Lord for a scripture, so I could know I was really hearing his voice:

"Where is it in your word?"

He told me to read James Chapter 3. Turning there, I found my answer in verse 17:

But the wisdom that comes from heaven is first of all pure; then peace-loving, considerate, <u>submissive</u>, full of mercy and good fruit, impartial and sincere.

It was true; God was willing to submit to my husband for the sake of keeping peace between us, and to protect me from being torn between two masters. I received a new insight into the heart of God that day, understanding more fully how gracious He really is.

Please understand that on another day under other circumstances the Lord's answer might have been different. But that day, knowing Ron's heart and mine, he knew that this was the most wise and righteous thing to do. Apparently, it was more important to the Lord that day to keep peace between Ron and I, and to reveal more about his gracious goodness, than having me do specific tasks. Relationships are fluid, living things, best handled with wisdom and loving care, not rules and doctrines. We have a thing or two to learn from the Lord.

Do I submit to an abusive husband?

Absolutely not. The Bible never gives a man permission to use any means to force a wife to submit to him. Physical, verbal and emotional abuse are wrong; they betray the trust and responsibility God gave to man to protect women. The mature man has a desire to protect his wife and a leadership style that focuses on loving and serving rather than asserting his authority. Submission is voluntary; we are commanded as wives to give it, but that does not infer a husband has God's permission or approval to enforce it by any means.

Generally I would say that God does not expect a woman to submit to a man who harms her or their children. If you are being verbally abused seek professional help through a pastor or qualified Christian counselor. If you are being physically abused in any way, and are frightened for your life, then get to safety. This is not to be construed as counsel to get a divorce, but do take steps to get help. You are the best judge of whether you or your children are in physical or emotional danger.

It is helpful to determine what constitutes genuine abuse. I have seen women married to harsh husbands with bad tempers, who may have slapped them or shoved them against a wall on rare occasion during a fit of anger.

This does not necessarily constitute abuse. Anyone can experience such rage that they lash out physically; over the course of our marriage Ron and I have both been guilty of slapping a face or twisting an arm a bit on very rare occasions. Again you are the best judge of whether your husband is dangerously abusive or just harsh, but if you're not sure, seek mature counsel to help you decide.

If a man's disposition is simply being bad tempered or easily angered, then you need to pay attention to what triggers his anger and live wisely with him. You might spend some time in prayer to discover the source of his anger and ask the Lord to heal him. For a long time my husband was an angry man, until we discovered that he had longstanding wounds of rejection. I often unwittingly said or did things that felt like rejection to him and triggered his anger. Because of prayer, counseling and personal growth Ron is no longer an angry man. But while he was in the process of healing, I sought and received wisdom from the Holy Spirit and others about how to avoid bringing out that anger and harshness in him.

The Bible does counsel us to bear up under harsh treatment if we can. The Apostle Peter introduces his comments on submission by saying, *Wives, in the same way be submissive to your husbands...* What "same way" is he referring to? The answer is found a few verses earlier where Peter has already been discussing submission to authorities, saying: *Slaves, submit yourselves to your masters with all respect, not only to those who are good and considerate, but also to those who are harsh. (1 Peter 2:18).*

This verse is not at all giving God's approval to slavery or harsh treatment, only that since God knows that both will occur in this fallen world, he tells us how we should respond. While harsh treatment does not belong in a marriage (and I think it breaks God's heart), it is commendable, Peter says, if a person can bear up under unjust treatment because of his devotion to God. He points out that Jesus endured harsh treatment:

> *When they hurled their insults at him, he did not retaliate; when he suffered, he made no threats. Instead, he entrusted himself to him who judges justly. (1 Peter 2:23)*

It is immediately after this that Peter says, *Wives, in the same way be submissive to your husbands....* The bottom line is that we must each follow the Lord personally. Like Jesus, we need to know the Father's will and obey, because therein lies safety.

Is divorce okay?

No, it is not, and we should do everything in our power to avoid it and help others avoid it. It is not God's will for women to suffer in marriage, but we must resist the modern trend to easily flee from difficult marriages. But we must be careful to cultivate the same heart for people that God has, which means that while we condemn and hate divorce, we also join him in his hatred for the abuse of a relationship.[3]

It has been observed that the church could forgive a person more easily for murdering a spouse than divorcing them. We need to hate divorce but we also need to quit acting like it is the unforgivable sin. To condemn or harshly judge divorced or remarried people is to treat the blood of Jesus as if it is ineffective in regard to this sin alone.

On one occasion the Pharisees asked Jesus if it was lawful for a man to divorce his wife for any and every reason. Wives were often put away by their husbands for frivolous reasons.[4] Jesus told them that divorce was not the Father's will. When the Pharisees pointed out that Moses permitted divorce,[5] Jesus responded that Moses allowed it because their hearts were hard.

A hard heart is one that is unresponsive to God. Why would Moses, the lawgiver and most faithful observer of God's law, permit people to divorce? I suggest that it is because he knew the heart of God. He saw that husbands were no longer faithfully loving their wives and had already broken faith with them in following the whims of their sinful, hard hearts. We haven't changed much since then.

There was a time when I thought God would never permit a woman to leave her husband, but years of counseling under the guidance of the Holy Spirit has shown convinced me otherwise. I hasten to say that it is rare, but God has given me a deep respect for how unique every relationship is, and has put the fear of God in me to refrain from counsel or judgments that say "God never" or "God always" wants a person to do something.

We must never lay upon others a burden beyond what they can bear, or force them to stay in a relationship that continually subjects them to abusive or sinful behavior, or even heart-breaking, spirit-crushing behavior. To insist

---

[3] Malachi 2:16, see NIV footnote translation.

[4] Matthew 19:3-11.

[5] Deuteronomy 24:1-4.

that God's will is for two people to remain in a relationship in which one or both is continually sinning against the other is to make a mockery of all God stands for, which is righteous relationship between two people.

Jesus blew the minds of the religious experts when he told them what true righteousness looks like. They thought if they did not murder, they were righteous; but Jesus said that if they lived in anger or scorn towards another they were in as much danger of hell's fire as if they had killed the person![6] We make murder, divorce and lust the big sins, while in God's sight the biggest sin is our betrayal of one another, especially in covenant relationships. Let us not condemn what God does not condemn. Let us be for people as God is for people, and treat them with the mercy and grace our Lord so clearly delights in.

A large part of our work as Shammah Ministries has been counseling others, a gift we have freely shared over many years and across various cultures. We hold these assignments very carefully, never forgetting that hurting people are very vulnerable, and that God has entrusted these hearts to us in hopes that we will listen with His own heart and faithfully share what He would say to them. We are committed to counsel in a way that is faithful to the Word of God as we understand it, and with the ears of our spirit listening to the true Counselor, the Holy Spirit.

In Zambia I counseled two Christian women in the same afternoon, but separately. Both of their husbands had taken second wives, a common problem in their culture, a tradition from tribal days. As I listened to the first woman and inwardly asked the Lord how to advise her, I sensed strongly that it was God's will for her to abandon her adulterous husband. However, I did not tell her what I thought the Lord was saying. Instead, I asked her what she thought the Lord wanted her to do. She felt in her heart that God was permitting her to leave this man who had essentially already left her for another woman. I felt it right then to confirm what I also thought the Lord was saying about the matter.

When I counseled with the next woman, she described an almost identical situation. However, this time I sensed a very different guidance from the Lord, and that He wanted me to encourage her to stay with her husband, in spite of the situation. As I listened to her broken heart I felt

---

[6] Matthew 5:21-22.

some doubt and inwardly asked again, *"Am I hearing you right, Lord?"* The sense of God's will did not change in my spirit.

When she finished speaking I asked her, as I had the first woman, *"What do you think the Lord wants you to do?"* She said she wasn't sure, but was being pressured by her Christian friends to leave her husband. I took a deep breath and said, *"I can only counsel you as I feel the Lord is leading me. I think he wants you to stay with your husband and work on the marriage."* The woman burst into fresh tears, and I assumed she didn't like what I said; but when she lifted her face again there was joy and relief in her eyes. She admitted that she had also sensed this is what the Lord wanted, but had been confused and afraid to trust her ability to be led by him.

At the end of the day I pondered my experience in new amazement. In two adulterous situations, the Lord led one woman to leave her husband, but encouraged the other one to stay. Why? Because he knows the beginning from the end, and we do not. He knew which husband would repent and which would not. He knew the measure of strength in each of the women, and how much each wife could bear up under.

We are not all alike; our psychological makeup is as varied as our physical body types. When you factor in upbringing and environment, each woman is totally unique in her capacity to respond to distress. Behavior in a husband that would totally crush one woman could be tolerated and might even spur strength and maturity in another. Only God knows. We cannot measure another woman's ability or inability to stay in a difficult situation by our own strength.

We should encourage women with the knowledge that the Lord knows what we can bear and will not ask us to endure more than we can. If a woman simply cannot bear up under the treatment of her husband, and has not learned how to receive the comfort, strength and counsel of the Holy Spirit, let us remember that God is rich in mercy, compassion and understanding, and offer the same to her.

We should avoid divorce by every means and help those in troubled marriages learn to love one another faithfully and righteously. The conclusion that a marital situation is hopeless should be a last resort, not made in haste but only after much prayer and effort has been made to avoid it. Do not be in a hurry to end your marriage, even under the most difficult circumstances.

A woman who feels her safety or that of her children threatened should take whatever legal steps are necessary to protect herself and the children, to acquire and enforce financial provision, but not for the purpose of ending your marriage unless you are convinced that no other choice is possible.

Isn't ministry a higher priority to God than family?

Only my penchant for avoiding the word "never" in speaking for God keeps me from saying never in answer to this question. Let's just say this kind of call from God would be extremely rare and under the most unusual of circumstances. Few things bear more negative consequences than seeing a Christian woman leave behind her home, husband and children (emotionally and spiritually, if not physically) to pursue ministry instead of honoring the ministry they are called to at home. I have seen too many women out ministering to others who have undisciplined and untaught children, messy or chaotic homes and miserable husbands who resent God.

How often we've noticed the same women who are in church every time the doors open, are the same ones constantly asking for prayer for the bitter husband, the unruly children or her empty marriage. I love to see women use their gifts for God's service, but every woman's God-given priority is to minister first to her husband and immediate family. As long as those areas are fulfilled, a woman can freely offer herself for public ministry if the Lord is calling her out. Frankly, if every woman would turn her desire to minister towards home first, a good number of these ministry needs might not arise in the first place.

Similarly, some women get the idea that they are pleasing God by being totally preoccupied with the things of the Lord while at home. More than once we have had to counsel with couples where the husband resented the neglect of home and family because his wife spent all her time reading spiritual books, listening to tapes, and watching hours of Christian television.

One woman dragged her husband to counseling in the hope that we would correct his intolerance of their messy house and urge him be more spiritual like her. He complained that the house was always a mess with piles of dirty dishes in the kitchen and was embarrassed to bring anyone home. She complained she didn't have enough time for her work and was always behind in home schooling their children. She was shocked when we advised her to cut down the six hours of Christian TV she proudly boasted of watching every day, to one, and that to be enjoyed after her work was done and her house in order. The Bible says that if a woman wanted such a lifestyle of pure devotion to God, she should have stayed single![7]

Can a woman teach men?

The answer to this is yes, and no. First, the yes.

In interpreting Scripture I have always preferred to be too literal rather than explain away God's more difficult truths. Therefore, I shrank back from public ministry for years because of the following scripture, even though I felt a persistent calling from God to be a teacher to the Body of Christ:

> *A woman should learn in quietness and full submission. I do not permit a woman to teach or to have authority over a man; she must be silent. (1 Timothy 2:12).*

After years of agonizing, studying, praying and seeking the counsel of godly men, I believe it is appropriate for a woman to teach or preach to an audience that includes men as long as she remains willing to be held accountable to the local male authorities in the Body. In this way a woman is teaching under the umbrella of authority shared with her, not usurping. The authority of her teaching is legitimate because *she has received it from God and men*, not taken it.

Furthermore, I've realized that God has given me a call to teach the Body of Christ the importance of loving Him with all one's heart, and I have received authority from him to do so. In exercising the gift and the calling I am not exercising personal authority over any man; I am simply teaching God's word, which has authority over all men.

In doing so, I feel ever accountable to God for how I affect the souls of those I teach, as to whether I am faithfully teaching sound doctrine or sliding off into error. The men who cover me and the pastors responsible for guarding their flocks share that accountability. I invite such men to correct me, publicly if necessary, if I teach something they do not believe is right. (Of course, as was pointed out to me once by a very wise man, any male who

---

[7] 1 Corinthians 7:34.

stands up to teach should acknowledge that same accountability to those in leadership!)

In keeping with God's prophetic promise in Joel 2:28-29, the obvious outpouring of the Holy Spirit upon women today as a gift to the whole body of Christ makes it impossible to interpret 1 Timothy 2:12 in the literal sense which has held sway for decades. Sound principles of Biblical interpretation should keep us from making the assumption that a woman could never teach in the presence of a man based on this one scripture.

Now to the "no." As has been well established, no woman should presume to teach any man in a way that has the effect of taking authority over him, the family or the church. This would violate and usurp Christ's place as the personal authority over a man according to 1 Corinthians 11:3.

It is valuable to note that the words "woman" and "man" in 1 Timothy 2:12 are translated from the same words used for "wife" and "husband." Young's Literal Translation of the Bible renders it so: "*...and a woman I do not suffer to teach, nor to rule a husband, but to be in quietness....*"

There is ample evidence in the culture of Paul's time of the necessity of making such a statement, whether to husbands and wives uniquely, or to men and women in religious settings together. When Paul wrote these words to Timothy, a religious revolution was taking place. Before Jesus came, women were not permitted to publicly worship or study with men, if at all. The traditional structure of the synagogue was completely centered around men who were raised in a completely patriarchal or father-ruled society. But after Jesus came and the curtain in the temple came down that separated men from God, soon the barriers between men and women also tumbled, as they met together in the early fellowships. All the old traditional rules had been shattered, and when Paul wrote these words, women who had been released into an amazing new freedom of religious expression with their men, needed some guidelines.

I assure you that when God wants a woman's gifts used, then he will make a place for them. Any student of Christian history knows that God has used women mightily. Kathryn Kuhlman, one of the greatest evangelist/healers of this century, denied God's call to her ministry at first because she was a woman, until one day he revealed to her that he had called numerous men to that ministry and each of them had refused! And to further shake your theology, God used her powerfully even though she was divorced.

Furthermore, it is clear that a man can seek a woman's counsel, when he needs the benefit of the gift of wisdom that God has poured into women as well as men. In the distribution and operation of God's gifts there is truly neither male nor female, although that does not make gender irrelevant. A woman should walk in the authority, gifts and calling of God and still rightfully display a disposition that honors, upholds and yields to the headship of men. We see this clearly in the story of Deborah of the book of Judges.

Deborah served Israel by judging important matters, acting as the prophetic, guiding voice from God. God even called her to lead the army in a certain battle because the men were not willing. She did not seek power, but attempted to get the male leader to do the job instead of her. When he refused, she accepted responsibility to lead, but even then she insisted that he help her carry it out. She was mightily anointed by God to lead men in that situation. God had to get a job done and apparently he was willing to step outside the general norm to accomplish it, because no man would obey him like Deborah would.

But while this story liberates us to follow God in the exercise of our gifts, let us not assume that it is a license for women to take over when they think a husband or pastor is in error. God has made it abundantly clear in the New Testament, after the cross, through the Holy Spirit, that his will is for man to bear the burden of headship and for woman to be under the protective covering of that headship. God can and will give authority to a woman, but the fact that God will use whosoever he will to accomplish his work does not negate His will for women to honor the protective headship of men.

The bottom line.

Our job is not to follow rules, our job is to follow a Person, the Holy Spirit. Our goal is not to legalistically interpret the law but to understand the heart of God in submission and every matter. And in the wisdom of his heart God has given to women the unique privilege of portraying for the world and the church how a a Bride submits to and honors her Bridegroom, in public and in private. That is the bottom line.

Reflecting on Chapter 20

In providing answers to common issues regarding submission of a wife to her husband, this chapter underscores the need for wisdom in understanding and applying the scriptures.

❖ *How and when you say something is as important as the words themselves. Consider these scriptures in how you communicate with your husband:*

Psalms 141:3

Proverbs 13:3

Proverbs 14:3

Proverbs 18:6

❖ *Ask your husband how you can support him in leading your family. Journal his answers. Make goals to help you become consistent in these ways.*

❖ *Ask the Holy Spirit to help you become wise in relating to your husband.*

Deeper work

❖ *As you continue to work out issues in regards to honoring your husband's leadership, watch for areas that give you trouble. Talk to the Lord about them and always ask Him for the specific wisdom you need to live wisely with your man.*

Chapter 21

In Summary

The woman God designed is a living reflection of the loving God who made her. Because she gazes at the Lord continually with the eyes of her heart, she is able to live her life as a response to his love:

> *...for your love is ever before me, and I walk continually in your truth. (Psalms 26:3).*

Because she walks in God's truth, she is free, liberated to the uttermost.

The glory of the woman God designed is that she knows Jesus. She is intimately acquainted with his gentleness, his patience and his joy.

The woman God designed is holy. She has set herself apart as a gift to the Lord, because she understands the profound way that God has set himself apart as a gift to her.

She loves the Lord's will and lets Jesus choose her path because she knows he would only lead her one place: to abundant, victorious, eternal life.

She is not perfect, but because she trusts her Lord completely and hates displeasing Him, her heart is ready to obey him without fear.

The woman God designed is utterly dependent upon Him, fully aware of her need for His gracious Spirit and power to live. She continually refills her thirsty soul in the Spirit's waters by paying attention to him, seeking the Wonderful Counselor's guidance in all of her ways.

The woman God designed is a lover, a healer, and a strengthener. She shows off God's glory in her femininity, rejoicing and resting in his role for her on this earth. She is not ruled by her emotions, but lives at rest in the sovereignty of God.

The woman God designed enjoys God supremely, satisfied in his love and content in His goodness. God really lives in her heart and she lives in His. Her life shows that Jesus can be trusted.

APPENDIX A

THE BAPTISM IN THE HOLY SPIRIT

The Power to Know and Love God With All One's Heart

Scriptures are from the New International Version. Some are abbreviated, amplified or paraphrased by this author.

Ephesians 3:17-19: I pray that you may have power ... to know the love of Christ.

Galatians 5:22-23: But the fruit of [walking with and being controlled by] the Spirit is love ...

Ephesians 5:18: Be filled with the Spirit. (The Greek verb tense means "continually.")

Matthew 3:11: The baptism in water is for repentance. Jesus baptizes us with the Holy Spirit and fire. (See also Mark 1:8, Luke 3:16, John 1:33.) As he prepares for his crucifixion, Jesus teaches his disciples that when he returns to the Father the Holy Spirit will take his place as their Counselor and Teacher, to live within them to personally guide and teach them just as he had been doing. (John 14:16-17; 16:7-15).

John 20:22: After his disciples had been baptized in water [Jesus] "breathed on them and said, "Receive the Holy Spirit." This is their "born-again" experience, only possible after the resurrection of Jesus.

Acts 1:4-5: Jesus told them to wait in Jerusalem "for the gift my Father promised...you will be baptized with the Holy Spirit...you will receive power when the Holy Spirit comes on you." Then Acts 2:4 verifies: "All of them were filled with the Holy Spirit ..."

Acts 8:15-17: Peter and John pray for believers who had only received the baptism in water, that the Holy Spirit would come upon them: "When [Peter and John] arrived, they prayed for them that they might receive the Holy Spirit, because the Holy Spirit had not yet come upon any of them; they had simply been baptized into the name of the Lord Jesus. Then Peter and John placed their hands on them, and they received the Holy Spirit."

Acts 9:17: Ananias prays for Saul, now Paul, that he may be filled with the Holy Spirit: "Then Ananias went to the house and entered it. Placing his hands on Saul, he said, "Brother Saul, the Lord – Jesus, who appeared to you on the road as you were coming here – has sent me so that you may see again and be filled with the Holy Spirit."

Acts 10:45-48: Peter and the disciples are amazed that the gift of the Holy Spirit has been bestowed on Gentiles who've never been baptized in water. They baptize the believers in water also, to make their conversion and obedience to Jesus complete. "The circumcised believers who had come with Peter were astonished that the gift of the Holy Spirit had been poured out even on the Gentiles. For they heard them speaking in tongues and praising God. Then Peter said, 'Can anyone keep these people from being baptized with water? They have received the Holy Spirit just as we have.' So he ordered that they be baptized in the name of Jesus Christ."

Acts 11:15-16: Peter is sent to share the gospel with a Gentile believer and while speaking the Holy Spirit comes upon the believer and his household; seeing this, Peter then baptizes them in water also. "As I began to speak, the Holy Spirit came on them as he had come on us at the beginning. Then I remembered what the Lord had said: 'John baptized with water, but you will be baptized with the Holy Spirit.'"

Acts 18:24-19:7: A Jew named Apollos is zealously preaching the gospel and making disciples for Jesus in Ephesus. When Paul goes to investigate these disciples, he finds they have received only "the baptism of John ... for repentance". After learning this, Paul then prays for them to be baptized into the name of the Lord Jesus, and they are filled with the Holy Spirit.

Scripture is clear that whenever the apostles realized a believer had experienced only one baptism or the other, they saw to it that the believer was instructed in and received the baptism left undone. Note that these are the men who had been personally taught by Jesus.

Some do not believe in the need for this baptism because of Paul's statement that "There is one body and one Spirit - just as you were called to one hope when you were called - one Lord, one faith, one baptism; one God and Father of all..." (Ephesians 4:4-6) But Paul was not asserting that only water baptism is necessary for believers. The subject he addresses here is the unity of believers under one Lord.

This is an argument Paul further clarified in his letter to the Corinthian church, where he criticizes the tendency of people to follow the person who actually baptized them rather than follow Christ:

"My brothers...there are quarrels among you. What I mean is this: One of you says, 'I follow Paul;' another, 'I follow Apollos;' another, 'I follow Cephas;' still another, 'I follow Christ.' Is Christ divided? Was Paul crucified for you? Were you baptized into the name of Paul? I am thankful that I did not baptize any of you except Crispus and Gaius, so no-one can say that you were baptized into my name." (1 Corinthians 1:11-15).

He later concludes, "For we were all baptized by one Spirit into one body—whether Jews or Greeks, slave or free—and we were all given the one Spirit to drink."(1 Corinthians 12:13). So Paul established in his first letter to the Corinthian church and in his letter to the Ephesians that there is only one Name in which we should all be baptized (Jesus Christ) and one Person we should follow, one fountain we should drink from: the Holy Spirit. His actions as seen in the book of Acts clearly reveal that he practiced leading new believers through a baptism in water and a baptism in the Spirit.

Romans 6:3-4: Baptism in water is a believer's public ceremony of being "baptized into his [Christ's] death." In true covenant fashion, the new believer symbolically dies and is raised into new life with God (the "new covenant in my blood," said Jesus in Luke 22:20). Colossians 2:11-13 seems to connect water baptism with one's spiritual circumcision, the removal of the old flesh sin nature.

Jesus asks the believer to go the next step and receive God's power to live this new life, which is likened to putting on a new garment. Jesus called this baptism "being clothed with power from on high." (Luke 24:49)

Galatians 3:2: The baptism in the Holy Spirit is received by faith just as salvation is. The disciples demonstrated the difference vividly. Baptized in water, as devoted followers of Jesus, they still lacked the power to love Jesus enough to even watch with him through his suffering in Gethsemane. They love Jesus in the power of their own hearts. After the Holy Spirit outpouring, their lives and witness become incredibly powerful, their love effective! Miracles and gifts beyond their own natural abilities operate freely in them.

APPENDIX B

MY SHEEP LISTEN TO MY VOICE

Biblical Evidence That Born Again Christians Can Hear the Voice of the Lord

(All scriptures are New International Version unless otherwise noted.)

My sheep listen to my voice; I know them, and they follow me. (John 10:27).

The "new covenant" Jesus died to give us includes the promise of personally being taught by God. Hebrews 8:10-11. If Old Testament people heard God's voice, how much more should we!

Before he was crucified, Jesus taught his disciples about the role of the Holy Spirit for born-again believers: "But when he, the Spirit of truth, comes, he will guide you into all truth. He will not speak on his own; he will speak only what he hears, and he will tell you what is yet to come. (John 16:13)

Even in the Old Testament, anointed men of God record times of being personally taught by him: "The Sovereign Lord has given me an instructed tongue, to know the word that sustains the weary. He wakens me morning by morning, wakens my ear to listen like one being taught." (Isaiah 50:4).

King David records that the Lord said to him: "I will instruct you and teach you in the way you should go; I will counsel you and watch over you. Do not be like the horse or the mule, which have no understanding but must be controlled by bit and bridle or they will not come to you. (Psalms 32:8-9). In fact, the Lord is called the Wonderful Counselor! (Isaiah 9:6)

We are commanded: "Do not be anxious about anything, but in everything, by prayer and petition, with thanksgiving, present your requests to God." (Philippians 4:6). And to pray continually. (1 Thessalonians 5:17).

We are told to "find out what pleases the Lord (Ephesians 5:10) and to "understand what the Lord's will is." (Ephesians 5:17).

Colossians 2:3 says Jesus is the one "in whom are hidden all the treasures of wisdom and knowledge." If Jesus is the personification of Wisdom, then he is the one speaking to us in Proverbs: "If you had responded to my rebuke, I would have poured out my heart to you and made my thoughts known to you ... but whoever listens to me will live in safety and be at ease, without fear of harm." (Proverbs 1:23 & 33)

"Now then, my sons, listen to me; blessed are those who keep my ways. Listen to my instruction and be wise; do not ignore it. Blessed is the man who listens to me, watching daily at my doors, waiting at my doorway. For whoever finds me finds life and receives favor from the Lord. But whoever fails to find me harms himself; all who hate me love death." (Prov. 8:32-36).

Jesus complained to the religious experts, "You diligently study the Scriptures because you think that by them you possess eternal life. These are the Scriptures that testify about me, yet you refuse to come to me to have life." (John 5:38-40).

Jesus taught this also: "If anyone has ears to hear, let him hear. Consider carefully what you hear," he continued. "With the measure you use, it will be measured to you—and even more. Whoever has will be given more; whoever does not have, even what he has will be taken from him." (Mark 4:23-25; Matt. 13: 9-16).

James says: "If any of you lacks wisdom, he should ask God, who gives generously to all without finding fault, and it will be given to him. But when he asks, he must believe and not doubt, because he who doubts is like a wave of the sea, blown and tossed by the wind. That man should not think he will receive anything from the Lord." (James 1:5-7). James 3:17 describes what "the wisdom from above" will sound like so we can recognize it.

"Now what I am commanding you today is not too difficult for you or beyond your reach. It is not up in heaven, so that you have to ask, 'Who will ascend into heaven to get it and proclaim it to us so that we may obey it?' Nor is it beyond the sea, so that you have to ask, 'Who will cross the sea to get it and proclaim it to us so that we may obey it?' No, the word is very near you; it is in your mouth and in your heart so that you may obey it… that you may love the Lord your God, listen to his voice, and hold fast to him. For the Lord is your life…" (Deuteronomy 30:11-14 & 20).

He humbled you, causing you to hunger and then feeding you with manna, which neither you nor your fathers had known, to teach you that man does not live on bread alone but on every word that comes from the mouth of the Lord. (Deuteronomy 8:3, also quoted in Matthew 4:4).

APPENDIX C

What The Holy Spirit Does With & For You

Romans 8:16: Reassures you that you are God's child, and he is your Father.

Psalm 32:8: Teaches you, counsels you when you don't know what to do.

1 Corinthians 2:6-16: Reveals the thoughts of God (the mind of Christ) to you. See also John 14:26; 16:5-15.

Isaiah 46:16: Leads you and lights the way when you're blind (walking in a dark place and can't see the way).

Isaiah 57:18: Heals your physical/emotional wounds. Restores comfort when you've been hurt.

John 6:63: Gives new life. See also 2 Corinthians 1:3-4.

Isaiah 58:11: Satisfies all your needs, waters your thirsty soul.

Mark 13:11: Tells you what to say when needed. See also Luke 12:12.

Luke 10:21: Gives you joy. Reveals God the Father and Jesus even to little children (or those who trust Him in a childlike manner).

John 16:13: Tells you what will happen in the future. See also Acts 20:23.

Acts 9:31: Strengthens, encourages you when you feel weak or discouraged.

Romans 5:5: Reveals God's love to you; helps you love God. See Eph. 3:17.

Romans 14:17: Gives you gifts. Gives you righteousness. Gives you peace. Gives you joy. Also 1 Thessalonians 1:6.

Romans 15:13: Fills you with hope.

Romans 15:16: Cleanses you when you "get dirty" (do something offensive to God, violating his holiness and purity). See also Titus 3:5.

Romans 8:26-27: Teaches you how to pray.

2 Corinthians 1:21-22: Makes you stand firm in Christ.

Philippians 2:13: Energizes, empowers and motivates you.

About Shammah Ministries

Dr. Ron Woolever spent his first 20 years in ministry as a local church pastor and counselor before forming Shammah Ministries with his wife Tonia. Since 1990 they have taught across the U.S. and overseas with all streams in the Body of Christ through seminars, retreats, counseling and one-on-one mentoring.

With the ancient history of covenant-making as a backdrop to Scripture, Ron and Tonia offer a powerful Bible course entitled *Covenant, God's Pattern for Righteous Relationship*. This course unlocks the Biblical history of God and man from Genesis through the New Covenant of Jesus in a way that empowers faith in God's love and faithfulness, then reveals the nature and power of having "a covenant heart" like God's.

A sequel to *Covenant* called *Spirit Life* is a course on how to live life by the Spirit — knowing the Father, hearing His voice, doing His powerful works. The student learns how to follow the Apostle Paul's admonition to "walk by the Spirit" and discover one's spiritual gifts.

Detailed information about these and other teachings and projects of Shammah Ministries can be found on their website:

www.shammah.org

Resources Available from Shammah Ministries

Books

Leader's Study Guide for The Woman God Designed

Can I Really Hear God?

Finding the Heart of God in Every Book of the Bible

Teaching on Audio & Video

Covenant: God's Pattern for Righteous Relationship

God's Plan for the Family

Entering God's Rest

Spirit Life

What Kind of Woman Will I Be?

Grace: God's Ability Within Us

The Tabernacle of Moses: A Pattern for The Priesthood of Believers

Are you Satisfied With God?

To learn more about these and other products, log onto www.shammah.org

Seminars Available by Shammah Ministries

Covenant: God's Pattern for Righteous Relationship

Spirit Life

A Course for Christian Lovers

What Kind of Woman Will I Be?

Entering God's Rest

For more information on how to schedule a seminar, retreat or leadership training event for your group, write to Shammah Ministries at:

shammah@charter.net

Breinigsville, PA USA
14 February 2011
255492BV00004BA/20/P